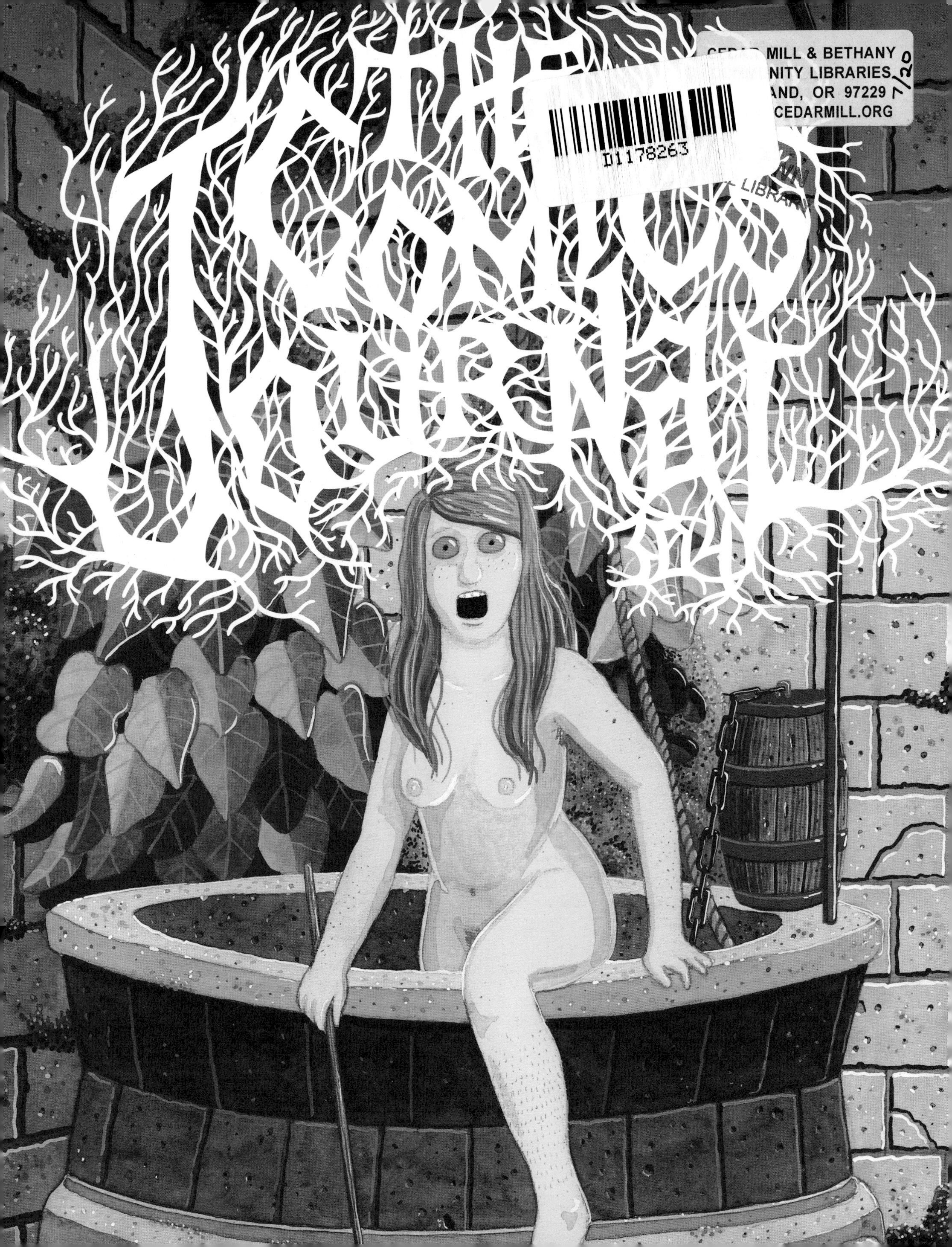
THE COMICS JOURNAL

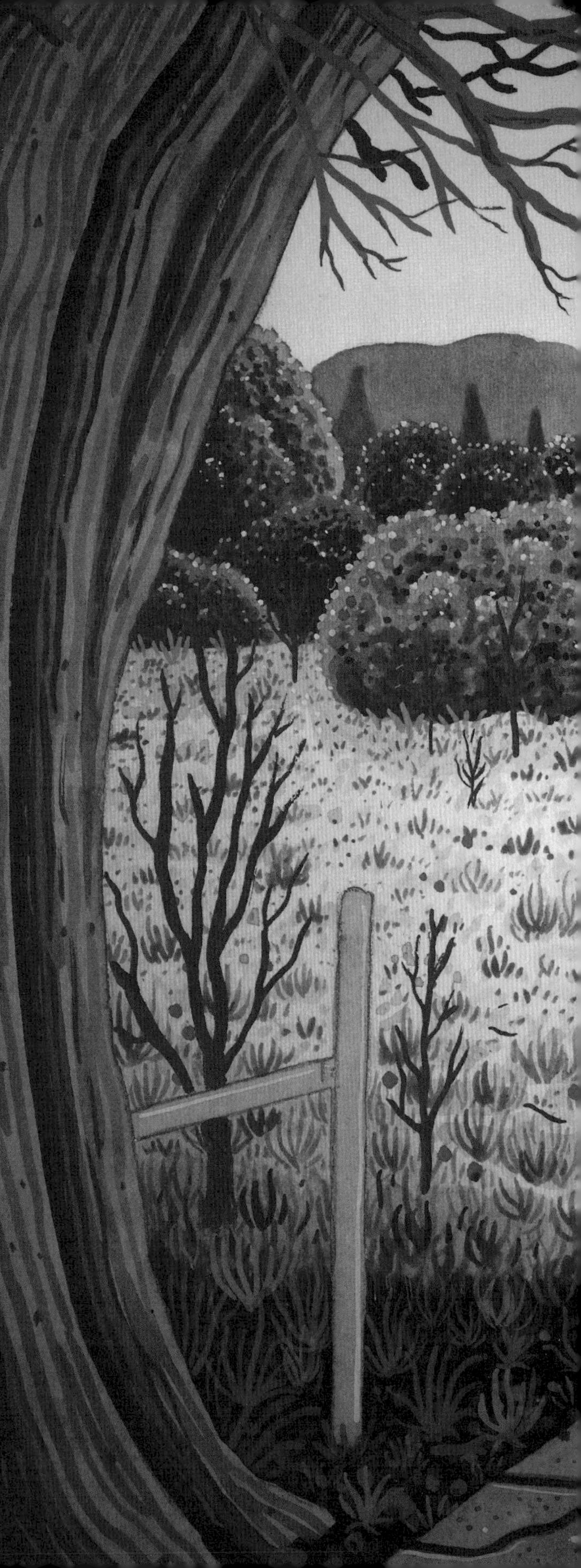

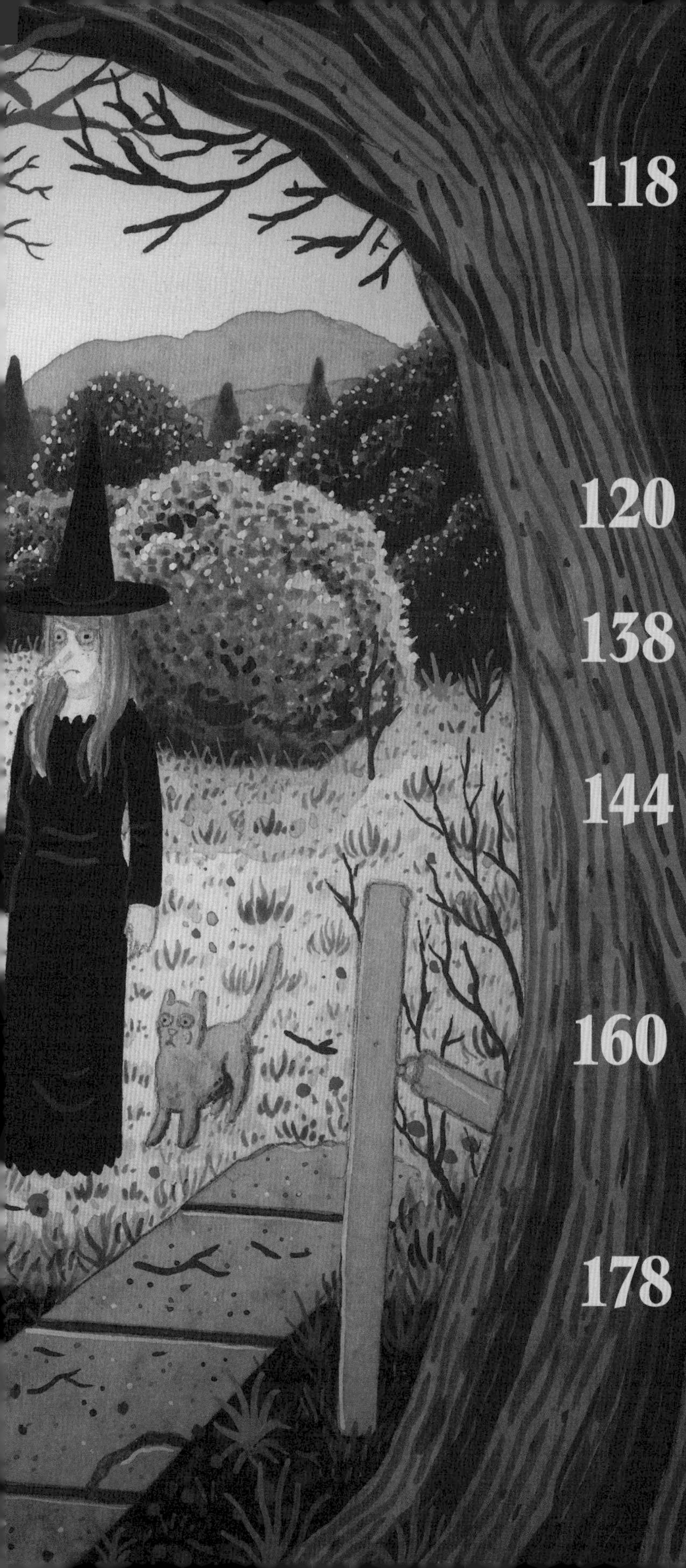

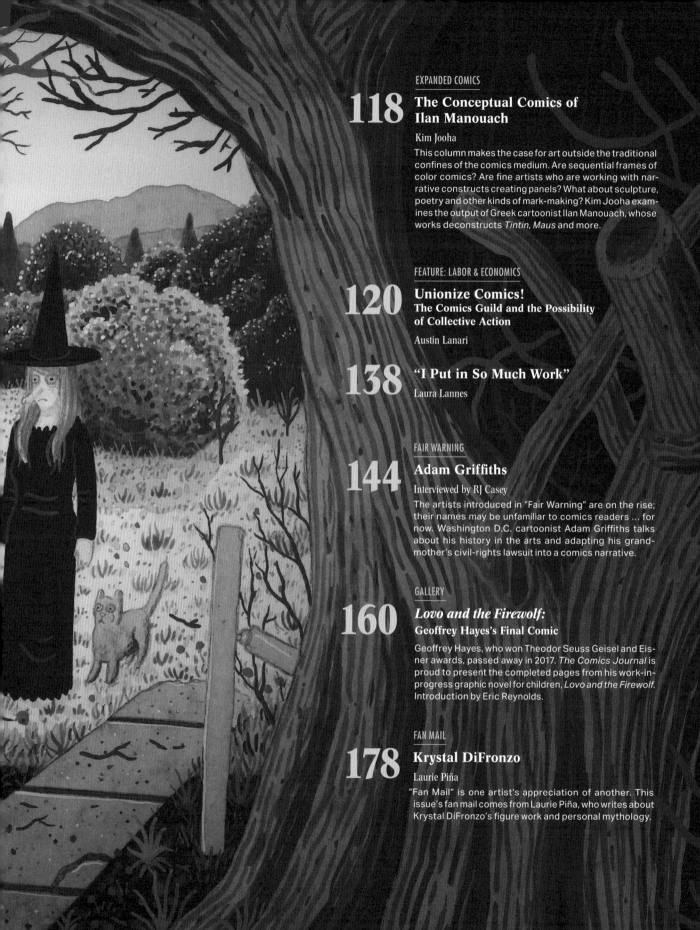

Contributors

Fantagraphics Books, Inc.
7563 Lake City Way NE
Seattle, WA 98115
Fantagraphics.com
Facebook.com/fantagraphics
Twitter: @fantagraphics

First Printing: October 2019
ISBN: 978-1-68396-264-9
LOC Control Number: 2018949537
Printed in: Korea

COVER: Photo of *Bad Gateway* exhibit at the Bellevue Arts Museum, 2019. Courtesy of Simon Hanselmann.

TITLE PAGE: From *Bad Gateway,* by Simon Hanselmann 2019.

CONTENTS: From *Bad Gateway,* by Simon Hanselmann 2019.

ADAM BUTTRICK is a Los Angeles-based cartoonist and illustrator. Buttrick has been nominated for an Ignatz Award and his art has been featured in *Kramers Ergot, Best American Comics* and *The New York Times*.

SOPHIE FRANZ is a cartoonist and educator from Portland, Oregon. Franz's comics have been published previously by Retrofit and ShortBox.

SHAENON K. GARRITY is a writer, editor and cartoonist. Garrity's webcomic, *Narbonic,* ran from 2000 to 2006, where it won the Web Cartoonists' Choice Award in 2005. Garrity has edited for Viz Media and has contributed to *Nickelodeon Magazine* and tcj.com. She currently lives in the Bay Area.

GEOFFREY HAYES (1940–2017) began contributing to underground comix anthologies with his brother, Rory Hayes, in the 1970s. In the following years, he became one of America's most celebrated children's books authors, winning the Theodor Seuss Geisel Award in 2010 and an Eisner Award for "Best Publication for Early Readers" in 2012. Hayes passed away in 2017 in Asheville, North Carolina, at the age of 69.

KIM JOOHA is a writer living in Toronto, Canada. Jooha is a contributor to the sites *Your Chicken Enemy* and tcj.com, and is the associate publisher of 2dcloud.

AUSTIN LANARI is a writer and web developer residing in Los Angeles. Lanari has previously written about comics for *Loser City, Your Chicken Enemy* and *Comics Bulletin*.

LAURA LANNES is a Brazilian cartoonist and illustrator living in New York City. Her work has appeared in *The New York Times* and *Entertainment Weekly*; and she has been published by Retrofit and 2dcloud.

LAURIE PIÑA is a cartoonist, DJ and poet from San Diego, California. She has been self-publishing comics and chapbooks since 2013.

ERIC REYNOLDS began his career at Fantagraphics in 1993, first as the *Comics Journal* news editor, then as director of marketing and public relations and now as associate publisher. He lives in Seattle, Washington.

Editor's Note

In our previous issue, I wrote that one of our new goals for *The Comics Journal* was to give artists and writers a platform where they are able to hoist up their real-world concerns in a frank and genuine way.

In this issue, the *Journal* attempts to propel labor and economics to the forefront. In the comics community, and the working world at large, this isn't something normally talked about in the open, or at all – and that is a major problem. The silence around money – sometimes insidious and specifically devised by the powers-that-be, other times innocently based on perceived niceties or even shame – is all equally damaging. To change this, each person inside comics – from creator to reader and everyone in between – may need to reevaluate certain long-held traditions.

We reached out to comics creators for this issue's "Blood & Thunder" letters page and asked them to discuss their economic goals. We asked contributors to write honestly about their fiscal concerns and how it affects them. And if we at *The Comics Journal* are going to put our money where our mouth is, so to speak, we also want to be transparent. I can start the dialog:

> Last year, working at Fantagraphics, publisher of this magazine, my net income was $28,257.61.

> My family moved more than 40 miles away from our Seattle offices so that we could afford a place to live. I am fortunate enough to own a car to make that commute every day.

> I am only able to stay employed in the comics industry because my wife works in the medical field.

Why not have these conversations? With so many people in the comics field feeling the crushing burden of the freelance/gig economy, why not? When many of the medium's greatest artists are forced to leave comics to secure a living elsewhere, why not? And when stories about insolvent cartoonists in their twilight years are all too common, why not?

You may not agree with everything written here (and the *Journal* wouldn't have it any other way) but several of this issue's contributors take the stances they do because many people in comics literally can't afford not to. Not all hope is lost, however. With the comics industry still being relatively small and fluid, real difference can and should ideally be possible. Let's add to the conversation right here. Why not? ☼

– RJ Casey, Managing Editor

Editor in Chief: **Gary Groth**

Managing Editor: **RJ Casey**

Series Design: **Sean David Williams**
Issue Design: **Justin Allan-Spencer**

Production: **Paul Baresh** and **Preston White**

Promotion: **Jacq Cohen**

Editorial Assistance: **Sena Crow, Conrad Groth, Christina Hwang, Emma Levy, Katherine Thomas**

Editorial Consultant: **Mike Dean**

Advertising: **Matt Silvie**
For advertising information, email silvie@fantagraphics.com

For more thoughtful criticism and reviews, visit **tcj.com**

Much of this issue is focused on labor issues and the economics of comics. We reached out to cartoonists across the medium, and asked them: "Do you have specific art-making financial goals? As an artist, what are your money-making expectations?" Here are their responses:

Illustrations by Max Clotfelter

I MENTALLY DIVIDE my work in two: paid and personal. "Paid work" is anything with a contract and for that, I negotiate aggressively for competitive pay to meet concrete financial goals. My monthly expenses are pretty high, and I need to be able to cover a big chunk of my family's childcare bills and mortgage. I'm the staff cartoonist for a monthly children's science magazine, but most of the work that fulfills my financial need is freelance illustration for print publications.

"Personal work" is comics, for which I have no money-making expectations. If I sell books at a con or get an advance or something, that's obviously wonderful, but I don't (and, frankly, can't) rely on it to support my family. Divorcing financial expectations from my art practice works for me, and if I didn't have to keep track of expenses and income for taxes I wouldn't look at the money side of my comics practice at all. The kind of work I make has pretty niche audiences, and my output is really slow (especially in these hard years of raising little kids), so this mental division frees me from feeling guilty when it inevitably makes little to no money.

Marnie Galloway

LUCKILY, I stopped losing money making comics around *Epoxy* #4 [2014]. I went back to self-publishing and printed it on a Risograph machine I bought a couple of years prior. I also had a good day job that let me take a few creative risks with the book. In other words, it didn't have to sell in order for me to eat.

Pricing became a tricky decision, since I had decided to sell it for what I really thought it was worth, fighting every self-critical instinct I had for the actual work. And that was a bit of a risk, too. It worked out and now the comics are a nice supplement to the family income.

John Pham

MORE THAN ANYTHING ELSE, I'd really like to have more time and space to work on comics and art. I still report for duty to a full-time day job, which is a privilege, but I'd be lying if I didn't say I'd love to make enough from cartooning to live on. I hope I will at some point. I do almost all of my comics on paper from start to finish and have stacks and stacks of original work. If I could sell my pages one day for a pretty penny, I guess that'd be one way to make money! But I'd also be sad to part with them. It's such a guessing game when it comes to what the next job will be, how much it will pay, how long it'll take to get paid and on and on.

When I was little I'd watch *Garfield and Friends* on TV and see Jon Arbuckle, the cartoonist, portrayed as such a down-and-out loser of a human. I remember I distinctly thought being a cartoonist must be such a thankless job. So, I guess my expectations have always been pretty low! And actually, it isn't thankless at all.

Katie Fricas

I'M LUCKY TO HAVE a good day job that doesn't wreck me so I'm able to not depend on drawing for food and rent. I don't expect to make money at all from my work that I publish, though I hope to maybe make enough to cover any printing costs. For work that others are publishing, I go a lot harder trying to make sure they recoup as much of the costs as possible, partly out of gratitude that they would bother publishing my work and partly to encourage them to continue publishing at all.

A silver lining in making work that isn't financially lucrative is that one can be free to do anything. There's (almost) no one looking and you aren't depending on it to survive so it's OK to go crazy and do dumb projects and books and stories that have no hope of generating "R.O.I." LOL R.O.I. It's OK to not make products. There's a Philip Guston painting of a sidewalk scene – people's legs going by, and in the gutter is a dog licking a garbage can and he is ignored and not part of the busyness but he is so happy. It's OK and even good to be that dog.

Warren Craghead

MY MAIN FINANCIAL GOAL is to never have a landlord, or deal with black mold, or poorly insulated windows or get my rent increased ever again.

After almost four years of full-time cartooning, my financial expectations are pretty low. Right now, I'm still young and can work a lot and live off of a small income. It might be occasionally creatively fulfilling, but it's not responsible in terms of saving money or developing a healthy work ethic.

Comic shows are my main source of income, but those are unreliable for a variety of reasons (not to mention exhausting, especially if I do 10+ every year). I'll probably always draw comics, but I don't see it as a sustainable full-time career unless it's supplemented by some freelance animation or illustration jobs.

Ben Sears

AS A FULL-TIME freelance sequential artist, I absolutely need to have realistic financial goals. The industry since the last run of *The Comics Journal* has had several financial relocations. Since I started buying the *Journal* from newsstands, the terrain is unrecognizable.

What used to be my safe harbors of a niche industry was bountiful with many species of fish and fauna. A few devout fishermen (and humans that fish) used to cast nets and return prosperous to a happy hamlet, to trade and bargain with known denizens of the town for tools and goods. It really was an eternal summer.

Where the same waters now are hardly swimmable, with giant trawling ships, full of social media noise, diesel and dragging infinite nets through exploited and empty pollution. OK, OK. I'm being a bit dramatic.

A sequential artist takes about a decade to start finding a foothold in the industry, another decade to get good if the work is steady and financially rewarding. I've heard and believe that drawing comics is akin to hunting and trapping as an occupation that takes a lifetime to master. Other peripheral art industries dream of "stepping down" to do a comic and most of them run right back to the bosom of steady hours, paid vacations and medical insurance. Anyone who has had the pleasure (or unfortunate proximity) of hearing my comic rants in a bar, after I'm good and filled with vodka, has surely heard, "There are more active duty Navy SEALs than artists that can hit a sequential deadline month to month." I've also heard someone exposing and comparing statistics of professional basketball players versus full-time comic artists.

So, to answer your question about money-making expectations: how is it that the aforementioned jobs can net millions of dollars, not to mention more in endorsements and book deals (including nice medical packages), and I keep running into offers that would net me less than unskilled employment such as washing dishes? So yes, I cry out my expectations to the sky: I am a highly skilled professional and I expect to make more money. More money!

Moritat

FROM EARLY ON, I pretty much had no financial goals associated with my comics career. Growing up in the 1950s and '60s, I saw little evidence that women were gainfully employed in comics. It became pretty obvious to me from the beginning of my experience in print that the work I was inspired to create was very far from the mainstream, and I had better cultivate other means of economic survival beyond writing stories and drawing pictures.

Even creating 40 issues of a series that was uniquely my own from a well-respected publisher that brought me good reviews and some very enthusiastic readers was not enough to keep a roof over my head without some (at least) part-time day job as backup. At least now I have enough retirement income from my various adventures in the workaday world to allow me the time for more creative work.

Roberta Gregory

MY FINANCIAL GOALS are simply to live as an artist year after year. I do this by working on various books a year. Outside of working on the writing or illustrations, I also help to promote the projects I am involved in by speaking about them at conferences and book festivals. I connect with librarians and teachers and visit many schools throughout the country over the school year, too. This not only gets my books into the hands of young readers but also helps to spread my love of drawing, which can be infectious, as well as my philosophy of creating works that are a representation of the diversity of our country.

Raul the Third

Power, Resources and Risk
The Present and Possible Future of Comics Festivals

Adam Buttrick

IF WE THINK ABOUT the artists that have made independent comics what it is today, it's not hard to find among them those who live in poverty or hover just above it. Young artists fare no better. Whether they're saddled with crushing debt from trying to get an education, facing dwindling prospects in the commercial arts that sustained prior generations or just struggling through day jobs that have come to be as temporary and contract-based as the worst of the comics industry, many find their options bleak.

At the same time that cartoonists come up against these frightening realities, independent comics festivals in America have proliferated. Under the banner of providing new opportunities for artists to highlight and sell their work, these festivals range from the small and community-organized to the large and institutionally backed. Smaller festivals undoubtedly provide this setting to cartoonists and their audiences. They are often artist-run, with focus placed on keeping overhead low for their participants. Some are also organized with the laudable aim of providing a platform for cartoonists who the medium has wrongly ignored or excluded.

Large independent comics festivals (which I'll hereafter refer to as "large festivals" for the sake of brevity) have a more nebulous character. What distinguishes them from smaller festivals – apart, obviously, from their size – are both their administrative structures and the things they do under the auspices of their missions. No two large festivals are the same. Some have boards, councils or individual managers. Some are established as non-profits and some put on symposiums. Some seek corporate sponsorships and take on paid employees.

All illustrations by Adam Buttrick, 2019.

In considering these distinctions, what seldom seems to be interrogated is whether these things that large festivals do — and even their size in and of itself — are done because they are broadly beneficial or are arrived at by some other means. It's strange because, without answering this question, it would seem difficult to justify the sizeable, ongoing expenditure of time, money and attention they demand from cartoonists, publishers and their audiences. To return to cartoonists in 2019 and their material standing, let's do exactly this. Let's consider the structure and operation of large festivals, how these qualities determine their outcomes, independent of our common understanding of their viability.

In their most basic articulation, large festivals exist as a pay-to-exhibit arrangement whereby cartoonists and publishers are required to help front the costs of holding these events and absorb the financial risks associated with their general performance. In exchange for their participation and money, they are given a set amount of temporary retail space to sell their work, as well as management by the festival's organizers of the aggregately collected fees. The festival's organizers use these resources, sometimes in tandem with others they've solicited from the public and outside organizations, to provide the retail space, host various programming events and more generally do something like put on "successful" shows. What constitutes this success doesn't seem to include the following:

- A formal commitment to exhibitors that their costs will be recouped in sales and that large festivals will be structured with this as their central aim.

- That they will provide a transparent and complete accounting of their costs, revenue and expenditures and the ability for exhibitors to have a say in how funds are used.

- That there will be a guaranteed means for exhibitors to exercise control over the location, hours and conditions in which they will sell their work.

I imagine some will bristle at these points. "Comics is meritocratic. We don't pick winners and losers. We're letting the market decide." Something of that order. I think any honest accounting of the history of the medium discredits these notions, not the very least its racism, sexism and discrimination against LGBTQ+ cartoonists. Nor does it seem plausible that events based on one's ability to pay for fees, travel and lodging or to take time off from work or caring for one's dependents could be fundamentally meritocratic. Nor that curation exists as an independent, inherently equitable way to establish markets. But even if we set my criteria and specious responses to them aside, the question would still remain: How is it that success is being determined for large festivals?

The answer, I believe, is that large festivals set terms, define their markets and determine success however they see fit. There is not an equal application of competitive pressure or shared decision-making across exhibitors and organizers. For example, do organizers, like artists, compete against hundreds of others to hold their positions? Do exhibitors decide who among them should be exempted from fees or compensated for their participation? These questions may seem absurd given what we accept as legitimate in the status quo, but they're important to consider. The answers reflect relations of power that have broader consequences, both for large festivals and the future of the medium.

> While it's true that cartoonists' labor has been intentionally devalued in the arts economy, many critiques wrongly ascribe this debasement to some cabal of institutional gatekeepers, who must be replaced with wiser, more benevolent administrators.

We must consider that if outcomes at all depend on who gets to construct what such markets mean, define their rules and determine who is subjected to them, then most exhibitors are in a poor, aggregate position relative to their contributions. After all, it is they who are providing a great deal of what's required to pull off these shows. Without their participation and embrace of the associated costs, large festivals wouldn't be "large," let alone happen at all. They do all of this without being given a formal, corresponding say in how these events are managed, nor demand that organizers be subjected to the same level of competition that determines their inclusion and financial returns.

How we arrived at the point where the resources exhibitors contribute exists in separate proportion from decision-making about their use would take a separate, even longer article. Suffice it to say that many cartoonists lead lives of tremendous insecurity, while simultaneously holding their peers in high esteem. This mixture of precarity and reverence discourages cartoonists from engaging critically with anything that promises "institutional stability," especially when these "institutions" seem to mirror our own values and estimations. This is compounded by popular narratives in comics that emphasize their being wrongly excluded from some bourgeois conception of "Art." While it's true that cartoonists' labor has been intentionally devalued in the arts economy, many critiques wrongly ascribe this debasement to some cabal of institutional gatekeepers, who must be replaced with wiser, more benevolent administrators. Instead of understanding this hierarchical gatekeeping for what it is – a structural outcome of an economy designed to atomize labor, make it cheaper and more expropriable, as true in the fine arts as anywhere else – and attacking it as such, they retreat to narrow, moralizing condemnations i.e. the bad curators/museums/universities who don't understand the real value of comics. What results from embracing these ideas is a pseudo-struggle. This pseudo-struggle rallies people to extract concessions of status from these institutions, but fails to dismantle the hierarchies that entrench their power, preserving their ability to atomize, devalue and expropriate labor into the future. This has several consequences, but, for our purposes, results in triumphalist celebrations of comics in the abstract or individual artists, taking the place of a real and durable solidarity among the medium's workers.

But regardless of whether we proceed with this understanding, large festivals will engage with exhibitors as a class. They will make decisions for all of them about how they will be treated, how exemptions and resources will be distributed to or away from what parties, and what details about

their operation must be shared or withheld. This arrangement is further premised on participants engaging with them in the opposite fashion: as individuals appealing for inclusion. By virtue of this imbalance, large festivals can choose to shift risk and costs onto their participants, while still maintaining control over resources and power.

Their markets, however, can only arrive at broadly positive outcomes when they are premised on transparency, when risks and costs are shared proportionally and inform the decisions of all parties. When someone can act on behalf of another with opacity and without their bearing the full consequences of these choices, they can become more likely to make risky decisions. This is, in fact, a well-documented phenomenon in economics, described by the related concepts of the principal-agent problem and moral hazard. In sufficient proportion and without regulation, circumstances of this kind can compound and imperil entire economies.

Through this lens, we should perhaps think about the growth of large festivals quite differently. Their increase in scale, activity and number might not be indicative of their health or how well they serve exhibitors. Instead, because their necessary resources can be drawn from one set of parties and used by another without the latter party sharing equally in the downside risks, they might simply represent a massively subsidized spectacle of administration, absent the checks needed to self-regulate. The more we consider how, again, those in charge of festivals can choose to operate opaquely and with insulation from competitive pressures, the more it seems possible that this could be true. And if our ideological defaults are skewed to always locate failure with the individual, while simultaneously rendering legitimacy as something externally derived, we would be blind to this danger. Masses of exhibitors losing money at large festivals would be unlikely to be understood as exposing their market's latent illness or irrationality.

If it is the case that large festivals exist in this form, it would seem only a matter of time before they suffer a correction. Whether this would be triggered by their combined and unchecked growth exhausting exhibitors' resources or some broader, external pressure is unclear. And we can't know when this will happen because, to paraphrase Keynes, large festivals can remain irrational longer than artists can remain solvent.

But if we want independent comics to weather whatever they might face in the future, it is imperative that we work to return a sane balance to how power, resources and risk are distributed at large festivals. To do so, we must learn to act as a class when treated as a class by institutions and those in power. This is no small challenge. There is no messianic figure or set of principles that will guide us to this solution. We will have to struggle together to resist the paternalistic legacies embodied in comics ideology and structures, as well as build alternatives to them that center artists' right to self-determination.

To close out and offer a step in this direction, I'd like to suggest a few ways we can begin to do this:

- Artists, publishers and their fans should work with smaller festivals to build an alternate base of power premised on transparency, cooperation and bottom-up, democratic control. As I said, many of these festivals are already artist-run, so this isn't some huge leap. It's just about helping them understand how their own example can clarify and improve the circumstances of others. Their risk profile is much smaller and can be

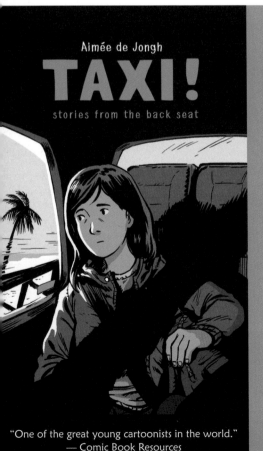

Aimée de Jongh

TAXI!

stories from the back seat

"One of the great young cartoonists in the world."
— Comic Book Resources

From one of the brightest new talents in Europe comes this debut auto-biographical work, focusing on taxi rides from four cities: Los Angeles, Paris, Jakarta, and Washington, D.C. As the drivers slowly open up about their personal lives, de Jongh does too, even when it means challenging her own ideas and prejudices. Through these vulnerable — and often humorous — moments, de Jongh finds common ground with the people driving her. *TAXI!* is an ode to taxi drivers everywhere.

"*TAXI* perfectly embodies the unique power of comics, as parallel narratives echo each other to craft an expansive, empathetic view of humanity. De Jongh is worthy of much wider acclaim as a quiet master of light and shadow, subtlety and environment. Highly recommended."
— Nate Powell

www.conundrumpress.com

made much smaller still by doing so, making them more likely to survive (and help artists survive) in the wake of some larger collapse.

- Artists and publishers need to share with each other a full account of the costs and revenues associated with large festivals. It's impossible to understand the long-term viability the large-festival model poses, nor assess their state of contradiction, if we don't have this complete, aggregate picture. Too much conspires against individual artists sharing instances of bad outcomes in the current landscape of comics, from fear of being blacklisted, sadists who delight in mocking the poor and people looking to brand themselves as "business gurus" doing more of the same. We must find safe and anonymous ways to gather and understand this information.

- Resist internalization. Our ability to create a better future depends in no small part on our refusal to believe that the status quo and its judgments are necessarily good or legitimate. It's admirable that individual artists or publishers can overcome the adverse position from which most comics begin (assuming they are not doing so by means of some outside funding or subsidy). But we shouldn't use survivorship bias to model ourselves after the best-case scenarios of a structurally dysfunctional system. We should instead work to construct new forms of meaning and value, while mitigating our exposure to harms of the present. The extent to which comics has become better and more inclusive is precisely because some of those who came before us took up this mission. ✳

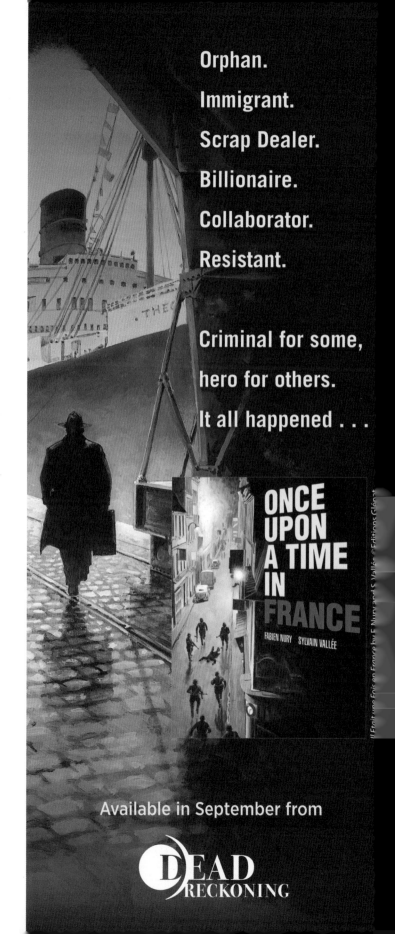

A Bad Gateway into the World of

Simon Hanselmann

Interviewed by Gary Groth

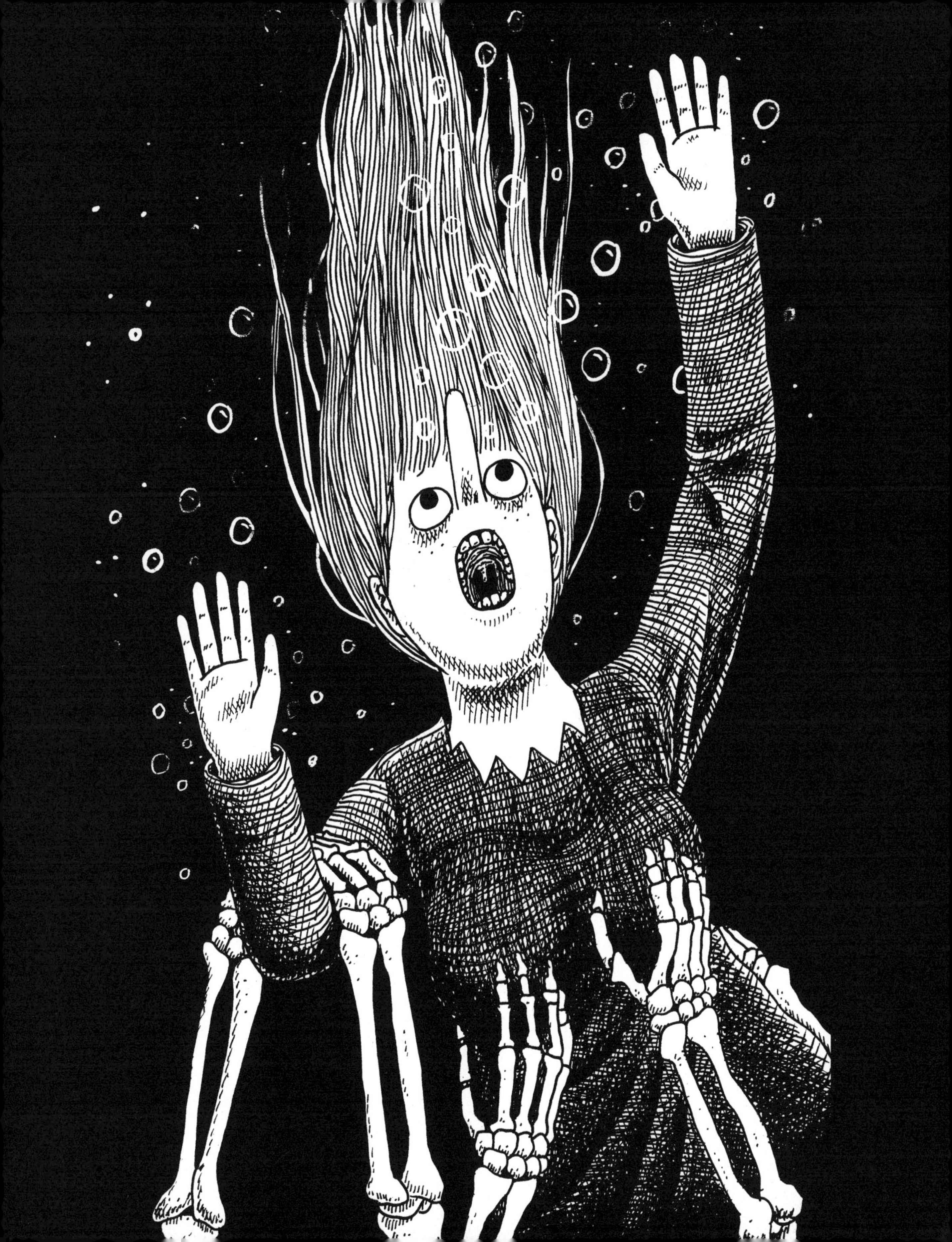

SIMON HANSELMANN WAS BORN in 1981, in the town of Launceston (pronounced Lawn-ses-ten – get it right!) on the Australian island of Tasmania. He lived there for 21 years, and – despite the fact that he describes it as a "cultureless, barren shithole" – he managed to cultivate a knowledge of and appreciation for comics (not necessarily a contradiction, now that I think of it), as well as a passionate interest in making them. His earliest influences include Carl Barks's *Donald Duck*, Morris's *Lucky Luke*, *Tintin*, *Asterix* and *Mad* magazine.

Launceston may have been colorless, but Hanselmann's life there was anything but. It was filled with extremes of love, pain, fear, confusion – out of which he seems to have learned empathy, discipline, self-reliance and an appreciation for the absurd. It also evidently served as the raw material he needed to transform incidents from life

into art. Even his high school experience was extreme. There is a generation of cartoonists (mine) whose high school years were fraught with misery and bullying and that left its mark on them and their cartooning. I can make no such generalization about Hanselmann's generation, but his high school experience was like my generation's on steroids. "I was pretty mercilessly bullied in high school. I had put quite a lot of weight on. People would spit on me at school. There were a lot of bullies that would just spit all over me. My back would literally be covered in phlegm. Once I was dragged through the mud by my legs, and even the teachers just stood around chuckling it up."

His mother worked at a bar and sold drugs on the side and became a heroin addict, which caused trouble with the local authorities, not to mention all the familial friction that would ensue therefrom. His father was a biker and quasi criminal who mostly vanished from his life when Hanselmann was 2 years old. Nonetheless he remembers his mother as loving and doing her best: "My mum did a really good job. I always had slick lunches at school. Nice sandwiches and Roll-Ups and muesli bars. She did provide a really good home." If it wasn't all roses, it wasn't all heroin, either.

At 21 or 22, he moved to Hobart, Tasmania's largest city (Launceston is the second largest), where his cultural horizons expanded. He met other cartoonists, including Grant Gronewold (aka HTML Flowers), who would become his closest friend and with whom he would occasionally collaborate. After four or five years in Hobart, he was growing restless. In 2008, he moved to Melbourne, where he lived in Gronewold's mother's garden shed. Throughout this time, he was drawing comics constantly – most prominently a long sprawling family drama titled *Girl Mountain*, never published and which the author now refers to as "shit," but which sounds like the kind of complicated, ambitious work a young artist needs to get out of his system before he can move on.

Hanselmann moved on to *Megg and Mogg*, starring characters he created in 2008. At the urging of his pal, Grant, he put some *Megg and Mogg* strips on Tumblr in 2012, which instantly attracted the attention of both fans and professionals, and which led to the fame and riches he enjoys today. I exaggerate, but he has achieved *New York Times* best-sellerdom, no small feat among those artists not drawing corporate characters. Megg and Mogg share the stage with Hanselmann's *dramatis personae*, most prominently among them being Owl, bourgeois, clueless, more conventional than the rest and often indignant at their shenanigans; and Werewolf Jones, a sybaritic beast, literally and figuratively, whose lifestyle revolves around self-inflicted damage and to whom the word *excess* does not exist. These, and a few other characters, provide Hanselmann the ensemble he needs to create an astonishingly wide scope of character dynamics and situational comedy — from the depiction of loopy *I Love Lucy*-like hijinks to drug-addled fantasies to solitary and unendurable pain. And it should not go unmentioned that Hanselmann's perspective on sexuality and gender, which permeates his work, is refreshingly liberating and latitudinarian. His characters' sexual appetites run the gamut from the conventional to the perverse and their gender preferences are fluid, and they are entirely unselfconscious about it. The secret,

I think, is that the author respects his characters' uniqueness, individuality and autonomy, and doesn't judge them (he leaves that up to the reader); nor is the openness about human sexuality presented didactically or as self-righteously enlightened. It merely is, and often hilariously so.

His earlier work, especially, was often referred to as "stoner humor." This is accurate, up to a point, but the description never sat well with me because I always thought of stoner humor as lazy and brainless and by this definition — my definition — it does a disservice to Hanselmann's work, in which there is usually (though not always) an underlying pathos and genuine connection to human feeling in these stories.

One of Hanselmann's narrative tricks, evident in even his earliest work, is to lure readers in with humor and weirdness, then whipsaw them with truth. Even in his first book, *Megahex* (2014), there is plenty of scatological humor, drugs and dissolution mixed in with a freewheeling nihilism, but all this, in a way, is a decoy. There are stories, for example, like the two-page "Silver Sequin Mini Skirt," about the futility of trying to avoid pain; the three-page "Bad Brains," which depicts an ineffable and inexplicable sadness (or melancholy or anomie) so powerful it hurts; or the two-page "Rimming," about the paradox of sexual incongruity between lovers — all deeply affecting as well as masterpieces of formal

RIGHT: From *Megahex,* 2014.

OPPOSITE: From *Megg and Mogg in Amsterdam,* 2016.

concision. (He couldn't achieve such effect without mastery of the formal elements of comics – timing, pacing, visual rhythms, all learned autodidactically.) He can also be expansive: His longer stories are intricately woven comedy dramas, balancing a fidelity to the internal consistency of the characters with plot-driven mayhem. Stories like "Amsterdam," "Jobs" and "Heat Wave" read like a mash-up between Preston Sturges and Frank Tashlin, with a little S. Clay Wilson- or R. Crumb-style transgression casually thrown in just to keep the reader a little uncomfortable.

Bad Gateway (2019) is certainly his most accomplished and humane work to date. His previous three books were composed of short stories ranging from one to 52 pages, but *Gateway* was conceived and executed as a single, stand-alone novel-length story. It's his most intensely autobiographical story, couched in the lives of the characters he's breathed life into for more than 10 years, proof of their protean, imaginative applicability.

This interview was conducted over two sessions in Simon Hanselmann's living room in his Seattle home in February and March. In person, he is funny, smart,

loquacious and opinionated – as you will see. He seems to accept the more distressing aspects of his upbringing with equanimity (though his work may indicate less sanguinity), he speaks eloquently about his creative process and is alarmed by the more punitive effusions of social media.

[Full disclosure: For those who are not aware of it, Fantagraphics Books is Simon Hanselmann's publisher.]

Gary Groth
April 2019

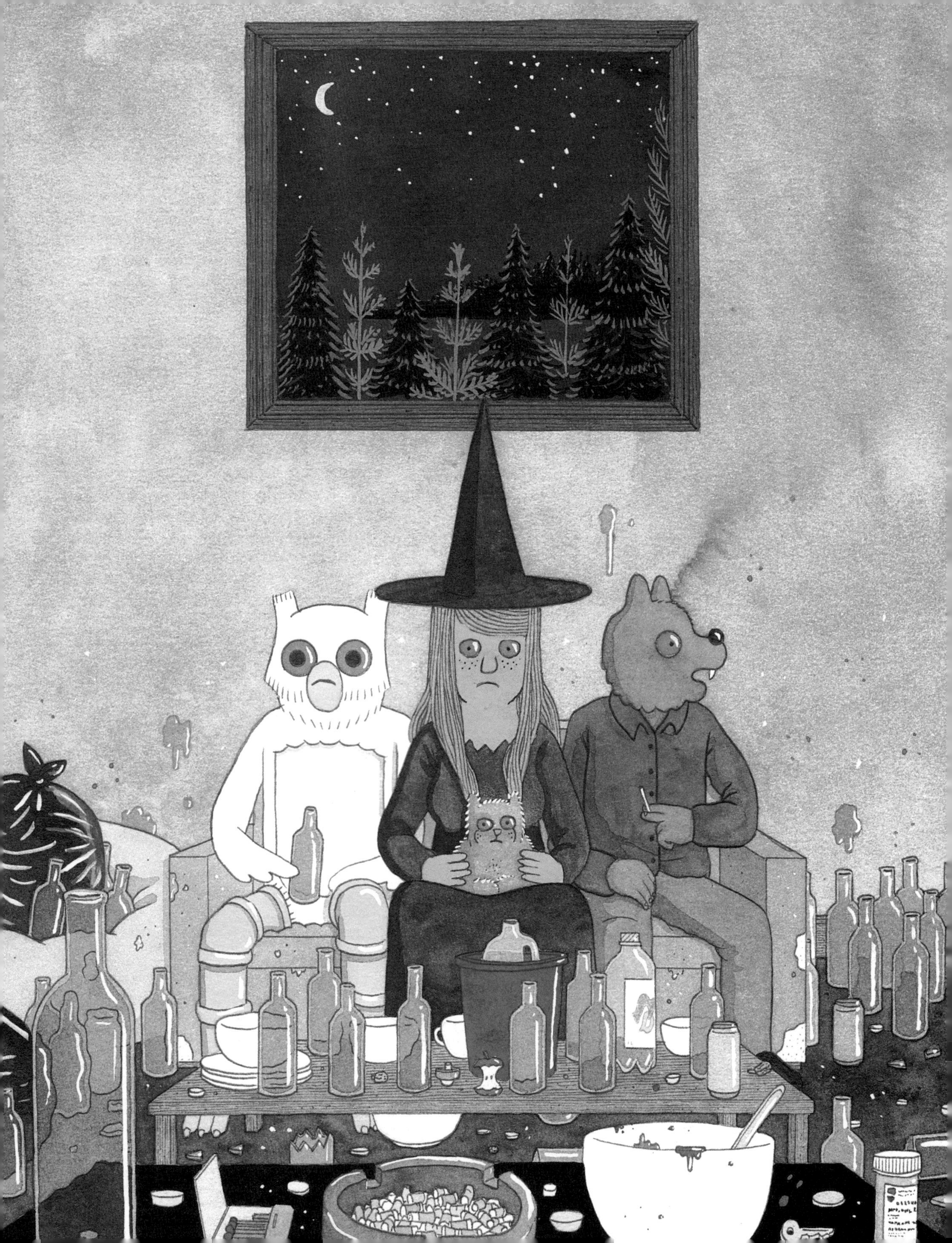

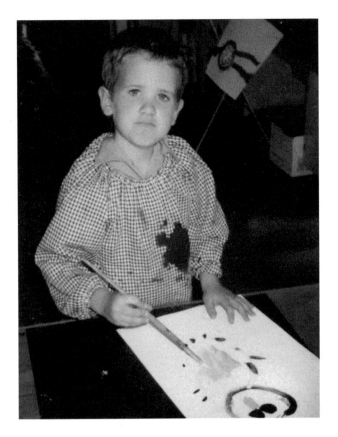

ABOVE: Hanselmann painting an owl in 1986.

Growing Up In Tasmania

GARY GROTH: I know a lot about your background, culled from a variety of interviews, but I'd like get to a fuller, more complete picture of your life. So, you were born in – Lawn-kes-tawn? [*Hanselmann laughs.*] How do you pronounce that?

SIMON HANSELMANN: Launceston. Lawn-ses-ten. [*Laughs.*]

What was Launceston like? It was a very small town.

A cultureless, barren shithole. I used to get bullied a lot. I'd wear a scarf around and I'd hear, "Hey faggot!" and I'd get beaten up.

Backwoods and rednecky?

Yeah, very rednecky, very racist. Very white, very homophobic and all that stuff. Just small town. There were no bands there.

There were no galleries. If you were a kid, there was a skate ramp at the park and you could go smash bottles there and finger each other. No gay fingering, though! We're famous for our Blockie Route [a system of city blocks where people cruise in their cars]. It's perfectly set up, the lights and the structure of the street so you can perfectly drive around. So, everyone drives around in their hotted-up cars and harasses people like me, that's what the kids do. But I was always a nerd.

You weren't driving around in such a car.

No, I've never driven. I still don't have my license. I never did that. I stayed home. I drew comics, I watched TV, I made puppet shows. I was a nerd.

My mother did some questionable things, but always kept a pretty clean house and always kept books in the house. I was a latchkey kid. I liked comics…I was exposed to a lot of roughness, but I somehow maintained a level of weird poshness. Somehow.

Were you a nerd because you felt alienated from the culture there?

Yeah, I remember my mother did a lot of bar work and I was stuck at the bars and played with my G.I. Joes under the pool table. And I'd hang out upstairs with the biker kids and we'd watch porno and horror films when I was like 5. I recently tracked down what the porno was – my friend Leon tracked it down. It was this prison porno where this kitten gets stepped on by this busty blonde with high heels, and it stuck with me forever. And just creepy serial-killer horror films, y'know.

Biker kids – those were the children of bikers?

Yeah, biker kids. There was Josh, this big-bearded tough biker.

You were a biker kid, weren't you? Your father was a biker.

Yeah, my father was a Satan's Rider. "Chopper" Reed was around. You've heard of "Chopper" Reed? He was a friend of my father's. He used to come to the house and my mother was like "Ugh." His ears were all chopped off from prison. This guy took me to the snow when I was 5, what was his fucking name – Sid! He got shot by "Chopper" and put into a car boot and driven around.

What did he actually do for a living?

He was just a biker. A criminal, I guess.

But that doesn't pay well, does it?

I think the Clubhouse is pretty well off. Organized crime does all right.

He was actually a criminal?

Yeah. They were killing people. I'd hear about bodies and bags of lime. They'd put them up near the old prospector's mill or something. I'd overhear scary things when I was a kid. My mother's boyfriend for a time, Graham Lee, he used to go down to the park where the gay people hung out, and reportedly – this is what I heard – he used to force them to blow him at gunpoint. The *power* really got him off. He became a born-again Christian wicker-furniture salesman, but he used to terrify me. He touched me a bit as a kid as well, I remember that. No penetration, just a bit of finger diddling. He was a terrifying, terrifying man.

He was abusive to you?

Yeah, he diddled me a bit. Touched my dong. Which, I don't think has really messed

ABOVE LEFT: Drawn in 2008 and appeared in the first *Megg and Mogg* minicomic in 2009.

ABOVE RIGHT: From *Werewolf Jones and Sons* #1 by Hanselmann and HTML Flowers, 2015.

me up – I don't worry about it. But I got touched a bit. Nothing too bad. People have it far worse, if you were born in Ghana or something. And there were a lot of dog fuckers around as well. I tell my dog fucker stories. But I'm trying to save most of that for *Megg and Mogg*.

Literally?

Three separate instances of me witnessing dog fucking.

Between humans and dogs?

Some local junkies and friends of my mother – [a] mulleted, bespectacled man and his poodle-haired wife. We went around to score some pot or something, me and my ma, and went around the side of the house – and saw Judy in the window. She was up against the wall getting fucked by their big Afghan dog while Ross was watching in the corner. And it was like, "We'll come back later!" And another thing at some biker man's house. Weird shit like that. But it's all grist for the mill, I'm thankful for all this weird shit. I've got this all written down and it's gonna make great comics.

But anyway, my dad left when I was 2.

Did you ever see him again?

[*Deep breath.*] Very briefly. He became a police informant and narced on the Satan's Riders. And they blew his bike up with a pipe bomb. He moved to Western Australia and became a miner. Iron ore. He drove the Haulpak machines, I think they're called, the big fucking trucks with the big fucking wheels the size of buildings. So, he'd drive those around.

My mother and I moved when I was 6 or 7 to Newman, a tiny mining town, all red dirt and dingoes. We lived there for like a year, maybe. He was abusive. I think they'd fight and he'd hit my ma. I'd hide under chairs. I think my ma started fucking some friend of his up there. There was some woman who was trying to kick-start her bike – Trudy, or

some tough woman – slipped her leg off the kick stand and it came back and tore her leg up, blood everywhere. That sticks in my mind. And just playing in the gutters, getting beat up by this little Aboriginal girl at the swimming pool. And she stole my *Star Wars* figures. There's a big Aboriginal community up there and they walk around naked with big sheets of $50 bills at the Woolworths, all this government money. And just racial tension in this small, weird town, with all these rich miners coming in.

How big was this mining town? Was it actually a town?

There was a Woolworths and a chicken shack and a bar where all the prostitutes had their caravans out back. And you'd go to the town dump and it was all new televisions, boxes of *Mad* magazines, Barbie Dream Houses in full working condition. The miners would just come, make the money, dump everything, all this great stuff, and leave. They weren't gonna take it with them. My ma would always say, "Go and do it. Go work in the mines for a couple of years, and you can make a lot of money." But I was way too much of a pussy to do that. You can make a lot of money doing it. But I think my dad almost died a few times. Like getting drowsy and almost driving off a cliff in the quarry.

You were about 6 when you moved to the mining town in Newman?

Yeah, I remember when I first got there, there was a mix-up with my luggage, and I took the wrong suitcase. I was a little kid. "Oh, I'll grab my suitcase." I go home with my dad, just me alone – my mom was coming later, I think – and it was all girl clothes in there. This plays into all my gender stuff. And he freaked the fuck out. Screaming at me, and screaming on the phone to my mother: "What the fuck are you doing to him, dressing him in all this shit!?" And my mother was like, "Dude, wrong suitcase. Like, what the fuck?"

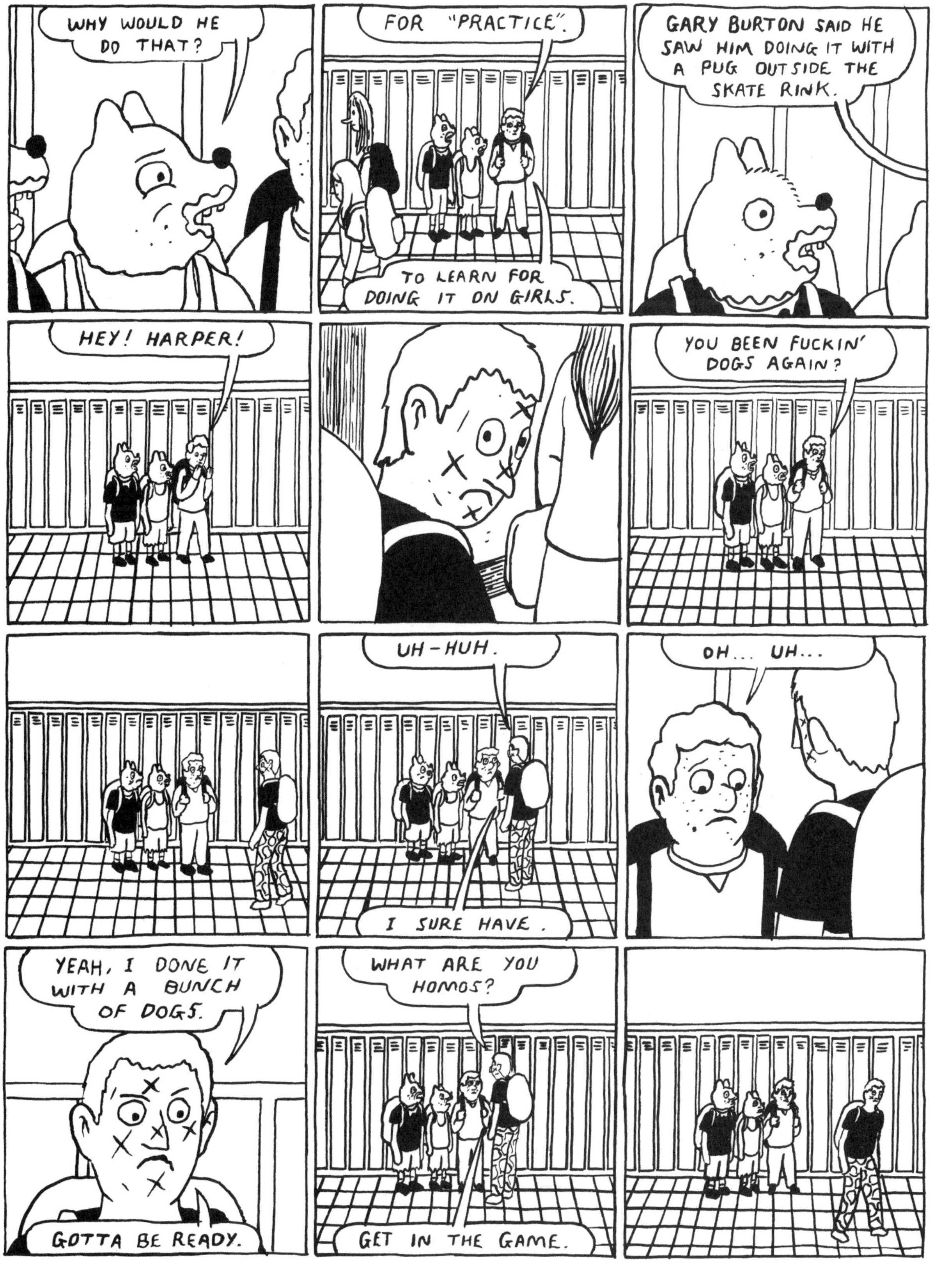
WHY WOULD HE DO THAT?
FOR "PRACTICE".
TO LEARN FOR DOING IT ON GIRLS.
GARY BURTON SAID HE SAW HIM DOING IT WITH A PUG OUTSIDE THE SKATE RINK.
HEY! HARPER!
YOU BEEN FUCKIN' DOGS AGAIN?
UH-HUH.
I SURE HAVE.
OH... UH...
YEAH, I DONE IT WITH A BUNCH OF DOGS.
GOTTA BE READY.
WHAT ARE YOU HOMOS?
GET IN THE GAME.

ABOVE: Hanselmann self-portrait, circa mid-'90s.

I guess he wanted me. He had a new wife, Beth. She was a music teacher. She seemed like a nice lady. I haven't seen my dad since I was 13. He with Beth and Amy, her daughter and my stepsister, we went on a family vacation to Bali, which I barely remember. I remember him drinking a lot and leaving me to walk home late at night, which was fucking terrifying. And apparently, I got really bitchy to Beth and said to her, "You're not my real mother!" I have no memory of that, but apparently, I was a real little shit.

And you were 13?

Yeah. They were like, "Drink! Kids drink here!" And I didn't want to. I was like, "No, no, no, I don't wanna." I was a nerdy kid. I was very fat at the time, just this little fat kid wearing a Hawaiian shirt. Just really fucking dorky.

Did you know your father from the age of 6 to 13, or was there an interruption because you lived in different places?

No, there was interruption. We were up there for a year in the mining town, then went back to Launceston and didn't see him again until that trip. My mother always said that he was a good guy and paid child support and he's always supported me. And then I found out later that he didn't. He never paid child support. She bought me a big letter-writing set and forced me to write to him, and he never wrote back. And we stopped talking in the end. I haven't talked to him in like six years. My ma would always say, "Come on, you've got to try." But he'd just talk about his off-road trail biking, like, "I broke my legs on the trail-bike track but I'm back on the bikes." He's a macho dude, and I'm like [*feigns a twee voice:*], "I like doing my little comic books. My Tumblr. And I work at a bookstore now." I think I called him for his birthday and then he didn't call back for my birthday, and I was just like, "Aw, fuck it."

He also sat me down and told me that my mother was a drug addict. He was trying to win me over to him—he was trying to steal me away from my ma. He told me that she was a junkie and a bad woman. I was like 6 and confused. I vividly remember him saying, "I've still got the needles, I can prove it." I told my ma that and she was like, "Why would he still have the needles? That's fucking weird." She told me when I was 9, officially, that she was a drug addict. It was all true. I mean, I knew, but...

He was trying to turn you against her. For the purposes of securing guardianship exclusively?

And he said some weird pro-Hitler stuff and I couldn't tell if he was joking. My grandfather's a Nazi, my dad's family is German. He came to Australia in the '60s and was naturalized, so I couldn't get German citizenship, which sucked. Anyway. I think that maybe he's actually a racist. We have nothing in common. I don't have daddy issues; I don't miss him. He was never there. My mother provided everything.

Is there a sense in which you regret not having a father around?

Yeah, I'd probably be more normal and less fucked up. But then again, I'm happy. I've made something of myself, and done what I set out to do. I've got a great wife and a decent house, and I've made a living for myself. So, I wouldn't really change anything. I don't believe in stressing out about the past. Like, "Ohh, what could have been?" That would erase what I have right now. You know, just roll with the punches …

So you lived in Newman for one year.

I think so.

And why did you move back to Launceston?

Because my ma and dad were screaming at each other, and he was probably hitting her and stuff. I dunno. [*Laughs.*]

Was your father married to Beth when you were living in Newman?

No, I think that must've happened after, in between me being 7 and 13.

Your parents were together in Newman.

I think they were trying again. Maybe for me. It's all blurry. I was a fucking kid. Secondhand blurry memories.

When he left when you were 2, you didn't know him. You can't really know your father when you're 2.

No. Not long distance as a 2-year-old to a 5-year-old, no. I just knew him at 7, and then the Bali trip, and then talking on the phone. He helped me out in 2008 when I wanted to move to the U.K. He gave me three grand, which was very generous at the time. I've never asked my mother for money. I give her a lot of fucking money. I've never relied on my parents. But I was fucking desperate. The internet was blooming, so it was like, "You can masturbate on camera for money!" I was desperate, so I thought that maybe I could do that.

I didn't want to have a real job. I was living in a garden shed and working on comics and trying to really make something of myself with that. So, I begged my dad. He got in trouble with the tax man, he said. He was still mining and was a helicopter rescue man. He was doing all right. He'd moan about his cars blowing up, and the tax man. But he gave me three grand, that was good of him. It got me to the U.K. I blew it real fast. Got some jobs.

All I know is that your mother worked at a biker bar. When did she work at a biker bar, and what did she do before and after that for most of your upbringing?

Well, fuck. She was born in 1960 to a very schizophrenic woman, my grandmother.

How old was your father when you were born?

He was like 10 years older, so 31 or so, something like that. My mother became a heroin addict when she was 18. Her parents broke up. My grandfather was an ad man or something. I imagine him like a '60s Don Draper type. And he started fucking his secretary and left my grandmother with five kids. So, my mother's experience in childhood was really brutal. She has the same birthday as my grandfather, she was the favorite, and he was always doting on her. When she was 5 he just left with the secretary and left the kids with their schizophrenic mother who was like, "The bad men are coming," and would lock them up in the shed all fucking night. "The bad men are coming! The bad men are coming!" Just freaking these kids out. And she'd eat cigarettes in front of them and was convinced that they were feeding her dead bodies. It was rough.

So, my mother went off the rails. She went to some Catholic boarding school. She was shipped back and forth, I forget the chronology. But she became a sharpie. There were skins and sharpies, so she wore the mod cardigans and had a shaved head and stuff.

> " I was this fucking pariah, and then I hated going to school. So, I wouldn't go. And my ma would say to the school, 'Look, he doesn't want to come. I'm gonna take him to the beach.' "

Is that the equivalent of a gang?

Yeah, basically. But a fashion kind of gang. It was big in Australia. She was living with her father, packed off when she was 13 at the airport. He gave her $20 and a pack of cigarettes, and sent her back to her schizophrenic mother. And my mother has not left Launceston since that point. She got with a shitty guy who got her onto heroin, and then she's been a drug addict ever since. She used to deal a lot. She'd work at the biker bars, and that's when she met my father – through the biker and bar scene. She was hanging out at the bars. Met my father, a biker. Started working at the Trades Hall.

A little biker bar networking.

Yeah, she went to lots of different bars for years. And then she got out of that scene and, when I was like 13, 14, 15, she ran a video game arcade. This American dude,

Colin, moved to town and opened up the big arcade called Family Fun. I'd go in there after school with my friends. He had greasy, slicked-back hair and had these stocking socks with sandals and walked around with a plastic cup of coins giving out change by hand. I think that was the first day it opened. And the next day, based on me talking about this arcade, my mom went down and asked for a job. And she worked there for like three years. Colin was in love with her, clearly.

My mother was quite hot back in the day. She kind of looked like Laura Dern: long blonde hair, thin, tall, wore heels, made an effort – a very functional drug addict. Liquid morphine was her drug of choice. And she was dealing a bit, that ramped up later. But she ran the games arcade. He was a shitty boss. She'd work 18-hour shifts, sleep out the back and then drive an hour to the second store that had opened up in Devonport up along the coast and sleep in the backroom there. She just worked to the bone for minimum wage. It was a shitty, unregulated cash-in-hand job. And she worked at some other shitty little milk bar take-away making rotten chicken sandwiches for some fat cunt who ran it. She used to scrub the urinals at the army barracks for a while. I used to hang out at the army barracks and read choose-your-own-adventure books when I was 8.

What was your life like? Did you accompany her to these jobs?

I would. After school, I hung out at the games arcade, and I would also sleep out the back. If I went to fucking school, because a third of the year I'd go to school but normally I'd just leave once I got there. But when she was working I could just go home. I could leave school and go home and draw and watch TV. Fuck it. Fuck school.

How did you graduate from one year to the next if you were only in school a third of the time?

Eh, it's public school, they just put you through. [*Groth laughs.*] It wasn't dependent on grades really. I dropped out of year 10. Elementary school, one through six, I went to enough. The first few years, I had a good time in school. It was fine, I had friends. In grade four or so was when I started getting bullied a lot. I still had a good group of core friends, and some of my friends were bullies as well. Just poor kids who were really abused by their parents and became bullies. But we had a close-knit group of friends. We'd make comics together. I'd sell my comics at school, self-publish them.

Did you have friends who protected you? Like one friend who would protect you from another bully?

Yeah, my big friend, Lockwood. He was my mom's junkie friend's son, and we were friends, and he would bully people like crazy. He went to jail eventually for manslaughter. But he protected me. All through grade six people called me a homo, the whole time. And they spat on me. This one girl, Carmen, who used to be my friend early on, just kept calling me a fag and a homo, and everyone started doing it. I was this fucking pariah, and then I hated going to school. So, I wouldn't go. And my ma would say to the school, "Look, he doesn't want to come. I'm gonna take him to the beach." My mother was very good early on. We'd ride our bikes around, we'd go hang out at streams and have picnics. It was nice. She was trying to be this picture-perfect, Hallmark mother, and she did manage it for a good long while. With all the weird shit that went on …

For how long did she manage it?

Until I left. Her downfall was me leaving. I think she wanted to marry me, basically, in a weird psychological way. I was her husband. Her special boy. And I left, I moved away. And I just saw her crumble.

Do you feel guilty about that?

ABOVE: Hanselmann drawings, circa early '90s.

Oh, yeah, constantly. My morals, drummed into me by TV, tell me I should go down and help her now. She's in the hospital. She's got no one – like fucking no one. I feel like I should go down there. But I've gone down before, put her in rehab, I've done all this shit. I can't fucking do it.

She's a grown-up and has to take care of herself.

Exactly. I don't need a daughter right now. It's fucking unfair. But it really haunts me. But she was really high functioning for a while and worked a lot of shitty jobs. She kept the house pretty good.

Let me go back to your school days. You were called a "fag." Was that a generic pejorative, or was that something specific about you – such as the way you acted, or your demeanor at the time?

I think it was mostly generic.

So, they weren't sensing gender issues and pouncing.

Melbourne. It was much better in the '90s, it sucks now. I went there, and I was talking to the clerk about some Marvel trading cards, and he called upstairs and said, "I've got this little girl here, she's asking about these Marvel trading cards." And I was just like, "I'm a boy! I've been talking to you for 10 fucking minutes!" I guess I had a feminine vibe. I was struggling with gender issues since I was like 5.

I wanted to wear girl's clothes, and I didn't know what was wrong with me. There was no internet, so you couldn't do research. You could go to the library, look up weird stuff in books … And my mother always called people derogatory names. And all the kids – it was a small town! So they sensed something. When I was 26 I worked in a primary school, I was a teacher's aide for a year. And all the kids would tease me about being a cross-dresser. I was like, "That's so astute, how do you know?" [*Laughs.*] They sensed it. I don't fucking know.

You said your mother was quite homophobic and "slurry."

Oh, still is. Yesterday on the phone she was like, "Guess who's in the hospital?" I was like, "Who?" "The faggot." And I was like, "I told you not to say that!" A bunch of her friends are gay, though. She has so many gay friends and still makes all these slurs.

Does she acknowledge they're gay? Or does she pretend they're not gay?

No, she knows they are. But it just repulses her. She's just a classic homophobe. "Oh, it's disgusting. I don't wanna see them kissing. It's fine, but I don't want to see them touching."

Do you simply avoid that subject, or do you lecture her?

Oh, I tell her off, these days. Back in the day I think I'd just go, "Ugh," but I wouldn't yell at her. But I have lectured her endlessly.

When I was 11 years old, I was in Birchalls, the newsagent in town where you could buy comics and pens, and I was looking at the magazines and comics. I could feel some boys staring at me, and I heard them whispering, "Oh, yeah. She's all right, but she hasn't got any tits." And they're looking at me! So, I was like, "What? I'm a boy!" I think I was always kind of feminine. I was a bit portly. I was growing my hair long at the time. I was into the Red Hot Chili Peppers, so I wanted to have long hair. I guess I looked kind of girly.

Another time, my mother and I went on a trip to Melbourne and these girls on the escalator – who clearly knew I was a boy – were like, "Ooh, is it a boy or a girl? Ooh." And I was weeping. We went to Minotaur, a really good comic shop in

To no effect, I assume.

Like, "I've traveled the world, mother, and know lots of different people. And I am respectful of people and diversity. Don't say that shit around me." There was a lot of negative reinforcement going on with that shit.

Is it safe to say that you retreated into pop culture because of your social situation?

It's escapism. That's what nerds do, you escape into *Dungeons & Dragons* or miniatures or comic books or TV, whatever you can find.

It's remarkable how similar your and my experience was. I mean, mine wasn't nearly as dramatic as yours, but the bullying, all of that.

It felt like *The Walking Dead* outside. It felt like there were just roaming, horrible fucking people who wanted to fuck you up, so you just wanted to stay inside and delve into fantasy. What's wrong with that?

Pop Culture

You said there was a lot of pop culture available in this miserable town. How did that happen? I mean, you had access to so many comics. You talk about *Mad* magazine, you read a lot of *Donald Duck*…

And *Punch*, I read a lot of *Punch* annuals. *Garfield*, *Footrot Flats*, anything I could get my hands on.

How were these available? Were there drugstores, newsstands?

Mostly secondhand stores. I think I read that back in the day *Hate* and *Eightball* were shipping 20,000 units per issue. My theory is that pre-internet, people were desperate for content. All these record stores were ordering this shit. And people needed

this shit! We needed analogue content, so it was everywhere. First I started going to secondhand stores that had all sorts of stacks of *Garfield* and *Mad* magazines. I started reading *Asterix* and *Tintin* in school.

Lucky Luke.

Yeah, all the kids wanted to read that shit. Like, "Oh, where's your Richard Scarrys and *Lucky Luke*s?" Trying to get the best ones. We all wanted that stuff. We loved comics. So, I was getting stuff at the secondhand stores, and one of them started ordering in American magazines and American superhero comics and displaying them. They were trying to become the shop. They later became Empire Comics when I was like 11.

And it was a front for drugs, as I found out because I had some friends who worked there. And Labyrinth was a front for drugs and Electric Adventures. They were all fronts for drugs, all these comic shops. And all those guys who worked there had crushes on my mother. She'd come in there all Laura Dern-y, and they were obsessed with her. This one guy Dean would come over to the house and bring me early comics issues, like, "Here's the new *Punisher: War Zone* #1. I brought it around for you, Simon. You look at that while I look at your mother's tits." And they'd just fucking hang around. So, I became friends with all the shop owners.

LEFT: From *Lucky Luke*
Vol. 8: *Calamity Jane*.
By Goscinny and Morris,
originally published in 1971.
Translation by Pablo Vela.

ABOVE: From *The Amazing Spider-Man* #339, Sept. 1990. Written by David Michelinie; penciled by Erik Larsen; inked by Randy Emberlin, Mike Machlan, John Romita and Keith Williams; colored by Mike Rockwitz, Bob Sharen and Gregory Wright; lettered by Rick Parker.

Were you aware that that was what was going on at the time?

Yeah. And I was always verbose and friendly, so they were like, "Who's this weird kid with the hot mother?" I was shopping at all these shops, and they started getting in all the American shit, and they had *Hate* and *Eightball* and *Black Hole* on the shelf. I made friends with some stonery dudes that lived down the road when I was like 13, and they got me watching *Twin Peaks* and showed me all the good comics. I mean, I saw them on the shelves and bought *Wizard* magazine. I read "Palmer's Picks" and saw Jim Woodring in there, and was like, "What's all this weird shit?"

That would have been in the early '90s?

Yeah, '92 or so, '93? We were all obsessed with superhero comics in school for a while. We had all the new Image comics in our desks. "Oh, [Todd] McFarlane's left Marvel and [Erik] Larsen and all of them created their own company! Ooh, *Spawn* and *Youngblood*!" But that lasted about two years, and those stoner dudes down the street were like, "You should check out this stuff. Check out Joe Matt and stuff." I was 13 reading *Peepshow* and *Hate*, and that set me off on my path, and I never looked back.

You said you started making your own comics at the age of 5. Is that right?

Yeah, I started drawing comics since about I was about 5.

And you said the first comics you drew were, quote, "A direct rip-off of *Spy Vs. Spy*," is that right?

Well, that was when I was 8. I self-published some *Spy Vs. Spy* rip-off books. But I think *Garfield* comics were the first comics I drew. Or maybe *Spider-Man*, my first comic might've been a *Spider-Man* comic when I was 5. I think in an interview once I said it gave me a boner, Spider-Man being tied up by Doctor Octopus. I found it erotic. I got an erection from Spider-Man being all tied up. I was also obsessed with some weird ad for a Marvel phone line. Doctor Octopus behind bars. All this imagery got stuck in my mind. But then I just went on a hard cartooning kick. It was all about the *Asterix* and all that shit. I loved *Garfield*. And I was obsessed with *Footrot Flats* by Murray Ball, the New Zealand newspaper thing. I liked *Snake Tales* by Sols, another Australian thing. I think my uncle fucked Sols's daughter for a while.

Is that why Mogg looks like a descendent of Garfield?

Oh definitely, the Garfield cheeks. And Owl has the Tintin puffs, his ears. Megg has the Lisa Simpson ripple on the dress. All the characters work in silhouette as well, that's the strength of the *Megg and Mogg* characters, they're all recognizable in silhouette. I've read that's a key feature for good characters.

So at the age of 5 you started drawing comics, and at the age of 8 you start self-publishing comics and selling them in school?

Yeah. I think I might've gotten the idea from my friend Luke. He was my rich friend, his parents owned a wood heating store. They had a nice big house. We're still friends, I guess we talk every couple of years. He moved to L.A. to work at Dreamworks. He actually got out of Tasmania as well. We both dropped out of school at the same time and we both fucking worked our asses off and got where we wanted to be. He used to sell these drawings. When he was 6 or 7 he'd go to his dad's store and run off all these bootlegs of *Transformers* coloring books, and he'd go out into the streets and say, "Hello, Sir, would you like to buy one of these coloring sheets for your son or daughter?" Like a lemonade stand. He was an enterprising young man.

So we were both into comics and collected comics together, and I guess we put two and two together and thought that we could print our own comics on his dad's office machine and sell them at school for a buck a pop – free Garfield Band-Aid taped on the front of every issue. We weren't exposed to self-publishing culture. I think when I was maybe 12 or 13 I discovered a local dude in Launceston who self-published comics. Like, he put them in the comic shop. And I was like, "Wow, there's someone else!" I met him years later, and he was a nice guy. But yeah, we just got the idea and fucking did it. Just flat sheets, stapled them through, nothing fancy. Later on, in high school we figured out how to fold booklets and use a long-armed stapler.

ABOVE: From *Bad Gateway*, 2019.

And then the Hobart years, every government office there was required to provide you water, telephones, fax machine, free Xerox copies. So, the whole fucking scene was in there doing their band posters and their zines. Big 100-page zines, just people in there all day utilizing those services. That was a golden era. The comics scene in Hobart was fucking great.

Do you still have some of those?

I do. I've got them somewhere. It was like Dune, the [drink-and-draw group] they have [in Seattle]. We did a 24-hour thing, like everyone, every month would get together, and we'd just get fucked up, blotto, draw shit for 24 hours and go to the government office to print it all up.

You also drew funny animal comics?

Yeah, I had a bunch of characters.

ABOVE: *Footrot Flats* strip by Murray Ball, 1979.

And that was based on what? What funny animal comics were you exposed to? I guess *Garfield* could qualify.

Just all that crap like *Footrot Flats*.

What *Donald Duck* did you read? Was it the Barks *Donald Duck*?

Yeah, fuck, I was buying a lot of *Donald Duck*. I can't remember the brand, was it Gladstone? The imprint in Australia didn't say who it was. I remember years later in my teens thinking how weird it was that it didn't have a proper publisher on them. Like we had a weird Marvel sub-distributor in the '70s or '80s. There was a relaunch of Disney, in the '90s on the newsstands. They were everywhere. And newer stuff like *Goof Troop* and *Junior Woodchucks*. They were reprinting classic Barks stuff and also newer stuff. They actually did credit the artists in there, which was not usually Disney's thing.

There could've been Don Rosa in there too.

Oh, there would've been a lot of Rosa, yeah. I was reading a ton of that stuff. I had a shirtless whale character called Omar, and a cat called Mogg-Mogg, and there was a now super-racist Mexican bird character called Taco Pedro that wore a sombrero. Stuff that wouldn't fly now. They were full of blatant small-town homophobia and just rampant shit, just bad. I mean, TV back then – I was really into bawdy Australian

sketch comedy, there was a show called *Full Frontal*. And *Fast Forward* and *The D-Generation*. Shaun Micallef I think is still brilliant, and Eric Bana, who played Chopper in the *Chopper* movie, he started out in these Australian sketch comedy shows.

Was *The Mysterious Cities of Gold* a big influence?

Yeah, I used to watch that and *Astro Boy*, all those things. But I feel like I was lucky. I've rewatched some of this Australian comedy from the '90s, and it still holds up. It's good. I think it's almost as good as the American shit that was happening over here. Alternative, edgy comedy like *The Kids in the Hall*. I was exposed to a lot of that, and that influenced me as well.

***The Mysterious Cities of Gold* was manga essentially, or manga derived. Was manga any kind of influence?**

No, it wasn't. That came generations after. I mean, all the kids now in their 20s were just pumped full of that. I remember it coming along, I remember when anime started to be distributed because I was looking at *Previews* since I was like 11, just pouring through this big phone book.

You'd see these in comic book shops?

Yeah, I'd get them and go through them. I knew what *Ren & Stimpy* was two years before it came to Tasmanian television. I knew what it was, because I just kept up with pop culture. You could buy *Previews* and figure out what everything was. You read *Wizard*, you read all these fucking magazines, and you knew what this shit was.

Peers

I think you said that your adversarial position with your peer group started in the fourth grade.

I guess so.

How did it that conflict evolve through high school? It's my experience that it only gets worse, more violent and more damaging.

Oh, yeah. In high school I was brutally beaten and spat upon. I'd go to science class, I remember, and these kids would just sit behind me and hock up big loogies. My back would be covered in phlegm. The teacher, Mr. Button, he was a fucking moron, I don't think he liked me anyways, so he just let it happen. I played soccer for a while on the B team, and this one bully dragged me around in the rain, just soaked me. And the teachers were laughing. I'd go home and be soaked and muddy for the half-an-hour-long trip. It's like, "We're driving past my house pretty much, can you drop me off?" "No, no, we have to go all the way to the school." "Oh great, I just have to come back to the bus circle and wait for an hour to get home." The cunts. Just injustice, you know. But I was a fucking nerd, like I was saying earlier.

And you were treated like this for what reason?

I was a tubby kid with long hair who wore Hawaiian shirts, collected comic books and played Pogs. And I got into painting the little *Warhammer* miniatures, the little

goblins that you paint. I was a nerd. I wasn't getting any pussy.

ABOVE: From *One More Year*, 2017.

You weren't into sports [*semi-sarcastically*].

I was periodically popular because I could draw. I'd draw pictures of Nickelodeon characters fucking each other, and people were like, "Ahh, that's so funny. Now draw Ren fucking Stimpy, ha ha ha." I saw that in Chester Brown's *The Playboy*, the jocks getting him to draw posters for the mixer. I was that person. I used drawing and comedy to ingratiate myself.

And mitigate the horror.

And I got in trouble for selling books. The principal sat me down and said, "You can't do this. You can't just self-publish." And I said, "Well, there's the *Riverside Gazette*, a community newspaper, that's a local self-published thing. Yes, you can. You can't stop me from doing this." I was doing all these comics about fucking and violence. I was reading Buddy Bradley and stuff, and I was trying to imitate that. I was trying to do this raunchy, sexy, violence funny animal thing. And obviously, the teachers didn't like me trying to sell pornography

to people. [*Groth laughs.*] But that was the last straw. I dropped out of year 10, I was like, "Fuck this." But I did go back. I went back for year 11, which was like college. It's still high school, but it's separate. In Australia, seven through 10 is high school, and college is 11 and 12. Private schools do it all together, public schools separate them. So, I went back for 11th, and started doing 12th, but dropped out. I passed 11th grade, but dropped out of 12th.

So you dropped out twice.

Yeah! And I did actually go back to TAFE, as well, which was a community college type thing. I went to learn about IT when I was 21, but that was me and my stoner friend, John. We'd drink vodka and cordial and get fucked up, and go to these computer classes and just look at pornography on the computers. But college was all right. I didn't get bullied in year 11. It was me and my friend, Luke. We would fight all the time, but we were good friends. We were drawing comics, working on the school newspaper

as the cartoonists, we were having a good time. We were stoners, we'd go get stoned. We'd try to call in bomb threats to the school to get out of class so we could just go home.

Did that work?

No, it didn't. We had to sit in class really nervous just waiting for them to tell us we could leave. And we had to stay, so we were like, "Fuck! It didn't work!" and just get paranoid and stoned.

I understand you started smoking pot at age 13?

Fuck no, I was like 8 when I first smoked pot. I had a psychotic episode. My friend Lockwood, my tough bully friend, I stayed at his house on his 8th birthday. And his parents weren't there, so he got into all their bongs, and we smoked drugs. Apparently, I went crazy and was running around in the dark. I wouldn't stop shouting and maniacally laughing. Nobody got any sleep.

And there was this guy called "Jason the Poofter," that was his nickname. He was a gay gentleman, and he lived out in Lockwood's shed. And there are all these drawings he'd done on the wall of his shed, good drawings, of women shoving crucifixes in their pussies and bleeding everywhere and ants eating their shit. Quite amazing outsider art. We'd hang out in the shed and bash bullets with hammers and get shrapnel on our hands. Anyway, he was supposed to be coming back the night of that party to watch us, but he never showed, and someone was trying to break into the house. We were these stoned 8-year-olds with butcher knives from the kitchen, and we chased off these creepy men, over the fence. Great party! And then I tried to smoke again when I was 12 or 13. It was the classic thing where it didn't really take, didn't really do anything. I had started to drink a bit. Luke and his parents had a nice beach house because they were well off, so we'd drink rocket fuel and like weird cooking sherry and get fucked up in the woods and lurk around and spy on girls on the beach with binoculars. Just creepy kids.

But you didn't smoke pot between 8 and 12?

No, I just experimented when I was 8 because I was at a party. And yeah, it wasn't a good experience. When I was 13 or 14 I made friends with the older dudes down the road and was good friends with them until I was 18 or 19. I guess 15 was when it was full on, when I realized, "This does something. I like being stoned." And that's when it became a problem. I mean, my mother was dealing, lots of junkies passing through, so it was around.

What was she dealing, pot?

No, she was dealing liquid morphine and tablets and stuff. She'd get stuff off of cancer patients, I guess. So, a lot of junkies and sex workers always came around the house. To my credit, I've never once used needle drugs ever. I've seen all the women crawling down the stairs, and my mother blowing her veins out and doing it between her toes. Like at Christmas, my mother would be shooting up.

And you witnessed this?

Oh, yeah. She'd ask me to help. She'd be like, "Can you help me with the belt?" Because you have to tie the belt up and get the pressure, and then you have to loosen the belt once you shoot it. She was like, "This'll go a lot easier if you help me. I say go, and you pop the belt." I was like, "Whew, OK."

Boundary issues.

It is. I was opening up my presents while she was opening up her veins, six feet away. But it was easier for me just to do it for her.

LEFT: From *Minihex*, 2016.

But I think the standard thing that people would think is that I would become a junky, since I was exposed to that, but I did not.

Or the opposite.

Well, I became a big pothead. But I always kept it pretty manageable. Except when I started pawning stuff. Like I used to have a whole run of *Groo the Wanderer*, and I pawned them all. I hocked them. Me and an ex-girlfriend trawling around selling all our stuff so we could buy some more weed. She'd get in a funk and couldn't function, so I have to walk two hours across town. And then they're sold out. So maybe we can drive down the coast, and we're calling and we're waiting, and it gets dark … No, no pot. Usually I'd just want to go to bed and read and just wait it out until the stress subsided.

Thank God you didn't put any of this in your comics! [*Hanselmann laughs.*]

High School Sexuality

I have to ask you about your sexual identity in school.

Ehhh …

How did that evolve? You said you were confused at a very young age.

Super confused. I just assumed I was gay or something, because there was no information out there. I like all these girly things and I'm secretly dressing up in my mother's

clothing and lingerie at any opportunity when she's out of the house. It felt like a drug. It was like this weird rush. Like, "Whoa!" Trying to understand that as a kid with no information … There were these ads late at night for a sex store called The Black Rose. I was always a TV kid. I had a big VHS collection from taping everything and I'd be up late and I'd see ads for The Black Rose pop up. There was a guy dancing around in lingerie and a wig, men in leather. It was like, "The Black Rose for you. For *you*." And I was like, "For *me*." And then *Priscilla, Queen of the Desert* came out and I saw a bunch of the "real" drag queens on TV. I was 6 or 7. And they were talking about how the movie was based on them and about their lives and about being kids and wanting to dress in their mothers' clothes, and it was just like, "Ahh. Ahhh! Yes!" And then always looking through books and trying to research and figure out what the fuck was wrong with me.

Did you conclude at any point during school what your identity was?

Well, in high school I started reading about transvestism, and I saw *The Rocky Horror Picture Show*, and I just surmised that there were straight men who liked to dress as women and that that was probably it … Like I read about paraphilias, like necrophilia, pedophilia, you know. At that time, which didn't make me feel great, my thing with wearing women's clothes was listed alongside necrophilia and pedophilia as one of the paraphilias. So that made me feel [*sad aww*].

But that was demonizing what your inclinations were, so that's not quite right either.

But it was kind of cool. There was a rebellious kind of punk nature to it as well. I started lurking around department stores when I was 13. I'd wag school and then sweatily lurk around department stores buying women's clothes. It was a rush!

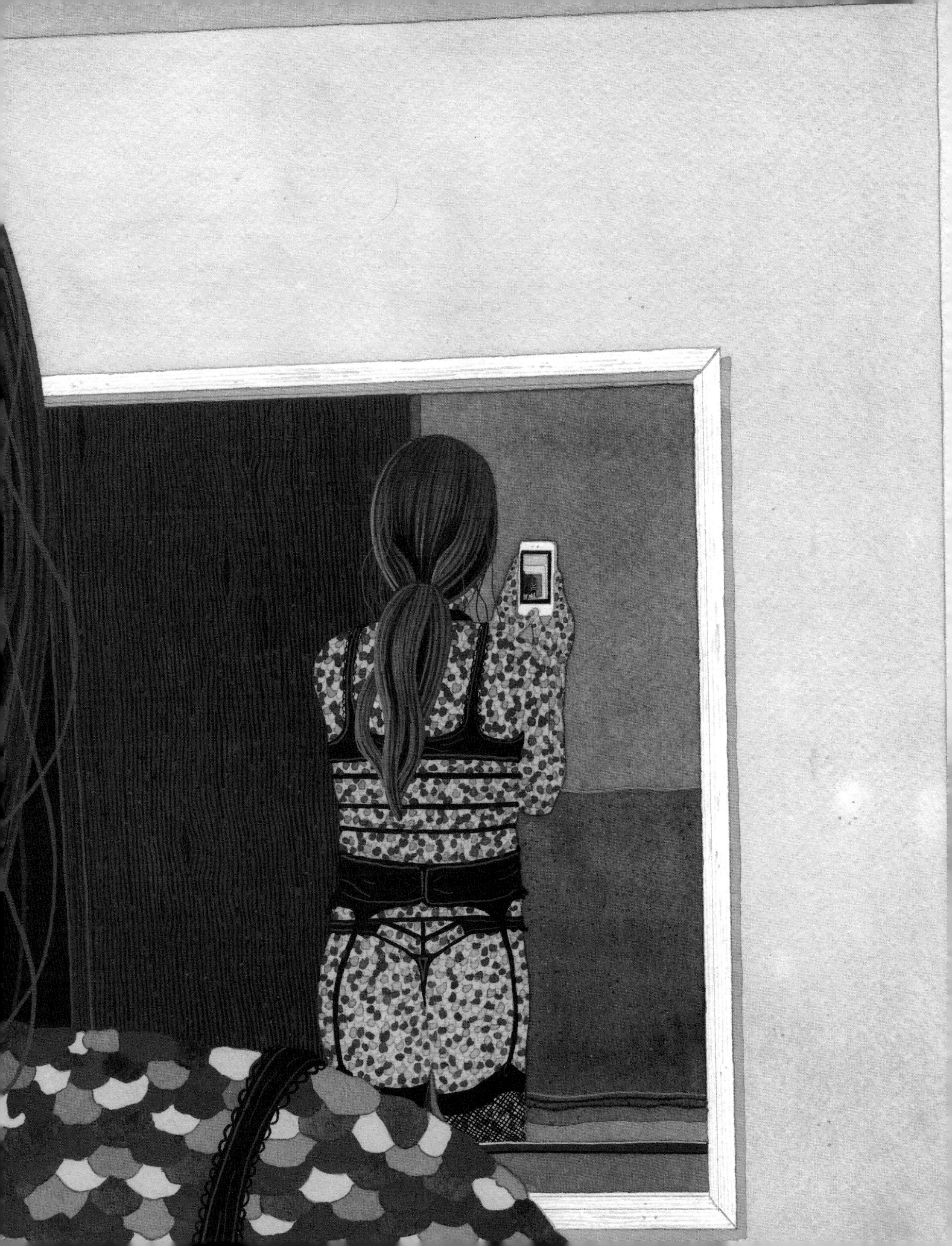

EVERY DECEMBER, BACHELOR EPPS GOES CHRISTMAS SHOPPING. "IT'S FOR MY WIFE," HE SAYS, "SHE'S A BIG GIRL, AS TALL AS I AM…"

ABOVE: From *Eightball* #17 by Daniel Clowes, 1996.

I don't know what they thought. It's not like at 13 I could say, "It's for my girlfriend. It's for my wife." There's that Clowes comic, "Gynecology," where Epps, the main character, uses Christmas as the perfect time to get them – "They're for my wife, she's a big girl." I remember reading that when I was like 14 and thinking, "Ohhh."

Did you ever try to wear your mother's clothing?

Oh, yeah. That's when I was first exposed to it. And she was like a slutty, tarty lady, so there were always garter belts and stockings around. And I'd prance around when she was out of the house and just think, "Why does this feel so good?" But I knew it was bad. That everyone made fun of it, that it was wrong. But that made it feel kind of naughty, kind of punk.

Did you date?

Not until I was like, fuck … I always had crushes on girls. But I was a nerd. I was sweaty and tubby and lame.

This was in high school?

Yeah … I lost my virginity when I was 18, I think. I dated a friend's sister earlier who dumped me real quick and broke my heart. My mother was like, "You should buy her 12 red roses." And I thought that was just fucking weird, that was too much for some 15-year-old girl in a small town. She'd just be like, "What's this, you fag?" – which she pretty much did when actually presented with them. It was always very awkward. I had a crush on a girl I worked at McDonald's with. I would just stare at her when she was on the McChicken station, just lusting. I went on a date with another girl, I was 15, we went to see *Grease*, and I never saw her again. There was this girl at the supermarket that I thought I got along with, so I asked her once, "Do you want to go on a date?" I was like 16 or something. And that was a terrible date. She brought a friend and it was just a fucking train wreck of awkwardness.

I was just an awkward teenager, with all that pent-up sexual energy and nervousness and desperation.

Did you ever feel like asking out a guy, or exploring that side?

No. I remember feeling really horny when I was 16, hanging out with my friend Luke. I was so sexually pent-up and horny, and I remember thinking, "Maybe we could fuck each other …" But I know that he wouldn't have been into that.

Were you attracted to him?

No, just horny. I remember me and a bunch of friends all blew each other when we were like 11 or 12. We went and bought a bunch of condoms and tried them on. And then we "pretended" to blow each other – with the condoms on, so it wasn't gay. [*Laughs.*] Just stuff like that, just floating around. I think me and Lockwood would get pictures of naked ladies, his dad's porno, and put them under a foam mattress with a hole cut into it and take turns humping the hole in the mattress at the picture of the ladies.

We were 6 or 7. Oh, when I went camping with my friend Daniel, when I was about 7, we used to take turns with the good stuffed animal. When my mother was away we'd hump the stuffed animal in our sleeping bags and then talk about it afterwards.

It sounds like you were more attracted to women than men.

I always have been. I'm into the feminine. That's why I like to cross-dress, because I'm attracted to femininity. I always thought that cross-dressing was an aspirational worship thing. That makes sense to me. You find women pretty and that's what your attracted to, why would you not want to be that thing? It's the societal build-up of femininity though, it's the lingerie and the makeup, this projected kind of falseness. Because I obviously wasn't born with this, let's say, affliction. You're not born being into lingerie and makeup, it's a social construct. You're warped as a child.

When I was 2, apparently, my flight attendant aunt came over, and she and my mum dressed me up in my aunt's sexy frilly knickers and threw balled-up stockings at me, and apparently, I got a boner. My mother doesn't remember this story. I've told it to her, "You did this to me, basically." And she's like, "No, I don't remember that." And I'm like, "I vividly remember you telling me this story, and I think about this stuff all the time. So, you did. You dressed me up in my aunt's underpants and threw fucking stockings at me." And I used to cross-dress around the house a bit as a kid. My mother would dress me up when I was 8 or 9 for fun. It was just a funny thing to dress me up in one of her dresses and do makeup. I think my friend Lockwood came over once and she dressed him up, like "Ha ha ha."

But I don't think she thought it would become a thing. And I don't think she wanted it to be a thing. But when I told her about it, eventually, she was quite accepting of it. Like friends of hers will come over, there's a framed picture of me in the local newspaper that's got me dressed up, and her creepy friends, her junky friends will be like, "Ah, he's a poofter, is he?" And she'll be like, "No, he's got a wife and stuff. He just likes dressing up like a lady sometimes. He's very secure in his sexuality."

> "I'd see ads for The Black Rose pop up. There was a guy dancing around in lingerie and a wig, men in leather. It was like, 'The Black Rose for you. For *you*.' And I was like, 'For *me*.'"

She's accepting of that but not of homosexuality?

Yeah, but she did make some cracks on the phone. Like a year ago, I got upset, because she was obviously out of it on drugs and made some cracks about me. And I was like, "Yeah, that's pretty fucking horrible. I don't like that." But what are you gonna do? She's a really fucking good person. She has a lot of empathy, helps old ladies in the neighborhood, genuinely wants to spread joy. To her detriment, because she's almost too giving of herself, and it's never reciprocated by the people she surrounds herself with. No one will help her. No one will do for her what she does for others. And that's really broken her, because she has given a lot, and she just feels used up and taken advantage of. And all the drugs don't help.

Career

So you dropped out of high school in order to draw comics. You wanted to draw comics.

Pretty much. I knew what I wanted to do. I had been self-publishing for years.

So you actually wanted to be a cartoonist? That was the goal?

ABOVE: From *Crap* #2 by
J.R. Williams, October 1993.

I had been self-identifying as a cartoonist since I was 12. Like, "I'm a cartoonist. I'm going to call myself a cartoonist. I want to be a cartoonist." And I think when I was around 15, I thought, "I am a cartoonist."

You were obsessively drawing every day?

Oh, every day. Yeah. It's all I ever did. I wouldn't leave the house. I mean, my friends and I would go out skateboarding or riding bikes, but there wasn't much to do out there. We made puppet shows, we made stop-motion videos with camcorders. When I was 15 or 16 my mum was dealing drugs very successfully and we had money, so I got cable. Then I could watch HBO stuff like *The Larry Sanders Show* and *Mr. Show*, decent American stuff. I got really into Conan O'Brien, late '90s, early 2000s. Just the comedy on that. It was really very surreal comedy. He was in this late slot, and he'd come off being a *Simpsons* writer, a lot of people say that he was one of the best *Simpsons* writers.

He was a little more anarchic back then.

He was. He's not anymore. I still like Conan, but back then some of the writers he had were so fucking great. See, I was just watching TV and making my puppet

shows and doing my comics. I used to make all these little sculptures, I did a lot of little things, like making music. But the comics were always first and foremost.

What kind of comics were you making in high school?

Funny animal stuff. But it was just a rip-off of *Hate*. I was really into *Crap* by J.R. Williams. That was my favorite comic when I was 14. I thought it was the bee's knees. *Crap* was big in Tasmania.

Little did I know.

Oh, we loved J.R. Williams. I finally met him at the Linework NW festival in Portland. He was down in the basement selling secondhand Matchbox cars. And I was like, "What are you doing here selling Matchbox cars?" He tried to sell me a CD-R, a burnt copy of all the *Crap* back issues for like three bucks. And I was like, "I've got 'em all, J.R."

You didn't buy it for old time's sake?

No, I've already got the floppies. I don't want a CD-R! [*Laughter.*] I don't like webcomics that much, it's not my preferred form. But yeah, shit like that.

And then when I was 16 I started to do these weird, trippy dream comics. I did these big sprawling adventure comics, like *Planet of the Apes* type shit. I started doing dick joke comics called *Cap'n's Schemes*. It was like *Tintin* but the Captain was just focused on getting free handjobs. I actually used a bit of that in the new book. I still think this one dick joke is funny. It's a classic fucking dick joke, so I repurposed it.

Did you experience any underground comics, like S. Clay Wilson, that would've possibly blown your mind at the time?

I was reading a bit of Crumb. There were old copies of *Weirdo* lying around at my friends' houses. But I never really got into

LEFT: From *Megahex*, 2014.

that stuff, it was a bit macho for me. It was a bit too expressive and crazy. I was more drawn to Clowes and Bagge. I loved Joe Matt. I love thinking about Joe Matt releasing *Peepshow* #1 now, in the current climate. "Greetings from Ipanema," where he hits Trish. That could never happen now! I'm not condoning it, but *Peepshow* was great. He spends a whole issue dubbing porn. Not even long play, it was EP, extended play, really stretching those tapes to their boundaries.

You dropped out of school; did you then devote yourself even more to writing and drawing comics?

Yeah, I just wanted to be left alone and draw comics. I was on government benefits.

At the age of 16?

Oh, since I was like 13 and had started to go see therapists. I don't know how it started. I guess I was a depressed teen.

But how could you get benefits as a minor?

Well, I started working at McDonald's when I was 14. I think at 15 or 16 you can start getting proper government benefits, not minor benefits. They have to wean you off your parents' benefits. I got on the benefit gravy train, and I had to go to a therapist every now and then. [*In a sad voice*:] "Oh, I'm depressed." And my mother would tell me, "Use me. Just tell them I'm a junkie and that you're sad." So I said, "Yeah, my mother's a junkie."

Which was true.

Yeah, I felt like I was hyping it up and lying and using the system, but I kind of wasn't as well. There was a lot of shit going on at home, and I was fucking depressed.

Did any of the therapy do you any good?

I was in therapy off and on up until like five years ago or something. I don't feel like I need it anymore. I feel like I went through all my issues. I think my main problem is that I just want everyone to fuck off so I

can draw these comics. I just want to work, I just want to be left alone. Fuck off.

That would solve a lot of problems.

It has solved a lot of problems. And a good relationship with someone who accepts all the gender stuff and supports it, so I don't have to feel fucking horrible about it. And my day job now is doing whatever the fuck I want with full freedom, full autonomy. What the fuck do I have to complain about? [*Laughs.*] And I'm older. I'm 37 next week! I've figured my shit out. I got through my teens and my 20s.

I thought you were 35. I didn't know you were getting up there.

Pushing 40. I think I signed my Fantagraphics contract the day before I turned 31. That was my goal, to be published by the time I was 30. I signed that fucking contract the day before I turned 31. So, just fucking made it. I have everything I want.

You went back to school at 11th grade, which is the equivalent to our first year at university. You went through about a year of schooling again?

Yeah, I did year 11 and then dropped out after about three months of year 12. My friend Luke dropped out. That's why I enjoyed going, because Luke and I would draw comics together and just get fucked up. And then he dropped out and decided to become a computer animator. His rich

BELOW: From an online
Truth Zone strip, 2013.

parents always had a computer at home. That was the route he wanted to take, so he was like, "I'm going to drop out of this graphic design shit. I don't care anymore." So I left. I thought, "Well, I don't have anyone here now. I hate everyone else in the class, they're all a pack of cunts. So why would I stay?" I knew what I wanted to do, just draw comics, so fuck it.

Was this in Launceston?

Yeah, I was still in Launceston. I did a few years after school in Launceston where I just got drunk by myself and watched cable. Just filled myself with all this entertainment, buying a fuckload of comics, drawing comics, making these puppet shows. Just making stuff! And then Luke moved to Melbourne. That's where you go. If you're in Tasmania and you make art or music, you move to Melbourne. It's the arts and fashion capitol. Just get the fuck out of Tasmania. I was scared. Luke and I's friend, Johnny, moved over there and started dealing drugs in Melbourne. And he just got shat out, like he just came home with his tail between his legs.

But you went to Hobart.

Yeah, I met all these cartoonists in Hobart. I would get on the bus myself and just go down to Hobart. They had a comic shop down there, and we didn't have one in Launceston. I'd go to the Hobart comic shop, hang out on my own, and in this vegan cafe I found all these local comic zines. And it was good stuff. I met people I'm still friends with to this day. They were all reading weird shit like Al Columbia, the same shit I was into. I became friends with them through the mail initially, and then I'd come down and hang out with them at parties. They were cooler than me, like I got laid down there. They were drinking on rooftops and listening to noise music and in bands, and I thought, "This is fucking cool! Why would I move to Melbourne where it's fucking expensive

and I have one friend?" So, I moved down to Hobart.

How far from Launceston is Hobart?

Two-and-a-half hours on the bus. Launceston's to the north, Hobart's in the south. Launceston's the second biggest population center, Hobart's the capitol. It was a great scene down there. I got a girlfriend pretty soon and had a shitty little flat. And we'd have all these comics parties.

How did you make money?

I was on the dole. On the government money. Everyone was. There was no employment to be had. So, I got $400 a fortnight from the government, had to go to therapy every two weeks. Occasionally, you had to do "work for the dole." You had to do a work scheme. So, for a while I worked at a music magazine. I was the cartoonist, I got real lucky with that one. My girlfriend did riding for the disabled. She had to go off and get the kids on the horses and wheel them around and scoop the shit up. But yeah, I did the music magazine, and then I was at a school for a year as a teacher's aide. I did art classes with the kids and hung out with them. I was getting stoned in the morning, and I'd roll up and start drawing with the kids. For three hours a day, Monday through Friday, I had to go to this school. And they actually legit hired me afterwards. I was so good with the kids, and I did all these comics courses with them, and they let me follow this curriculum that I made up, and I made this little zine about how to make comics.

And you were 21, 22, 23 at this point?

I think 25? I'd been in Hobart for a few years. I moved there when I was 21, 22. And then eventually they said that I had to do some work for the dole. You can't just be sitting around, you have to do some work for society.

ABOVE: From *Bad Gateway*, 2019.

There's a long, honorable tradition of cartoonists serving their apprenticeship on the dole. Crumb, Feiffer…

If you can do it. It's an arts grant. I always thought about it that way. There's a societal stigma against it, that you're a bludger, that you're just ripping people off.

But in a way, it helped you get your footing.

Exactly. In 2013 I finally got off the benefits. They'd say, "You've got to come in and do this seminar about working in a supermarket and hang out with all these scumbags and violent dickheads," and I was like, "I've just been contacted by the Fox network, I've got this Spanish book deal, I'm declaring 3,000 euros next month, I'm making something out of this. If you

leave me the fuck alone, I'll be autonomous soon enough." And I was, but they had a code to follow. They're like, "How the fuck do we code 'Spanish book deal'?" They weren't used to dealing with people who were succeeding, I suppose. [*Laughs.*] But I did that for years. I met a girl, I moved to the U.K. and I had to get a job there.

That's where you cleaned bird shit out of airport hangars?

Yeah, I couldn't go on government benefits, I had to work. I was breaking down art galleries for a while, I was scrubbing shit out of the airport hangar. Then I got into bookstores, I worked at a camping store for a while.

That sounds like your speed. Learning a lot about tents.

It was horrible. Just selling malaria pills. And all these rich kids would come in with their North Face jackets, like, "I need my Duke of Edinburgh." I lived in the posh part of London, like David Attenborough was a street over and Mick Jagger was just up the road with his glass elevator and Pete Townsend was a bit further up.

Melbourne

Did you move to London from Hobart?

I moved to Melbourne. I had been in Hobart for six or seven years, and I was feeling like I'd done everything I could. People were starting to move to Melbourne. New people were coming into the scene. All these rich art school kids with mummy and daddy's money were getting into the music scene, and it was getting less scummy and less exciting.

I met HTML Flowers [Grant Gronewold], who is still my best friend. He came down to Hobart to play a gig. I'd play a lot of gigs, I'd run merch tables. I wasn't going to go to a show, but a friend of mine gave me a CD from their radio show and it had one of Grant's tracks on it. I was listening to a lot of lo-fi, K Records folk shit at the time, and Grant's stuff was kinda like that. It was a sad kid singing about having cystic fibrosis. This weird American kid. Grant and I just fucking hit it off. We got drunk all weekend and slow danced at parties and stole booze from people. I asked him to be on my cassette label I ran at the time. I was trying to run this shitty cassette label. I paid him $20 to be on my label. And after that we just starting hanging out a lot. We'd talk on the phone all the time...

ABOVE: From *One More Year,* 2017.

What was the band's name that you had with Grant?

We didn't really have a band. I think we had a band called Double Mario for a couple months. We made like one EP and played a gig, but we didn't mesh musically.

But you and Grant became very close friends, right?

Yeah, just through art, comics, hanging out. And he's very funny, I guess he thought the same of me. We just got on, instantly. I think his outlook on life with the cystic fibrosis, constantly being told he's gonna die, he's very wild and untamed. He doesn't worry about the consequences of things. I love that. He's just funny. The sadness has just made him fucking funny. He makes all this dour music and sad art about being ill, but it's also very funny.

Would you say you share that outlook with him?

Yeah, I guess. We had similar fathers and our mothers both have substance abuse issues and similar abandonment issues from our fathers leaving them. We just understand each other. I'm not chronically ill though.

You once said you met Grant [HTML Flowers] and fell in love, you started touring together and moved into a shed.

Yeah, we toured. Plutonic Boyfriends. I'd go and hang out in Melbourne and play shows at his house. We went to Adelaide and Sidney and played gigs together. And he was really interested in comics. He was drawing at the time, and I really liked his drawings. The offer was there to move to Melbourne. He said, "Look, you can live at my mother's house in the garden shed. No rent. Get your fucking feet off the ground." His family was great. They were just so relaxed, such great people. They moved from fucking poverty in Chicago for the healthcare system in Australia. And his mother was like my second mother, I love Karen. And yeah, I lived in the garden shed.

I stayed with my mother for a few months to save money, I quit smoking weed and became a vicious alcoholic instead. I started drinking like eight liters of white wine a night. I think I always need some kind of intoxicant to distract from the noise. I lived with her for a while, that was when she was still doing OK, and saved some money. She drove me on the ferry, took all my shit over to the shed. The shed didn't lock, I just had a chain looped around. Cockroaches everywhere ...

Was it heated?

No, no. It was outdoors, like a car garage. It was filled with old doors and garbage, and I had to clean it out a bit. All my books warped. But it was free rent, and I got on the government benefits over there in Melbourne. I had to go to a therapist every month. Grant and I just rode bikes and got fucked up and drew comics and made music. And then I met this girl, and she was moving to the U.K. to study. I think I was in Melbourne for about eight months and then I moved to the U.K. I was there for about two-and-a-half years.

Was the band that you and Grant were in called Horse Mania?

That was my friend Karl von Bamberger, rest in peace. He died of a heroin overdose at the start of 2016. He's a Hobart friend. We met in 2003, and we hated each other. I was staying at a friend's house and Karl was staying there also, and he came out in this weird Jesus robe and his weird hair. He was always a cunt, that's what was so endearing about him. [*Groth laughs.*] He'd had the shit beaten out of him on a trip to Melbourne and his brother said it damaged him, made him different. He was just really forthright and would tell you what he thought of you. He was a real toxic cunt, but I loved that about him. But yeah, we

hated each other for a while, and then we became friends and started doing all these comics parties. And then we started Horse Mania in 2005 or so.

Was he also an aspiring cartoonist?

No, not super into it. He didn't have the drive. He'd just doodle about for fun. He wanted to be a proper writer and was more into the music. He was a fair-weather cartoonist. He mostly just liked being around cartoonists. But we were in Horse Mania for 10 years, off and on. We sucked. Grant was always a real musician. He could write melodies and sing properly, and I couldn't.

LEFT: Hanselmann and Gronewold (aka HTML Flowers) at the Fantagraphics Bookstore and Gallery, 2016.

OPPOSITE TOP: Album art for *Volcano Pimples*, the sixth Girl Mountain album, 2009.

OPPOSITE BOTTOM: From *No Visitors* Season 3 by HTML Flowers, 2018.

BELOW: *Horse Mania*, 2017.

You described Horse Mania as consisting of "Tasmanian ghost shitcore." What is that exactly?

Well, the "ghost" was added after Karl died. I kept on playing Horse Mania shows with him participating as an iPod. I'd have the backing tracks and vocals, and I'd play along and sing my parts. But we were always Tasmanian and shitcore.

Can you describe that style of music? I don't know what shitcore is…

Just no talent. Just two idiots…

…just bangin' away.

Yeah, with keyboards and a bunch of pedals, maybe one snare drum. We were shit. We'd play for two hours, refuse to get off stage, vomit into plastic bags – because we'd take all these pills and drink half a bottle of vodka before each set – have band meetings on stage, yell at the audience. It was a train wreck. But that's what was good about us. We had a dedicated, small group of people that would turn up with our cassette recorders and record our gigs. We were shit. It's a genre within noise, shitcore. Just bad, bad performing. [*Laughs*.] But we'd try to write pop songs. We'd try to play to waltz time, but we didn't know what that was…

Was that in Melbourne?

We started off in Tasmania, and once I moved to Melbourne, Karl was there as well, and we got the band back together. Karl was my angel, my songbird.

Girl Mountan to *Megg and Mogg*

When did you conceive of and draw *Girl Mountain*?

Girl Mountain, that was probably 2004. I think I was 22ish, I'd been drawing comics

for like 12 years already and self-publishing since I was 8 and blah blah blah, so I thought I was ready for like the big graphic novel. So, I took all this autobiographical stuff about the cross-dressing, my druggie mother and just some shit that had happened to me. Put it together with all this bad teenage poetry and weird shit I'd made up. Bunch of shit about black magic and sci-fi. Stuff from dream diaries. So, I put it all together and mashed it into this big five-different-families-small-town, *Twin Peaks*, space-opera, black-magic thing. It was quite sprawling. It was a learning experience. It was six years of working towards something, evolving as an artist and realizing that what I'd done was shit, and what I was doing was shit. It was garbage. I was a fucking moron. At 22, I wasn't ready for that.

But it sounds like it was laudably ambitious, like you really wanted to do something significant.

It was like my version of *Twin Peaks* or something. A big family drama with a big cast, with all the drug stuff like *The Royal Tenenbaums*. And I was gonna explore all the cross-dressing. It's what *Megg and Mogg*'s become. *Megg and Mogg* started out as a silly diversion with sitcom-esque drug humor, and I thought, "I like these characters and people seemed to respond to this. So, OK, let's put all this sad drug stuff into the *Megg and Mogg* stuff." And *Girl Mountain* sucked. I don't like human characters either. I've heard that people can more readily engage with anthropomorphic characters, because they can project themselves onto them. I have a thing with putting fashion in my comics. If you hate Nike [*Groth laughs*], you think they're a shit company, you hate Nike and you hate people who wear Nikes – if you read a book and the main character is walking around in a Nike shirt and Nikes, you're not gonna like that character. It's gonna distance you from them straight away. So, I feel like putting too many real-world reality signifiers

LEFT: The first *Megg and Mogg* strip, 2008.

and enhanced details makes the characters too fleshed out and too human. That's fine, but my personal philosophy, I like to keep the characters cyphers.

Tell me a little more about *Girl Mountain*; no one's ever seen it.

It was heavily autobiographical. Not heavily. It was all dreams, bad fiction and autobio, all mixed into a big ball. I was trying to do a big family drama, like a young nerdy kid, all based on me and his weird friend. There was going to be sci-fi portions of it. I had had all these weird dreams. In one dream, it lasted 30 years. There's this town square and this kid had been murdered under a train – and this big fucking train crash flashback. It was like a fully-formed sci-fi movie. I had big plans for *Girl Mountain*. I just never got there. I just was getting sick of it, and thought that I'd do this silly stuff. *Girl Mountain* had been my full focus for years. It was supposed to be my big main thing. I wanted to get a publisher, but I never sent anything to publishers. I didn't think it was good enough. It wasn't.

I couldn't quite figure out what year you actually conceived of *Megg and Mogg*.

Two thousand eight. I'd just moved to the U.K. Arrived the night Obama was sworn in. Terrible jet lag, like, "Whoa! Obama's getting in! Coool." I think a month later, I drew the first *Megg and Mogg* comic. I'd been drawing a lot of witches. "Ah, witches are cool! I like the hats, and all the green with big noses." So, I'd done some art show where I'd drawn some witches. And then, I just wanted to draw these silly comedy comics and, "Oh, I'll do the witches." And, "Oh, I'll make them Megg and Mogg like the kids' books, I'll nickname them Megg and Mogg." It just happened, yeah.

Which you presumably read as a child. I read about six of them.

[*Laughs.*] That's heavy research. One would've been enough.

LEFT: From *Meg and Mog*, illustrated by Jan Pieńkowski, 1972.

OVERLEAF: Artwork and pages from *Girl Mountain*, 2004–2006.

"GIRL MOUNTAIN"

CHAPTER ONE:

FRIDAY AFTER SCHOOL

HEY MICAH!

UGH, JEEZUS MUM!

SORRY...

HEY, COULD YOU REMIND ME LATER THAT MY BRA IS ON THE HOT-WATER CYLINDAR?...

...I'M GOING TO THAT PARTY LATER ON...

chapter 8

SO NO... I CANT.

WIPE

...OH. OK...

HEY, LET'S PLAY A TWO-PLAYERS GAME!

PLANET of the APES

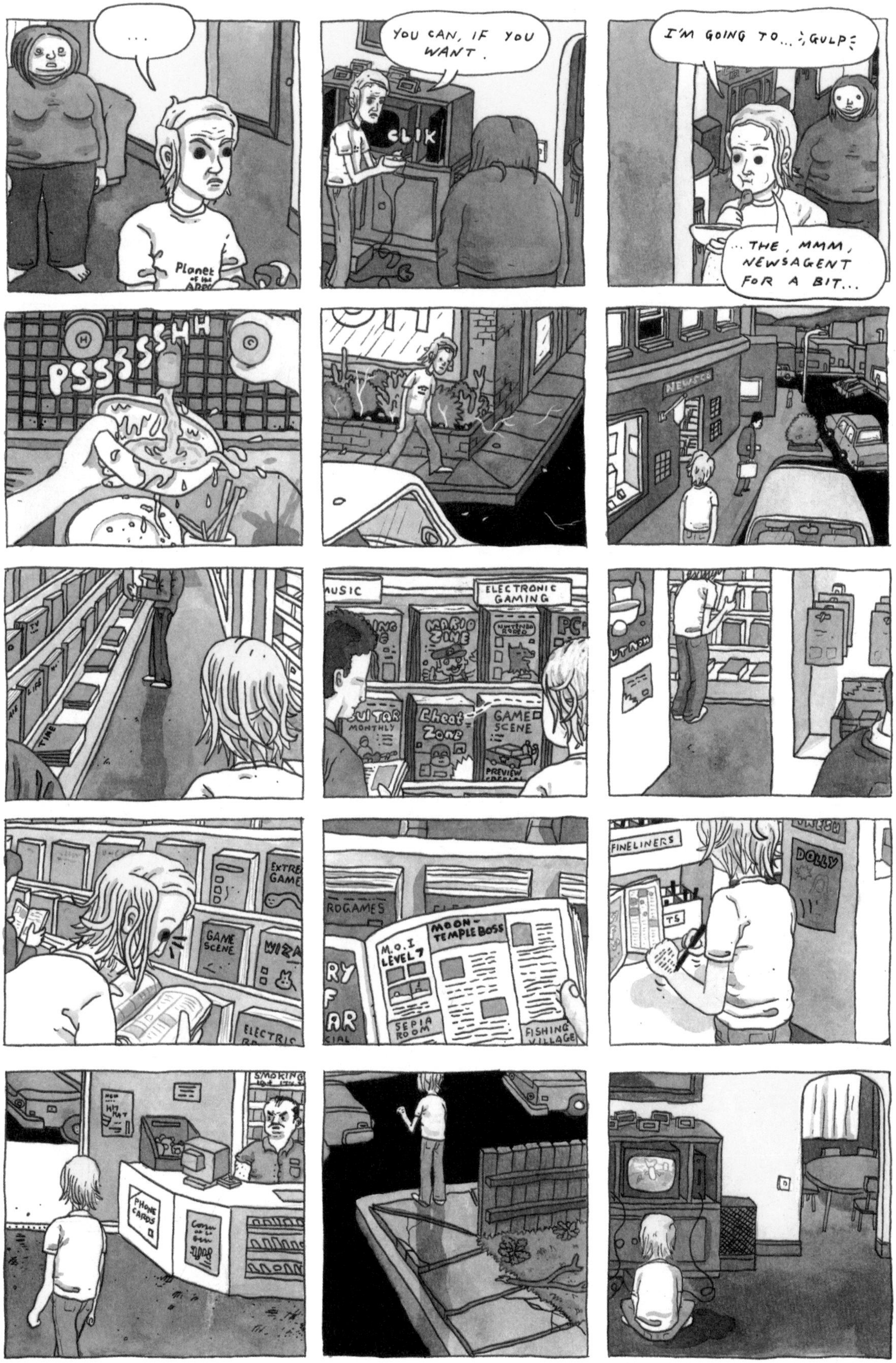
...
YOU CAN, IF YOU WANT.
CLIK
I'M GOING TO... ;GULP;
...THE, MMM, NEWSAGENT FOR A BIT...
PSSSSSHH
Planet
MUSIC
ELECTRONIC GAMING
MARIO ZINE
MONTHLY
Cheat Zone
GAME SCENE
PREVIEW
GAME SCENE
M.O.I LEVEL 7
MOON-TEMPLE BOSS
SEPIA ROOM
FISHING VILLAGE
FINELINERS
DOLLY
PHONE CARDS
SMOKING

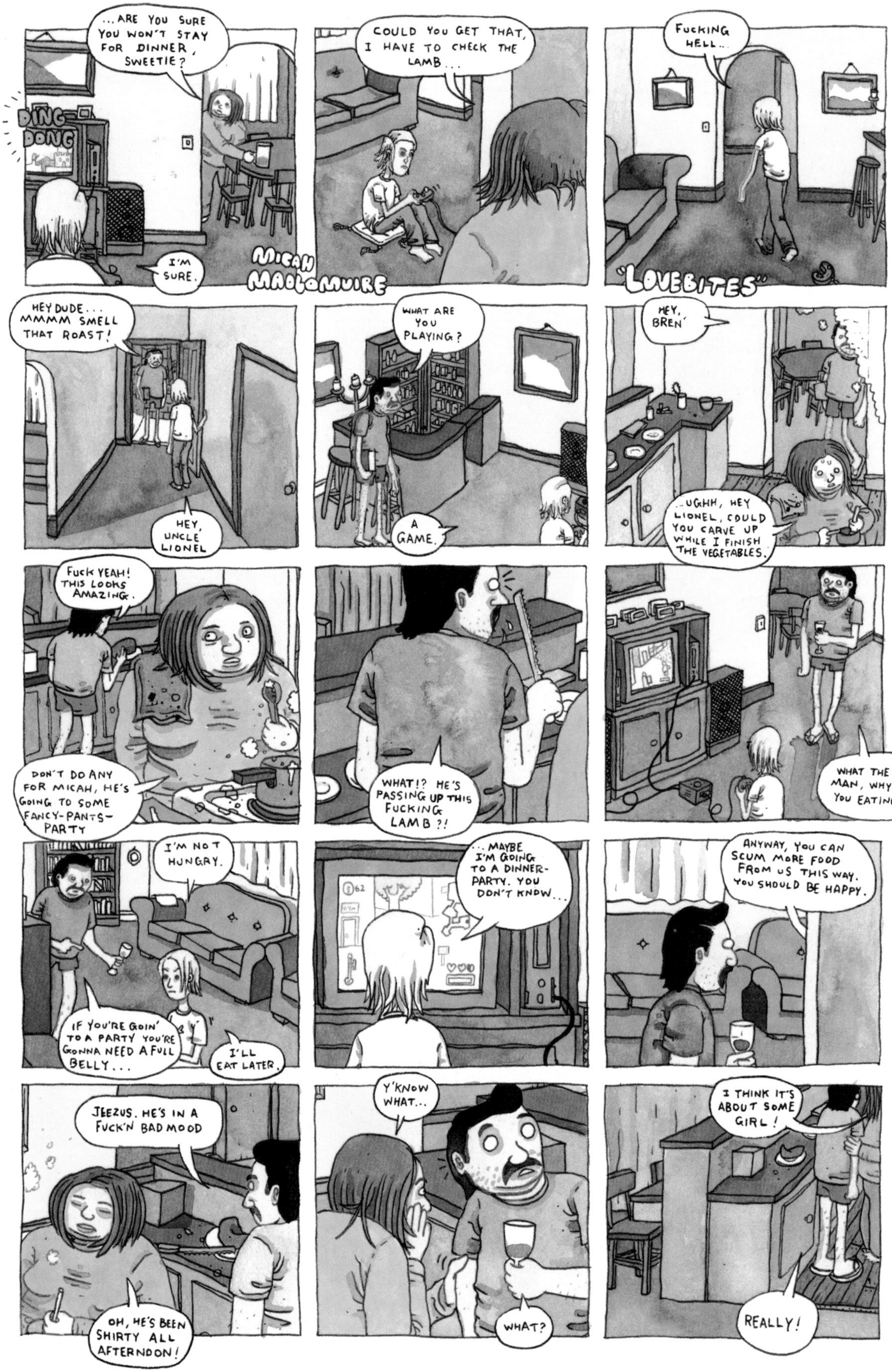
...ARE YOU SURE YOU WON'T STAY FOR DINNER, SWEETIE?
DING DONG
I'M SURE.
MICAH MADDOMUIRE
COULD YOU GET THAT, I HAVE TO CHECK THE LAMB...
FUCKING HELL...
"LOVEBITES"
HEY DUDE... MMMM SMELL THAT ROAST!
HEY, UNCLE LIONEL
WHAT ARE YOU PLAYING?
A GAME.
HEY, BREN'
...UGHH, HEY LIONEL, COULD YOU CARVE UP WHILE I FINISH THE VEGETABLES.
FUCK YEAH! THIS LOOKS AMAZING.
DON'T DO ANY FOR MICAH, HE'S GOING TO SOME FANCY-PANTS-PARTY
WHAT!? HE'S PASSING UP THIS FUCKING LAMB ?!
WHAT THE HELL, MAN, WHY ARN'T YOU EATING!?
I'M NOT HUNGRY.
IF YOU'RE GOIN' TO A PARTY YOU'RE GONNA NEED A FULL BELLY...
I'LL EAT LATER.
...MAYBE I'M GOING TO A DINNER-PARTY. YOU DON'T KNOW...
ANYWAY, YOU CAN SCUM MORE FOOD FROM US THIS WAY. YOU SHOULD BE HAPPY.
JEEZUS. HE'S IN A FUCK'N BAD MOOD
OH, HE'S BEEN SHIRTY ALL AFTERNOON!
Y'KNOW WHAT...
WHAT?
I THINK IT'S ABOUT SOME GIRL!
REALLY!

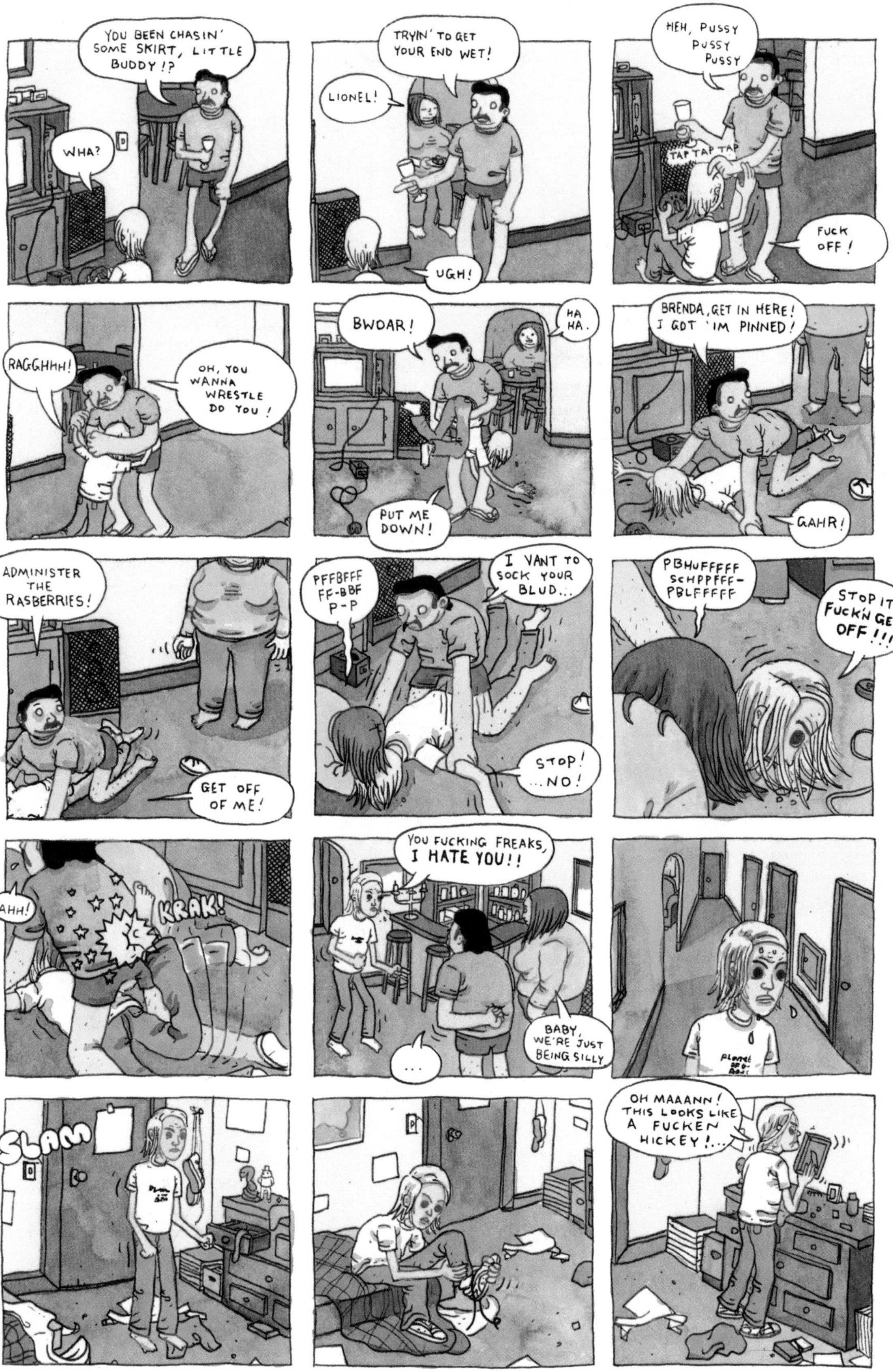

YOU BEEN CHASIN' SOME SKIRT, LITTLE BUDDY!?
WHA?
TRYIN' TO GET YOUR END WET!
LIONEL!
UGH!
HEH, PUSSY PUSSY PUSSY
TAP TAP TAP
FUCK OFF!
RAGGHHH!
OH, YOU WANNA WRESTLE DO YOU!
BWOAR!
HA HA.
PUT ME DOWN!
BRENDA, GET IN HERE! I GOT 'IM PINNED!
GAHR!
ADMINISTER THE RASBERRIES!
GET OFF OF ME!
PFFBFFF FF-BBF P-P
I VANT TO SOCK YOUR BLUD...
STOP! ...NO!
PBHUFFFFF SCHPPFFF-PBLFFFFF
STOP IT! FUCK'N GET OFF!!!
AHH!
KRAK!
YOU FUCKING FREAKS, I HATE YOU!!
BABY, WE'RE JUST BEING SILLY
...
SLAM
OH MAAANN! THIS LOOKS LIKE A FUCKEN HICKEY!...

ABOVE: From *BodyWorld*
by Dash Shaw, 2010.

They look like Michael DeForge books.

[*Laughs*.] I'm not sure that answers the question.

[*Laughs*.] Bold, colorful, cartoon-y lines. I quite like Jan Pieńkowski as an illustrator. It's simple and effective. He does all those paper cutouts and silhouette stuff as well.

When I made these *Megg and Mogg* comics, it was an offhand, stupid thing. I didn't imagine, 10 years later, *New York Times* Best-Seller, 14 languages, TV deals, on the go all the time. For years, I was like, "Is Penguin Random House going to fucking sue me?"

How soon after you created Megg and Mogg did you realize that these were the characters you could use to express what you wanted to express?

It took a while.

Were you self-publishing?

Yeah. Just zines. I never put any work online. I remember I got really inspired by *BodyWorld*, when Dash Shaw put that up.

What was it about *BodyWorld* that gave you a creative kick?

It was a *good* webcomic. I don't generally enjoy the aesthetics of webcomics. They *can* be good, but generally, there's just this stink of lowest common denominator and it's mainly twee nonsense.

Badly drawn.

Yeah. It was this weird thing I'd never seen — this infinite scroll — before. That you could just scroll through 200 pages of something. I thought it just worked really well. And it was color.

I couldn't afford to Xerox stuff in color. I was like, "Fuck it! I guess you can put stuff online. I'll just do it in color, anyway. And maybe it will be a webcomic, but for

[*Laughs*.] Now you tell me. I didn't find them to be exceptional. Is that because I'm not reading them as a child, or am I missing something? Why did they have such a big impact on you?

I grew up reading them, so it's that I learned to read on them.

But, qualitatively, do you think they hold up as children's books?

now I can just do the zines in black and white." And I was printing black-and-white versions of my color work. It just inspired me. "I guess everything's going to be online one day."

I haven't had a slump for like 10 years, but I think that, at that point, I'd had a bit of a slump. I wasn't enjoying *Girl Mountain*, I was moving countries. And *BodyWorld* gave me a real shot in the arm. Like, OK, I gotta get to work. And when I finally put 200 pages of *Megg and Mogg* online in 2012, in a month, I got PictureBox, Koyama, Jacq [Cohen, Fantagraphics publicist and Hanselmann's future spouse] from Fanta writing to me. It happened really quickly. I had that backlog of work.

And it was the online version, not the printed version.

When it was just online. I think I'd stopped making zines during that period.

When were you influenced by [the art collective] Fort Thunder and Paper Rad? Was that around the same time?

I think 2003 or so.

So, a little earlier.

Yeah. 2002 or 2003, which is a few years after they'd come out. I read like a *Comics Journal*. "Youth Quake! 2002!" I had this year-in-review issue that had interviews with Ben Jones and CF and saw a little bit of their work. Then looked at their website. I got way too into it. I started drawing like Ben Jones. I had to really beat that influence out. Early on, everyone called me a Paper Rad rip-off when I put the stuff on Tumblr, in 2012.

What was it about that that was revelatory?

I think it was just the humor. It was based on *Garfield*, all this pop culture stuff. All these icons – the nostalgia factor. They were using all these pop culture things.

But reinventing them.

Yeah. I'd riffed on *Tintin* when I was 18. I was interested in that kind of stuff. I did all my puppet shows with these weird pop culture figures that I'd rename. I was always remixing things. So, that aspect.

And, just the simple drawing. I think they'd stumbled upon this fun style of drawing. It was fun to draw like that. So, drawing the triangle noses and just the bubble lettering. It got bad. I used to bristle. I'm like, "Ooooh, I'm not a ripoff." But I was. I was visually aping that stuff. All the Europeans were.

I remember Sammy Harkham saying something like, "Oh, a new *Kramers Ergot* will be out soon, check out what all the Europeans will be ripping off next year." I think those guys haven't owned it well. They're all my age, the Fort Thunder guys, and they're hugely influential. I don't think they've been able to own it, because I guess everyone ripping them off was their age. Like, it's fine to rip off dead guys and stuff, but ripping off living people, it's not cool.

Well, they're all older than you.

A few years. Not that much older. One or two years.

I had to beat those influences out. I've always told my own stories. The *Girl*

ABOVE: From *Horace* by Ben Jones, circa 2001.

ABOVE: From *Megahex*, 2014.

Mountain stuff, it was always about cross-dressing, my mother. I was always doing the heavy watercolors, I always had a real sense of space, of trying to draw full backgrounds. Those guys never really did that. They're more minimal. But that stuff, I got really excited about it. I feel like kids don't know them anymore. I feel like all that stuff — it did influence Net culture, it was very early, within all this internet art.

I think you're right. I think they've receded in public memory.

Megg and Mogg

In 2011, I moved back to Melbourne. I thought it was the end of *Megg and Mogg*. I thought I'd done everything I could with them, or there'd be one more book. It was going to be this really harsh, really brutal ending, where they faced reality. And then it'd reboot into a magical teenage kind of thing, they'd go back in time to high school, and it would have magic in it and it would be completely different. I figured that I wasn't going to do *Girl Mountain* anymore, I wasn't ever going to get back to it. So now I had this wealth of material, all this shit I could put into *Megg and Mogg*. There were times I thought early on that it's jumped the shark, I've run the course of what I can do with *Megg and Mogg*. But now I have six more books planned, with notes.

The characters are spooling out. Like, more family members and all that.

I think you've said that there are aspects of yourself in all the characters.

Yeah.

Megg and Mogg and Werewolf Jones treat Owl like shit.

Yeah.

I assume that there's a lot of Owl in you. A lot of you in Owl. Being bullied.

Yeah, I've been bullied a lot. But also, in Hobart there was a social hierarchy. There's one strip where Werewolf Jones pushes Owl in the trash. He says, "You belong in the trash and fucking stay in the trash. Fucking stay there!" And Owl does. That was my friend Andrew. He did that to Scott. Andrew was the "King of Hobart." He was older than all of us, the big man. Scott was this young new kid on the scene. "You get in the fucking trash, Scott." There was a lot of bullying. There's always a loser in the group. If there are three kids, one of them is going to get teased. It's not great, but it's what fucking happens. That's reality. That's social structures. Owl is the George Constanza. He's the straight man, the loser. The whipping boy.

What of you is in Werewolf Jones?

LEFT: From *Megg and Mogg in Amsterdam*, 2016.

The hedonism.

He's a pretty despicable character.

He is. He's disgusting. He's a composite of numerous people from the Hobart noise music scene. Bipolar alcoholic fuckups. And junkies that my mother used to hang out with. But there's bits of me. He's the hedonistic, wild, destructive bits... Also bits of Grant, the way Grant can be so involved in his own world because he's stuck in this mode of being told he's going to die. Everything seems futile. If he wants to spit in a restaurant, he's gonna fucking spit in a restaurant. Fuck it. [*Laughter.*] And Megg's the feminine depressed side. Mogg's this weird perverted cold little lump. He's a cold character. In regards to him and Megg in their sexual relationship.

Oddly, Werewolf Jones defends Booger against homophobes.

Well, Werewolf Jones is gay as fuck. He's always getting fucked and fucking people. He's omnisexual.

I was going to say he's not just gay, he's bi or omni.

He'll fuck anything. He's omnisexual. Of course, he's going to stick up for Booger. He's got no prejudices, I don't think. He's just a cunt. [*Laughter.*]

The way you've talked about *Megg and Mogg*, it reminds me of *Peanuts*, which is this tight cast of characters with which Schulz could do anything he wanted.

They are versatile. I have a sci-fi thing I want to do with them, and I might do someday. But for now, I'm *Gasoline Alley*-ing it. Like *Love and Rockets*. I want them to grow up. I know what happens to all these characters, like Werewolf Jones's kids, how they grow up, what they're like. I've thought about it all.

It's all been intensely autobiographical.

Yeah, pretty much. I tease it up. I think all writers draw from their own life. How can you not? You're given these gifts, and you riff on them. It's pretty heavily

autobiographical. I can't write fiction, I'm not a talented writer who can make stuff up. [*Laughs.*]

Is that true?

Well, I can make stuff up, but I consider myself a comedy writer. So there's lots of *Megg and Mogg*s that are just like … There's the ram raids one, where Werewolf Jones picks up Owl at the dick doctor, and he's ramming into buildings and stealing things. That's just made up. That's Grant and I.

Were there such a thing as ram raids?

Yeah, there's a big ram raid culture in Australia.

Did you ever go on a ram raid?

No. But there's this girl I banged on tour once. She was a bit crazy. I saw her a few years later, and it's like, "Oh, wow. You look really good. You're wearing a fur coat. Wow, you're doing well." "Yeah, I'm squatting with these guys, doing all these fuckin' ram raids." Oh, god. Anyway, you'd have friends who were doing ram raids. They'd crash the fucking Subaru through the shopfront, jump out and grab all the stuff. Grant and I riffed out this comedy bullshit story about Werewolf Jones doing that. So that's not autobiographical. But it is, in a way, because it's something people I knew did. But I was able to riff on it and make jokes up. I can write jokes. Essentially, yes, it's heavily autobiographical. What's not, you know?

I'm interested in how you transform your life experience and your anecdotal experience into art. There was that long story where Megg and Mogg go out late at night, and they break into the deli and steal food, but the wrong food. How autobiographical was that?

Well, I don't know if, legally, I should talk about it.

The statute of limitations is probably over. [*Laughter.*] And it was a different country, I don't think they're going to extradite you.

It was like 10 years ago, it's been a decade or something.

You're safe.

That was a nutty ex-girlfriend who was really hungry late at night and didn't want to walk over the hill to McDonald's. She says, "I'll take my mother's drill set and break into the fucking corner store that we shop at every day." Awesome! We were really drunk. Let's do it. Then we buried all the stuff in the woods the next morning out of paranoia. She was a crazy girl. She was lovely, but she was crazy. I was drinking a lot at the time. She stabbed me once.

So you actually did that?

Yeah, yeah. We broke into the corner store, and smashed through the back with the drill and stole a bunch of food, because we were hungry late at night. Then buried it all the next day out of paranoia. We didn't buy everything [that we'd stolen]. At the end of that *Megg and Mogg* story, they go back, and the theory is that if they *buy* everything that they stole, people will think that there would be no need for them to have stolen those things, because they're buying them.

Yeah, that made no sense to me at all. Which was part of the humor of the story, which is that it was ridiculous.

Yeah, it was their stupid logic. But we just had to go back to the store. We went there the next day, because we shopped there every day. But I don't think they had cameras there.

They even buried the drill with the food.

I don't think we buried the drill. I think her mother would have been upset if the drill

had been missing. [*Laughter.*] But I remember, she'd go off. She'd slide under trucks with her knife and cut all the sparkplugs out of the trucks. Just vandalism. I guess she was crazy at the time. That was when I was hanging out with Grant, very early on, when we'd first met. We made friends with these two girls, and we were like fucking one of each of these girls. Then I started fucking Grant's one, and it got really messy.

So, when you extrapolate from a story that you've either lived, or you've heard

OPPOSITE: From *One More Year*, 2017.

BELOW: From *Megahex*, 2014.

about, how do you go about transforming that into art? It's more than just transcribing the story. You obviously have to invest it with a great deal more humor than was evident at the time.

Yeah, it wasn't funny at the time.

So you give it that slant. What are you trying to do by transforming that story or that anecdote into art?

It's just a quality anecdote. I'm desperate for content. I'm always writing, and I need squalid stories. It's a quality anecdote, and I beat it up into shape. I just go through, A to Z, what happened, what's the point of this, what's the run of events. It's just a sixth sense, being able to tell if something is a decent anecdote that can be spun into a little concise story.

BELOW: Hanselmann's thumbnails, circa 2010.

Construction

I'd to like to know how you go about literally constructing a story. I think a good example is the long story, "Jobs," which is a 30-page story from *One More Year*.

Yeah, that was 2013. That was the longest thing at the time. I think since then there's been a 50-page one, and the longer swimming-pool one ["Heat Wave"] and a few other ones.

"Jobs" impressed me, as your most elaborate story up to that point. Walk me through your process. Do you write the entire story out first?

I just rough it out. I block out the scenes. At the end I thumbnail everything. I get in there in each scene. It's like being a theater actor on stage with all the characters, and

I draw really fucking quick. That's how I do it. Try to make it fluid and like it is reactive. Like someone says something and you're like, snap, what does the other character say and *buh buh buh*, really fucking quick. It does feel like acting. I make the motions and I'm shouting things. I get quite shout-y when I write sometimes. Grant and I write on Skype as well. He helped me out on one of the chapters in a writing session we did. The other day we were just writing, snapping things back and forth and just wrote a great story about one of Werewolf Jones's children getting a vasectomy at 14. That's going to be a great one. [*Laughs.*] But, yeah, fucking do it like a robot. Thumbnail it all out, make sure it's all good to go, refined and as good as I can get it. And then start penciling.

Do you do that in chronological order?

Yeah. Very staunchly chronological order. When I have the panel, the pages, I won't skip to a later panel. It has to be drawn, like panel one through 12. No fuckin' around. I'm weirdly shamanistic and kind of afraid of tradition. What's the word? Superstitious. Like baseball players with their fucking dirty jockstraps.

So if you hit a panel that you're not keen on drawing, you don't move onto a panel three pages later that you'd prefer to draw and then get back to it?

No, I just have to soldier through. I'm always stuck on scenes. It's like, "Fuck, they're in the restaurant scene, I'm stuck in the sports bar. Fuck, fuck." I'm just pushing, three days in the sports bar. I'm desperate to get out, I want to get outside so bad. [*Claps.*] I'm outside. Fuck, there's like trees and cars. I'm stuck outside. I just want to get back to the house. It's always just wanting to get back to the house. The house is fine. I love drawing the TV and the couch and the little bottles. That same fucking standard shot, that stock shot, I can draw that a million times in a row. But, yeah, it's just scene to scene, bleh.

Is this done on 8½ inches by 11 inches paper?

Any paper I can get that's lying around. Usually the shitty old computer paper. But I feel it's like staging. I do it so quickly with thumbnails, it's like putting characters on a stage. And they all talk to each other, and they all wrestle within your mind. I just act it out. Like, OK, this has to happen. This is the scene. Just fucking write it out, get in the heads of the characters and what would they say to each other. It's like writing a play.

> " I don't want to have fancy layouts that confuse people. I can't read Chris Ware comics anymore. I'm sorry, they're too fucking confusing. I don't want to put together a board game. "

When you're in the thumbnail stage, how completely written is it at that point?

Pretty much done. I'll do a few passes on it. I should do more passes probably, but I find that just muddles things up. If you overthink it … I mean traditionally, fuck, only two passes and it's done. And I'm just like, "It's not going to get any better. It's all there." Maybe punch it up for a few extra jokes. If I'm desperate, I'll get a friend or two to read it, like, "Is something missing?" I know when something is not working. When something is fine, it's working, but it's just a bit off or dead. Or totally shit, you know. I turn out a lot of shit work that I'm not that happy with. It's passable, I may as well put it out. Spent the time on it. [*Laughter.*] What the fuck am I going to do? I don't have the luxury of endless fucking time. So sometimes you do a shitty one.

I don't understand people that just make it all up. I don't understand how you can work that way. It's going to be shit. There's a good chance it's going to be shit. You're going to dig yourself into a real messy hole. Works for some people, I guess.

Do you allow yourself any space for spontaneity? In other words, if on page 82 an idea suddenly strikes you while you're drawing page 81, do you have the latitude to change it up?

It's in the writing, I think. I have to pull the trigger while I'm writing. Like I said, I'm acting. There's always spontaneity and shouting. That's when it has to happen, and then you do a few passes and clean it up. And of course, there's late-stage edits. I think I've read Clowes say that nothing's really set in stone until you ink the final text in the bubbles. That's kind of the final change, the turn of phrase, a bad joke that you can change into something else. In the new book, I did that a couple of times. Had one joke there, and then I changed it to something else. I said, "That's terrible," and changed it back. But not really. I like it to be set in stone and then make it happen.

Do you refine the dialogue in the final stage of drawing the strip itself?

I'll change it sometimes, but generally it's good to go. I've written thumbnails, I've blocked it all out with the script. I don't worry about page layouts, I just count the panels – like 1, 2, 3, 4, 5, 6, 7, 8, 9, 10, 11, 12. Dash, that's page one. 1, 2, 3, 4 – pshew. Sometimes I'll move something around. Like, I'll want a splash panel here, or I want this to appear on the left-hand side of the page, so I'll rejig something or cut something. But generally, I don't worry about that. I just want it to be fluid, and the story moves along, and people aren't going to notice, really. If they're engrossed in the story, all that shit doesn't matter. They'll just fucking follow the panels. I don't want to have fancy layouts that confuse people. I can't read Chris Ware comics anymore. I'm sorry, they're too fucking confusing. I don't want to put together a board game. I don't want to be like, "Where do I go next? Is it over here?" There's little panels here, some arrows, I have to – like, fuck off. [*Groth laughs.*] I like meat and potatoes, clear, immersive stories. Chris Ware is still brilliant. I had trouble reading "Lint," [*The ACME Novelty Library* #20] but it was brilliant. The one that follows the guy from life to death. The bully character. But yeah, I try not to

RIGHT: From *One More Year*, 2017.

think about it too much. I just try to be clear and concise. Keep the pacing smooth as I can.

Well, formally, you almost never break the grid.

No. Why would I?

But you do occasionally. There was that great story where Owl fantasizes about Megg in high school, where you have a very large panel.

Well, I'll do a splash panel occasionally. You've got to do a splash panel.

It's the exception to the rule.

I have no desire to do triangular panels, or big side swoosh slashes. I did a circular inset in one story, that was a big splash showing the ram raids where it pans out over the neighborhood. There's a little circular Jones. But that's the extent. I'm just not design-minded. I don't feel like a strong artist, I'm not a good drawer. I struggle at it. I'm very lazy, I cut a lot of corners. I mostly just want to produce the work and finish it. So, I'm not laboring over it. I can't correct anything if I make a mistake.

When you say you're not a good drawer, what do you mean?

I'm not technically skilled. I'm not imbued with talent. I'm not a natural drawer. I can't life draw. Drawing's fucking hard. [*Laughs.*] It's always a fucking struggle. I don't draw good hands. There's so many things I just can't draw very well. But it doesn't really matter. When you're barreling along through a story, no one's stopping to check the fingers. If something's really bad, it'll stick out.

The storytelling is more important than the drawing.

It is. It definitely is. It's the basis of everything. But yeah, ugh. I can't correct. If I

use a correction fluid, or Wite-Out, that'll soak up the watercolor. There'll be a big blank patch. So my comics are full of mistakes. I'd like to be like Charles Burns and do five layers and white things out, and then do color on the computer, but ugh. I'm stuck with my ways. I don't like the computer.

Do you practice drawing?

No. I don't keep a sketchbook. I'm always working, so I'm always in practice. I've just been coloring for four months now, like 16 hours a day, just coloring. I haven't really drawn anything, or penciled anything, for a while. I'll be rusty when I get back into it. But I feel like it's a waste of time to keep a sketchbook. I'm so obsessed with time management, and time wastage, that to travel to a studio would be a waste of time. To do a warm-up drawing would be a waste of time. Why would I do that? I just get into it. I'm shaky in the mornings. When I wake up, I'm like, "Ugh. Fuck. I feel sick."

Well, your work ethic is amazing, based on what I know of it. You're never not working.

It's very unhealthy, in a way. I'd like to read a book, or relax. And it's very difficult being a present spouse. When Jacq gets home, having to stop working. I did really well at the start of this year. I worked from nine till six. Get up in the morning, when Jacq left. Work until she got home, and then we'd be a normal couple at night. But the last few months, I've just had to work. I move my shit out here to the living room, we hang out together. I just have to work. I have to finish this book. I've got two weeks. I still got a lot of work to do. I don't have time for anything else. I just have to sit there and fucking work.

But you enjoy that.

I do. I want to put out a good book. I want to kick everyone's ass and make the best fucking book I can. I'm not taking any fucking shortcuts. I'm serious. I'm militaristic. Why waste fucking time? I'm trying to solidify a fucking career. I've gotten onto a good kick. I want to be Matt Groening. I want to buy my mother a house. I want to take care of the people I love. I don't need self-care, I'm not going to sit around like la-di-dah. This is self-care. This is fucking work. Getting shit done, taking care of my family.

You've talked about work as therapy.

It is. It's an escape. That's where the problem comes in, because it can just become an escape. Reality melts away when you're staring at the page, and you become a robot. Gender disappears, reality, form – humanity disappears, and it's just me producing. It simplifies everything. It's the one thing I have to do: I just have to sit here and do this. Life distilled down to its simplest essence, only one thing you have to do. I've worked so hard to get to that point where I can just sit there and do that. It's a sickness.

BELOW: From *Megg and Mogg in Amsterdam*, 2016.

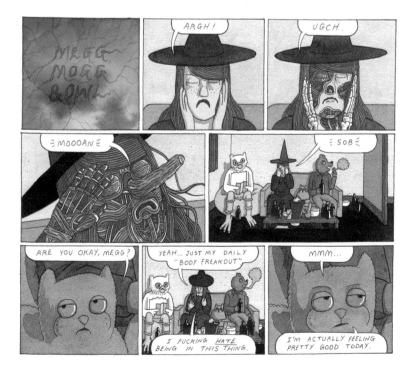

But you're engaging in humanity by transforming it onto the printed page.

Well, yeah. I'm creating fluffy entertainment for kids.

Wait a minute. Do you believe that?

Well, it's entertainment for the masses. It's art, but it's entertaining. I'm making it entertaining.

But all art should be entertaining.

It *should* be.

But all entertainment isn't art.

No, it's not. I'm purposely trying to make entertainment. I'm trying to entertain people. I'm not trying to change the world, or make great art. I just believe that in the scheme of things everything is fucking pointless. We're all dust floating around. We're ants. Everything is going to be dust one day. Everything we do is fucking pointless. We just distract ourselves in the fucking moment. So I know everything I'm working on is completely pointless.

I've read where you've said that before. But your own commitment to your art tends to contradict that. Why would you be so committed to it if it didn't mean anything?

Distraction from the horror. It's something to do because, in the moment, we have to distract ourselves. We have to pretend everything will be OK and we're not just going to die and be nothing. We have to pretend that things matter. We distract ourselves, we dig in. This has value to me, this makes me feel good, let's just keep doing this. I hold no illusions that it's this brilliant fucking thing. But then, kids come up to me and say, "Your book really helped me get through high school," or "It's made me feel better about being queer," or something. That's fantastic. It is affecting change in a very small way. When I read *Hate* when I was a teenager, it helped me understand dating and family strife. These things are informative. *Megg and Mogg* is very queer, or whatever you want to call it. But I try to do it in a really subtle, non-political-in-your-face way.

But in a way, you're having it both ways. You're creating art. You seem to be minimizing the aesthetic dimension of it. Do you not think there's a distinction between something that's just pure entertainment that has no aesthetic component whatsoever? The latest *Avengers* movie or something, and something that does have an aesthetic facet that you can grapple with?

Well, there's definitely better art. But it's also the same thing, really. Some stuff has more humanity or pathos in it.

But then it's not the same thing, right? It's something apart.

I still think they're the same thing, but one of them is more pure than the other.

Your work is becoming more and more serious. You'll do frivolous stories, like Werewolf Jones blowing himself, just short gag strips.

But that's about aging. That strip is about aging. [*Laughter.*] He can't do it anymore. His body is aging, he can't do that.

But you'll also do stories with an existential dimension. There's the "Sadness Mattress," for example, I think that was a three-page story, where there's a sense in which in that last panel Megg is coming to grips with her own dysfunction. And that has a deeper resonance to it.

Yeah, yeah. Those are real emotions.

Which indicates to me you were getting more serious in that story. You were using these characters to say something universal about what we all go through.

I write about anxiety and depression. It's just putting your feelings out there. It's trying to be pure, it's trying to be open. I remember when I was younger wanting to write about all the cross-dressing stuff. Thinking, "I should just be really open about it. People react to visceral, honest art." But I held back. I don't think you should hold back. I don't censor myself. I try to be "uncensored but not insensitive." Because my work can be very offensive and triggering to people. But I refuse to censor myself. It's all based on things that have happened to me, or friends. It's me processing things. I don't believe art should be censored in any way.

ABOVE: From *One More Year*, 2017.

RIGHT: From *Megahex*, 2014.

You once said, "I don't censor myself. You need to be honest. You need to not hold back. I hate twee art. [*Hanselmann laughs.*] I find it dishonest. A false, privileged construct. Life is not nice. Existence is sad and cruel."

I still feel that way. There's been this whole movement of self-care and stuff. [*Soft voice:*] "We just need to take care of ourselves." I find that so privileged. I didn't have that growing up. There was no opportunity for self-care. You just had to fucking work until you dropped to survive or get anywhere. You're surrounded by horror and people doing it hard. When people talk about their self-care – "I'm just going to have a hot bubble bath and watch

Netflix for six hours." It's like, fuck you. [*Laughs.*] There's people dying all around the world. We're in this privileged bubble, with no war – well, no major world war for a good time. I feel like people are getting soft. I think that's really bad.

What I sensed reading all your stuff from the earliest to the latest is that you're using the characters that you created more and more to face the reality of their situation. More and more to communicate the brutal dimension of what you've experienced.

That's what I wanted to do. I wanted it to be reflective of my own life, where, during youth, it can be quite frivolous and silly without consequence. And then we age, and reality starts to kick in, and you have to face the consequences of what you've sowed. They're growing up, as characters. The new book has a flashback, it shows where Megg came from and where she's gotten this behavior. The whole thesis of whatever *Megg and Mogg* is, is about redemption and change and how difficult that is. Breaking patterns and generations of failure.

RIGHT: From *Megg and Mogg in Amsterdam*, 2016.

It seems that you've been moving in that direction almost inexorably.

Slowly but surely. I mean, the book you're talking about, *Bad Gateway*, I started that in 2012.

Bad Gateway

Bad Gateway was the first book you conceptualized as a single narrative.

Yeah, it's the first like that.

Your longest previous story was 52 pages. Did you have to approach this differently structurally? Did you have to think it through differently, do more preparation?

Not really. I was excited to do this because it's what I'd wanted to do for a few years. It was the finances. I made money from the Galerie Martel show, and I had the money to say fuck off to freelance gigs and overly stressing about making zines to make money. I could pull a Clowes and just comfortably sit around and take my time. Patience, patience, and just work on this one book.

I assume that felt really good.

It did. It was also maddening, I think I had a mental breakdown on New Year's Eve. The insanity of just working on this one thing every fucking day, day in, day out.

That was toward the end, so that was OK.

Oof, it was really brutal, actually. Very fucking stressful. Long, long days. I wrote this comic from January to February, and that was fucking grueling just trying to stay focused and get into the thing. Then it took three months to pencil it all. Maybe four. I inked it in 40 days. I inked 156 pages in 40 days. That was four pages a day. I forced myself. I still had spare time at the end of the day to hang out with Jacq. But it added

up. Four times 40. I just said, "OK. I'm going to do four pages a day. I can get this done in 40 days." I fucking blew through it. But my hands were fucked. "Aaarrggg!" My back went out once.

I was going to say, has the arthritis hit you yet?

My back went out at one point. My friend Jordan came up, and I had to sign all these prints. And I was literally just walking around the house screaming. "Ahhhhhh!" Every time I moved. I think he felt really bad because he was here for the weekend. I had to paint all these portfolios. Anyway, I was in so much pain. But I just worked through it. I worked all fucking day through that shit just screaming. Fuck it. What am I going to do? Just lie there?

Bad Gateway is relentless. Did it feel relentless when you were conceiving it, writing it, drawing it – the whole process of producing it? Did you feel a weight that you hadn't felt with previous books?

When I started this thread of stories about Megg's mother back in 2012, I did cry while writing it. When I was thumbnailing it out. When I got back from London I hadn't seen my mother or grandmother for years, and I went down and visited them. And it was fucked. It was just like ... I'd been off having a nice time hanging out with normal, civilized people, and then I just went back to this den of schizophrenic junkies. It was really fucking upsetting. I just went to my old bedroom and wept. I was like, "Jesus fucking Christ!"

So writing about that and processing that was difficult, but it's like art therapy. It helps you to work through that and distance yourself. Once you turn it into fiction, you can look at it from different angles, and it becomes less oppressive and fucked up. Less real. I feel the book starts out very silly. I've sort of done the same thing as the previous books. It starts out a bit light and silly, there's dick jokes, but by the end it progressively gets more and more horrible and emotional and deeply depressing. [*Laughs.*]

It just spirals.

That's my trick, I think. I lure them in with the jokes and the *Jackass*-style slapstick, and then I hit them with the pathos and the bleak and utter squalor.

Well, you did say (I don't know when you said this), "I drew four pages of *Megg's Coven* in 2012 or so, and it was actually quite difficult. It was some very difficult material for me. I think I cried on one of the read-throughs." And you attributed that to the traumatic nature of the material. But you didn't have that problem with *Gateway*. Is that because you think you processed a lot of that stuff, had some distance from it?

The material wasn't as rough on me. It was the tame beginnings.

It's pretty rough. You have a high threshold!

The stuff I was upset about was my grandmother telling me she'd been raped in her kitchen. And my mother was in the kitchen shooting up. I was just stuck there with my grandmother telling me she'd been raped in the butt and how she didn't like it. "Not even a little finger, Simon, I don't even want a little finger up there. They raped me in my bum in the kitchen last night." It actually was the ghost man, the man in the painting. My grandmother for a while was wearing 14 wristwatches, seven on each arm, and three pairs of sunglasses. She was losing her fucking mind. So, with my mother shooting up and my grandmother telling me that, it was ... And I feel for these women, I empathize for them. These are lovely women. They've just been dealt bad mental hands and become drug addicts. I'm writing about that. But the stuff in *Bad Gateway*, the drug bust, the pee bottles, that's something I've been meaning to draw for years. I've always wanted to draw a comic about the drug bust with the piss bottles.

And that again is based on personal experience because you witnessed your mother being busted when you were 17, right?

Younger. I was 15 or something. Maybe 17, I don't know. They strip-searched me. The best bit of that that I couldn't put in the comic –

Why didn't you? When they saw you ... Oh, obviously, you couldn't put it in because it wouldn't quite work.

They found all my women's clothes. The guy was like, "Are these trophies, mate?" I was like, "What does that mean?"

I hope you said yes.

I did. I figured out what that meant, and I was like, "Aww, yeah. Yeah, mate. Trophies. Yes, I collect woman's underwear after I fuck them, and I keep them and sniff them." I couldn't put that in because it doesn't work. But that was a good bit. I could always have Booger get busted in the future. Their mother is also an addict, and they get busted and that happens.

There's a lot of pain in the book.

Pain, yeah. It's a depressing book. [*Laughs.*]

And I assume a lot of that pain was your pain.

Yeah.

Was it painful to revisit it and write about your own experiences?

Yeah, it was a bit. [*Laughs.*] I finished writing it the day of my mother's birthday, February 28, and started drawing it. I felt weird about that because I know this book is going to really upset her. So, I was feeling emotional about that. It was kind of creepy. I had to call her on her birthday, and she was having a really depressing, horrible birthday. I often find dates throughout all my work. I don't believe in astrology or numerology, but I notice weird things and numbers and dates sync up and it seems just weird. A few things like that. My dad got sick throughout the production of the book. I found out that he was dying of cancer towards the end of the book. All this weird family shit.

My mom was going in and out of the hospital at certain points throughout writing chapters and her house was demolished. In the flashback where Megg's back in the '90s at her house, that house was demolished while I was drawing the book, when I was penciling that story. So I was creating this mental version of my teenage bedroom that had just been demolished and doesn't exist anymore that I didn't get to say goodbye to. Semantic shit. It wasn't overly distressing, but a few things like that, it just feels kind of weird. I remember yeah, the first stab at this material in 2012, I broke down crying. I was writing about my mother and my grandmother, stuff that'll happen in the next book, but yeah, it was really hard. I was too close to it. I had gotten back from London and visited my mother and grandmother and it was fucking horrifying. I wasn't used to it anymore. I'd been off working real jobs and going to gentlemen's clubs. [*Laughter.*] Having a nice time in Piccadilly Circus and it was all pretty fucking normal. I was widening my horizon and getting out into the real world and then went back to the squalor of Tasmania and these small people consumed by drugs and schizophrenia. It was horrible. I tried to write about it a few months later and it really was quite difficult. But since then I've become numb to it. I've been kicking these stories around for years and planning *Megg's Coven* and this whole new movement of *Megg and Mogg*. When the time came it was like, "Let's just get it done." It's going to really hurt my mom. I don't want to send this book to her.

Do you think it will?

Oh yeah. I didn't even send her *One More Year*, the previous book, because of the story where Megg and Werewolf Jones are doing their music thing and it's Mother's Day. Megg can't contact her mother, and she's all paranoid and does some methadone or something that her mother's on – which is a true story, sadly. [*Laughs.*] But, yeah, the mother's calling up, asking her for money, and Megg's like, "Ugh." I didn't want to send that to my mum. I didn't want her to know that I do get pissed off when she asks for money too often. Obviously, she knows, but she's

ABOVE: From *Bad Gateway*, 2019.

ABOVE: From *Bad Gateway*, 2019.

sensitive. I help her out a lot, and I don't want her to know that sometimes I'm frustrated. I do vocalize that to her sometimes, but it's upsetting for her. She's already in such a bleak fucking black hole, I don't want to add to it.

Your depiction of Megg's mother in the book was not cruel.

BELOW: From *Bad Gateway*, 2019.

No, it's a human portrayal. I have a lot of respect for my mother and what she's done.

It's just the passage of time in the book … But at the end of the book, it's not nice.

It's tragic.

My mother's not going to read that. "You look nice, Simon. You look great." And then in the thought bubbles, "Oh, you're terrible, Mother. What happened to you?" She knows that she's been ravaged by all these drugs and by time. But she doesn't want to think about it. She still looks in the mirror and expects to see her 30-year-old self.

Did you own Gretskys?

I did. Yeah, I had some Gretskys.

Did know who Wayne Gretsky was? Did you follow sports?

I was briefly interested in roller hockey and, by default, ice hockey as a kid. I went through a baseball phase when I was a kid. We all played softball in school. I got vaguely interested in baseball. I think I went through a gridiron phase. I was never really into sports, though.

Did the skates have as much meaning to you as they did for Megg?

Yeah, they did. Because I did sell them years later and felt really guilty about it. Just like in the comic, sold 'em for drug money. That was a little different though, in reality. I think I was 9, and we had a track meeting at school. I was begging my mum for these shoes. "Everyone's got new shoes and my shoes are shit. I want the fancy shoes, Mother." And she bought them for me. She told me 20 years later how difficult that was because I wouldn't shut the fuck up about it. We were broke, and she needed the money for drugs, but she valiantly went without drugs and bought me those shoes. I was like, "You're a saint, Mother. You're a saint! You went without drugs for your child. Good for you."

That is the ultimate sacrifice.

In the comics, it got all mixed-up.

You conflated the two, that's all.

Yeah, yeah. That's what you do as a writer. You just take little disparate chunks of sadness and grift them together. And Megg's moaning about selling all the stuffed animals. That was something that happened when I was 15. "I don't need all these stinking, fruity stuffed animals." Then years later, I was like, "I loved those stuffed animals when I was a kid. My German grandma gave me one of those, and she's dead now." And just thinking about them ... Just thinking about someone not appreciating them and using them as rags. Just destroying them and putting them in trash bags. That's like attachment to physical things, though, which is really unhealthy.

My mother has a thing with baked beans. When she opens a can of beans, she can't leave a single bean in there. "All the beans need to be together!" She's anthropomorphized the fucking clothes pegs too. "They all have to be rotated. If one of the clothes pegs doesn't get a go ..." It's this unhealthy attachment. I've picked up some of that. I do get very sentimental about childhood bullshit. All that kind of stuff. Selling stuff is sad. That's just inherently sad. Growing up and selling your beloved childhood stuffed animals for drug money is horrible.

It plays nicely against Megg's usual cynicism.

Yeah, Megg's a huge cunt. She's horrible. But she can't help it. It's showing the genesis of what she is. I don't think that I'm as bad as Megg. [*Laughter.*] I said all this stuff is autobiographical – it is, but it isn't. You make things into fiction.

How old is Megg in *Gateway*?

Like, 30?

So she's close to your age. Are the characters, specifically Megg, going to age as you keep drawing them?

Yeah. This new book is a continuation of *Megahex*. Owl has moved out and boom, we're continuing. I'm stuck back in 2014. Werewolf Jones dies in 2017, so that would be two or three years on from *Bad Gateway*. There will be one more book after this, then the next one, the third in this new series starting with *Bad Gateway*,

ABOVE: From *One More Year*, 2017.

BELOW: From *Bad Gateway*, 2019.

RIGHT: From *Hate* #27 by
Peter Bagge, April 1997.

Werewolf Jones will die. I feel like George R.R. Martin taking forever to do this shit, but I'll get there eventually.

I thought it was interesting for readers to know that Werewolf Jones will die. It gives you a certain perspective as you're watching this person hurtling towards death. Like in *Hate*, there was the shocking death of Stinky. When I was a kid, I was like, "Whoa! Fuck!" It was shocking and crazy that this character I've been reading for years was suddenly dead. But with Werewolf Jones, you know that in the future he's going to die. It's slowly marching towards it. I did that in *Bad Gateway* with the overdose. I know that readers will be like, "Oh man." Astute readers who give a shit will be like, "Oh man, this is the moment he's dying." But no, he wakes up and he's off. He's got more kids and he'll be back. His wife and his father are going to show up in the next one and take over the whole house. I'm saving some good stories for that one. Some domestic battery in there.

I think it's great that we know he's going to die. It's not his death that's keeping us hooked, it's his life.

It's his antics. He's a complicated character. [*Laughs.*] I love Werewolf Jones. Grant and I are writing this new Werewolf Jones zine. We've both got bad dads, you know? Bad, absent, biker junkie dads. We're so good and adept at writing bad dad comedy. We're doing Jaxon's first driving lesson. Jaxon's vasectomy. This amazing beauty pageant

episode where Werewolf Jones puts the boys in a "Little Miss" beauty pageant to try to win easy money.

Is he easier or more fun to write than *Megg and Mogg*?

It's fun. It's just dumb-shit comedy. It's Grant and I trying to make each other laugh. We like this douchebag character. He's just this fucking hedonistic wrecking ball. A classic fucking trope.

It's a nice balance.

I think sometimes people are like, "Why don't you do a Booger solo comic? Why don't you do a Megg solo comic? Why does

RIGHT: Cover to *Werewolf Jones
and Sons* #1 by Hanselmann
and HTML Flowers, 2015.

Werewolf Jones have this spin-off?" It's because it's fun. I don't know. I feel like no one's writing dumb-ass filthy comedy anymore in comics. I'm really excited about *Werewolf Jones and Sons* #3 because it's going to be a fun, stupid comic. I'm just trying to make people laugh as much as possible. And make myself laugh. I was trying to think, "Who else is making just capital-C Comedy? Or attempting to do that?" I can't really think of anyone. *Bad Gateway* is full of wafty drama and pathos. It's full of it, but there are still some good dick jokes in there.

There are a few moments of levity, but not many.

No. So, I don't know how people will react to that who have just read *Megahex*, which is just full of *Jackass* pranks and dick jokes predominantly. It does have that acidic turn at the end and depression. #depression.

Well, it's quite moving.

I hope so. I don't fucking know. You get so deep into it. It's hard for me to tell. Just wait for the second book if you thought that was sad. Wait for Book Two and Three … Jesus. I don't think it's that bad. The few people who have read it have said that it's sad, but it seems normal to me.

Sad can be normal.

That's *my* normal. Well, not anymore. Through hard work and diligence, I've dug myself out of a big pile of shit. [*Laughter.*] I don't have to work at the gas station. Well, I'm happier now, but it's still a nightmare of feelings and emotions. There's a ton of bad shit with my mother and so much negative crap. It's hard. It's hard to get up and get moving. Like I was saying earlier, I don't really believe anything means anything. It does. In the moment, we have to take care of our friends and family and make things nice. I don't want things to be horrible right now, so we try to make things nice. But the more I think about it, everything's fucking pointless. Nothing is going to last. None of this is important. I'm pointing at all my books on the shelf. This is all landfill. None of this is important. None of this will mean

ABOVE: From *Megahex*, 2014.

anything in 1,000, 2,000, a million years. Nothing. I don't like to think about it too much. I just get upset.

I can see that you're getting depressed as I speak to you. [*Laughter.*]

Yeah.

But to devote that much time and effort and work and so much of yourself to something that is essentially meaningless…

What else am I going to do? I could just sit around and do nothing, but I have to make money. I have to take care of my mother. I need to buy her groceries and pay her rent when she needs it. It's a necessity. We want the creature comforts. We don't want to be living in squalor.

I have to believe it's something more than just utilitarian.

It makes me feel good. I discovered early on that sitting around making these little stories and distracting myself makes me feel good.

Do you think it's possible you feel good because you're doing something worthwhile? That it has some intrinsic value to it.

I don't really think it has value. It's entertainment. I'm making entertainment. It makes some people feel good. But how good? It's not as good as curing cancer. The work I do with the animal shelter is more important. Helping Jacq with the animal shelter and taking care of all the rabbits downstairs. Giving them their medicine.

They are living creatures that need love. That means more than me sitting around drawing some sad witch comics. I don't really see it as important. It's important to me, but I don't expect anybody else to think it's important. Why should they? It's important in our little world of comics. We attach importance to things. I was saying earlier, we are cursed with sentiment. We are talking monkeys. We've made this big complicated system of codes. We've built society and made it what we wanted. It's all a construct. It's all bullshit. Just roll along, find your niche. Roll along, do your thing. Try not to fucking think about it because if you do think about it too much you'll go fucking insane. That's why I envy dumb people. I really do. I don't think I'm the smartest cookie in the box, but I'm cursed with enough intelligence to be frightened by everything I see. [*Laughter.*]

It would be great to live life without being frightened.

There's always death. There's always going to be death. We can always be frightened of death. That's nothing to be afraid of though. That's a relief. Fuck. It was weird having all my friends die in 2016. It was weird that that finally happened. Experiencing that shit, that loss. It was devastating.

Deaths

You experienced several deaths recently.

Two in a row. My bandmate of 10 years died. Then Alvin Buenaventura killed himself, the dickhead. In the autopsy, they found 23 different drugs in his system, including crystal meth.

Jesus Christ.

He loved his drugs. He was a madman. He owed me a lot of money at the time. It was fucked up. Finally, that happened. You roll through life thinking you're invincible.

It's like how I smoke. My parents smoked and my grandma – they're all fine. "I'll be fine, I'll be fine." We tell ourselves we'll be fine, but then death comes a-knocking. You experienced that in 2013 when Kim [Thompson, Fantagraphics co-owner] died. That happened really fucking suddenly. It's fucked.

Quite a few people have died out from under me at this point.

I imagine. It kicks you in the balls.

But I don't think I've changed. I've kept doing the same things I've been doing.

That didn't change you?

I just kept working. When Jacq was like, "What do you want to do?" I was like, "I'm just going to keep working." What can I do? Just keep fucking working. I wrote a comic about Karl called *Drone* about our band. It's just me and Karl hanging out and doing our band thing. A little tribute. Then I just fucking moved on. I played some gigs where we sang together, and I wept onstage.

Do you think that affected your work in some way?

It will. Werewolf Jones dying. Actually, losing friends. I killed Werewolf Jones off in the future, in a previous strip, which is now in the past. That was about a friend of my mother's. A junkie guy who came over to the house and wanted to stay. She wouldn't let him stay so he went off some-where else and had an overdose. She was always feeling very guilty. "If I just fucking let him stay maybe he wouldn't have died." So, I did the Werewolf Jones comic about that. But now I've lost a really fucking close friend, and I'm going to change the way Werewolf Jones dies to process through that shit. I'll put that in the comics. It's directly changed the comics and the way I'll work on this shit.

But again, it's all pointless. Karl had a good run. He had a heroin overdose.

"HE WAS A REAL PIECE OF SHIT. A MAGNIFICENT, BEAUTIFUL PIECE OF SHIT."

♫ MUSIC: "TEENAGE DIRTBAG" - WHEATUS.

He went out happy. Under a bridge. Alvin wanted to leave. He'd been threatening to kill himself for years, and he finally fucking did it. I still think it may have been an overdose. But either way, he wasn't fucking happy so I can't be too sad about it. They went out fine. In the scheme of things, it's not going to matter. So many people have died. Like in the French Catacombs, there's all those fucking skulls and no one fucking cares. They're all faceless, all forgotten. No one's there caressing their skulls going, "Oh, you poor baby." No one cares. [*Laughs.*] That's nihilism!

Which is healthy, I think. I'm full of empathy and full of care for people. I truly believe we have to make things nice now, we have to make things comfortable before the end, but it's all so pointless. We can move on from this. It's very depressing. But it's a strength to me. It's a strength to not get too attached to anything and believe everything is pretty transient. Nothing means too much. Just try not to be a prick.

Is that comforting?

Yeah, it is. The cold embrace of death will come soon. Or the *warm* embrace of death. Maybe there is a fucking afterlife, I don't fucking know. I'm not going to go on faith, but maybe there is.

Do you think about your own death?

A lot.

It's quite a ways away, probably.

Yeah.

If you look at the stats.

LEFT: From *One More Year*, 2017.

I'm a heavy smoker. Chugging Red Bull down. My family is full of mental illness, but there's no heart disease or cancer, so I feel like I could probably weather that shit with good genes. Strong Nazi genes apparently, according to my dad. [*Laughter.*]

You seem quite robust.

I'm still pretty athletic. I'm 37, but people think I'm in my early 30s. I see other people not looking too good. "You're my age? Really? Fuck, what happened?" I still look good in a wig and some makeup. I still look OK. Maybe the nicotine stunted my growth. But it's all going to go downhill. The disease lottery is going to kick in.

I can't stay up like I used to. I used to stay up working for 40 hours nonstop. I think that's my record. But I can't do that anymore. Sometimes I say to Jacq that I'm going stay up and work, and I get to about 3:00 in the morning and I'm fucked. I gotta lie down.

There's that grim realization.

Time makes fools of us all. Still going, though. Still cranking it out and keeping the work up. Still trying to cement that foothold.

Truth Zone & Transgressive Humor

Do you think there are any topics that should be off limits to humor?

No, I don't think anything should be sacred. I try to be uncensored, but not insensitive – because my work can be very offensive and triggering to people. But I refuse to censor myself. I don't believe art should be censored in any way. I think artists should explore loaded terms. Take a risk and try to find answers. Obviously, I believe in artists playing with loaded fucked-up shit and experimenting with that.

Clearly, you're going to offend people by doing that.

I saw a mini-wave on Twitter of certain young, twee artists – very colorful, nice – and they were saying we have to get rid of the mean stuff. "There should be no mean art." They seemed serious. What the fuck are you talking about? Just sanitize everything, and I'm not allowed to write about what the fuck I want? My autobiographical work is not allowed by your standards? I write about something that happened to me, but you're offended by it? Fuck off. It's getting really weird out there. That's what that [*Truth Zone*] zine was about in part, internet outrage. And obviously, people got mad about it.

Did you anticipate that? How could you not, right?

I sold 600 copies direct to people. I wrote, "I've got a new *Truth Zone* zine out. People who like *Truth Zone* and *Megg and Mogg* can buy it." It wasn't heavily marketed to people. It was for a certain subsection of people. Most cartoonists fucking loved it. I got notes – "Brilliant. Very funny." But a different subsection of people think I'm a monster now. Someone called me alt-right, which I found absolutely fucking ridiculous. Someone who should know better.

But presumably, you wanted as many people to read it as possible.

No. I didn't. It's complete inside baseball. I was selling tons of them to Russian fans, and I thought they wouldn't understand any of it. It's like deep-web, hardcore inside-baseball comics shit for nerds. It wasn't marketed to the general audience.

You obviously felt strongly enough about whatever the subject was to write and draw a strip about it.

It was jokes that were going around. I talked to certain cartoonists and they'd be bitching about things. "Oh, that's a funny idea for a strip." It was overheard things. That's what *Truth Zone* always was. It was me digging around online and overhearing things and mashing it all up into this sketch-comedy thing.

Was it meant to be serious criticism, or are you just fucking with people?

It's both. It toes the line. It's just a joke, really. I pretended it was real criticism for a while and sometimes I thought it was. Tell me it's not. It's critical of things and it's writing about comics in a critical way.

What shocks me is that people got mad about certain things in there, but nobody talked about the comic in there that's printed emails from a certain publisher.

BELOW: From an online *Truth Zone* strip, 2013.

Would that be Nobrow?

It *might* be. I redacted those details of the publisher and the targeted individuals and publications. Your guess is as good as mine, Gary. No one fucking talked about it! Those terrible business practices! I thought that would be the bombshell. I thought a certain publisher might think, "That's clearly about us. Our shitty emails!" and try to send a cease and desist.

I thought everyone would be talking about it. No one said anything.

The problem is that you couldn't cite the publisher.

I could have, but I chose not to. It's so obvious who it is. It's so fucking obvious to an informed reader.

I think so, too.

It's really obvious. [*Laughs.*] I asked someone who I know that worked for them, I asked, "Did the other guys read that?" And he was like, "No, I don't think they know about it." Those emails have been passed around for ages, they must at least know they're out there.

You don't believe that, right?

I don't know. I was bitching to [Art] Spiegelman once at dinner in Copenhagen. I was bitching about their bad business practices and how they've ripped off artists and what cunts they were. Then from across the table, "Oh hello, I'm a guy from that publisher." I was like, "Oh no! Did he hear all that? Fuck!" [*Laughter.*] Spiegelman was eating it up. He was loving it. Everyone shared those emails around. That's some shoddy fucking behavior. Real cunts. Not just cheeky rabble-rousing. Just really shitty behavior towards artists.

I've heard about those emails but haven't seen them myself.

Well, I printed the emails there.

All of them?

That's the bulk of the emails, yeah. Adapted into a nice, breezy comic.

"Coat-Tailers."

"Coat-Tailers." I think this whole comic's good. It all got shit-talked, and I felt bad about it at the time, but I'm proud of that comic. I think it's a good comic. I think in the years to come, that'll be reappraised. Like, "Hanselmann is a genius. That's a good comic." It pre-dated all those Grammy-nominated stand-up routines. But some of those routines got in trouble online so that's nothing good to say. Like, "It predated these other offensive things. I was there first offending and alienating people." [*Laughs.*]

Where do you think your *Truth Zone* material lies in the spectrum of your art, relative to, say, *Bad Gateway*?

It's just silly shit. It's a zine I made for my friends. I printed 600 copies and sold them online just for dickheads and my cartoonist buddies. I made it for all the shit-talkers at the festivals.

> My autobiographical work is not allowed by your standards? I write about something that happened to me, but you're offended by it?

But you still consider it art?

It is art, obviously. But do I think it's great art? No. I don't feel arrogant about my work. It's fine, I put a lot of heart into it, but I also fucking hate it and I think it's shit. So many problems with it, I can see that. But then I just see this unchecked arrogance in other people. There's an arrogance to all these Twitter shit-talkers. This unearned arrogance with no solid skills backing it up. Now I'm seeing people saying that it's a right-wing thing: "working hard." But how else do you expect anything to happen? You can't just sit around saying you want something. You have to fucking make it happen. I mean, I've built myself up from nothing. I think it's unfashionable these days, "working hard." I've noticed a trend online, that is very anti-meritocracy. They think it's putting people down, it'll make people feel bad for themselves if they can't work at a certain set level. But I love the satisfaction of hard work. My mother grew up working all these fucking jobs. You have to work to survive, that's what I learned.

Is it that they don't believe that there's such a thing as a meritocracy or that there shouldn't be?

They don't want there to be, that's what I think. [*Laughs.*]

RIGHT: From *Spinning* by
Tillie Walden, 2017.

So they want a mediocracy.

A level playing field, yeah. They want to
break everything down so they can compete.
I make a lot of sports analogies when I talk
about the work I do. I work in a militaristic way. I've always liked the competition
aspect of art making. My friend Luke and I
competed in high school to see who could
do the most pages. It wasn't bad, it was just
pushing you. Like, "Oh, wow, Luke made
four really great pages. I've got to make
four pages." And then I got on the internet
and Michael DeForge was the big thing in
comics and he was up all night drinking
hot sauce and working like a maniac. And
he was the guy I looked to, like, "That's my
competition. That's who I've got to try and
beat." In a friendly way, it's motivation.

**Are they trying to eliminate all critical
distinctions between good and bad or
good and better? Is that the end goal?**

It can seem that way. It's being pushed that
there's value in all work. Which I do believe,
that there's value in all work, but some art
is frankly just better than other art. Some
people can put more time in or just be more
naturally talented. This is dangerous talk ...

What a radical notion [*sarcastically*].

Well, it shouldn't be a radical notion, I
think, but it is. I just believe in hard work
and focus. I'm sorry, but meritocracy
is real. You apply this to music – some
people can sing and some people can't.
Some people have natural talent and some
people don't.

**You're not the right person to ask this to,
but where does that come from? Trotsky
worked hard. Working hard and trying
to achieve excellence is not some sort of
right-wing conspiracy.**

No, it's not. Are you going to shit on the
Olympics? Is that next? All these people
training. "Anyone should be in the Olympics! A bunch of armchair slobs versus
Usain Bolt." Let's see how that goes. Can
Usain perhaps run a bit slower, as to not
offend people?

**I guess it has to do with a kind of perfect
equality where there are no differences.**

I can't help but see it as people just
demanding respect. "I want respect now!
I made *some* work. It's of a dubious quality,

but I think it's the best and I think it's important. I want kudos now! Why is no one publishing me?"

Let's talk about a couple of your *Truth Zone* strips.

Here we go.

The first strip is your critique of Tillie Walden's 400-page graphic autobiography. Your point, apparently, was that somebody who was, whatever age she was, 19 or 20 –

A young person doing a 400-page memoir.

Is *prima facie* fatuous.

Well, you say "my point." It's not necessarily "my point." I mean, it's what I'd been hearing around at the time. A bunch of older cartoonists saying, "Who's this young upstart doing a 400-page memoir? A kid doing a memoir?" I'm not going to discredit Tillie Walden. She's a fucking machine, she's a fucking workhorse. I like her Instagram posts. I don't like all of her work, some of it's a bit "nice" for my tastes. But I respect the fuck out of her. She's a fucking hard worker, incredibly talented. Better at drawing than I am!

In that case, what was the point of the piece, if you respect her work?

It's what people were talking about. In the comic, regarding her book, Megg and Mogg are just like, "Oh, cool. Good for her." And that's my personal opinion represented. I have no strong feelings one way or another. *Spinning* was coming out, I was like, "Good for her." But a lot of people were saying, "Who's this kid? A kid doing a memoir?"

But you don't think that particular point of view holds any water? That someone who's 19 shouldn't be doing a 400-page memoir because she doesn't have sufficient distance, or –

Here's the main point to me: The comic is called "Change." Owl comes in and says he's doing a shit autobio book about his masturbating habits with regressive macho action pastiches, and he's having trouble getting any critics to write about his series. This is about sad, pathetic white men who are moaning online that they're making this regressive sexualized shitty '90s work, and no one's writing about it. Because that's not what's cool right now. What's cool right now is young women making comics. That's what people are writing about. And that's what this comic is about. It's about how the scene has

ABOVE: From the *Truth Zone* zine *Portrait*, winter 2017.

RIGHT: From *Entertainment*, July 2018.

changed. I think that was a progressive comic!

But you also make Diesel's comic look ridiculous.

Well, yeah, it's a slight "roast" of Walden, as a public figure, also. It's a 400-page memoir about 12-year-old Diesel's roller-skating days from two years ago. He's bragging that it's already finished. On to the next project! Young guns.

You also have a shot at CCS [Center for Cartoon Studies], and how they tend to own SPX [Small Press Expo].

The CCS mafia. I didn't coin that term. Everyone talks about the CCS mafia. If you go to CCS, apparently you'll most likely win the fucking Ignatz ballot. It's a popularity contest. So, yeah, she went to CCS. And also she's really talented. I don't think it's a dig at Walden, it's a pretty fucking light ribbing, that she finishes work really fast and wins awards and has a supportive father. The biggest thing I got in trouble over that strip was me responding to someone on Twitter who I felt was actually being hugely insulting and dismissive of me as an artist and misinterpreting the strip that they had not read. They did the whole "no response but screencap and public shame" thing. I privately, facetiously referred to Walden as a "Daddy's girl" in a "direct message," because I'd heard people say that her dad escorted her to signings and stuff, and her dad made her website for her. Honestly, it was totally coming from

a place of familial jealousy on my part. It was intended to read as: "I am not as privileged as she is."

But I stand by this comic. I think it's a funny comic. I would hope and imagine that Walden wouldn't be super offended by the comic. I think what Tillie would be offended by would be the screencapped private conversations. I didn't want that flippant, early-morning, reactionary shit out there. I didn't want her to read that shit. So I think *they* did the fucking disservice by putting all that shit out there. This comic is pretty fucking tame.

So, you weren't condemning her comics.

No, I don't think I was. The main point to me was that I was condemning loser white males that were whining on Facebook that, "No one's reading my comics or writing about my comics." That's because your work sucks, mate. Because Tillie Walden's better than you and she's a fucking work-horse. But I'm also allowed to say Tillie Walden's work is not totally for me. It's for young women. Or whoever wants to enjoy it. I personally find it a bit too nice. People kept saying I was "punching down" as well, that I was punching down on Tillie Walden. I refute that. At the time, she'd been nominated for way more Eisners than me. She was way more popular. Big fucking book announcement from First Second. Super fucking popular online. She has a father who was present throughout here life. She has a nice, seemingly supportive family. She was a middle-class ice-skating girl when she grew up. I didn't fucking have that shit. I had junkies shooting up every-where. Getting fucking finger-diddled by Mum's boyfriends. I'm queer as well. I don't think I was "punching down."

I don't think you can legitimately be accused of punching down.

I thought that was just fucking stupid. I think she's socially far better off than me, but just because I present as male sometimes I'm a monster? Why didn't anybody come to Box Brown's defense? He was mercilessly spoofed in that book, really cruel stuff. Nah, he's a white male, "fuck him."

To what extent do attacks on social media affect you? Either personally or professionally.

Well, there was a third *Truth Zone* book I'd written, called *Orientation*, that I was going to bring out. I decided to shelve it. There was a somewhat fair but simultane-ously skewed online criticism of the *Portrait* book but it was the result of that, the un-nuanced hyped-up morons who just lis-tened to what some dipshit said, and took that person's account of what the intent of the piece was as gospel. Because people just did that, they were just like, "This was his intent. To denigrate this young, queer woman." Well, no. It's not, you douchebag. It's somebody's willful misreading of the actual intent. That's what bothers me, not the criticism, just when people are flat out wrong and zealously misrepresent you.

Do you think a piece like that can damage your reputation to such an extent where you don't want to put out another book?

It did, yeah. In this kind of climate, you cannot write about things like that. You cannot write weird, snarky, insider, slightly mean stuff. It's not worth the trouble.

Well, they would see that as an affirma-tion of what they did. They don't want

you to write and publish that, and they effectively prevented you from doing so.**

Exactly. Loud mouths shutting down work they don't like. Everything's infested with activism. It's all good in ethos. I agree with these causes generally, but a lot of these current comics are just bland activism. It's like, "Are you a cartoonist or an activist?" I can't tell. You don't seem to be trying to entertain me or put a solidly constructed narrative across. You're just trying to do a TED Talk and tell me something and bend me to your will. It's boring.

ABOVE: Back cover to *Megg and Mogg in Amsterdam*, 2016.

When you say you agree with it, you don't agree with the censorious aspect, do you?

No, I don't agree with the way they're going about it. But I agree with most of these progressive points and whatnot. I just think some people go about things a bit violently, and get a bit too excited. It's the #Metoo thing. It's a good thing, but I think people are becoming addicted to the dopamine hit of the next one. "Who's next? Who's next? Oh, we're going take them all down." So, people are out looking, hunting. They're looking for *anything*. Everyone's going through everyone's Twitters and digging things up and calling people out for very little things. There's nuance to these situations, though. It's getting fucking weird and you can't even say it's getting weird and complicated without being labeled alt-right or something. But I'm getting really sick of this shit. I'm genuinely sick of it, I don't think I'm a bad person. I'm a leftist. I'm queer. But yeah, I'm seeing more and more people getting out of these cliquey scenes, getting out of the more toxic queer scenes and just finding it all fucking silly. People are just pinning their whole lives on this stuff, just obsessed with gender politics and whatever activism they choose to follow. Well, go and do that, then. Why are you messing with comics? You think you're going to save the world by making a comic? Comics are just entertainment and they've got a very small reader base. You want to get out there and change something? Get out there with a placard, get out to your local parliament. Don't try to convince me, and shit all over me, and stop me from making what are intended to be fun, entertaining comics. [*Laughs.*] You're not fixing anything, it's embarrassing.

Their answer would be that you're making comics that are destructive. Hurting people. Triggering people.

Well, it apparently did trigger people. People were upset by a comic. The Crumb one in there, it's dicey.

I was going to bring up Crumb. He's a lightning rod, now.

Oh, definitely. "Boooooo!" That was a sarcastic boo, by the way.

And you essentially ridiculed the idea that someone could be triggered by either a Crumb comic or an anecdote about Crumb. Is that fair?

That's a bit broad. That comic was about a particular instance. That was a very particular instance.

Specifically, a woman posted something somewhere about how horrified she was when she read an interview that I did with Crumb, as a matter of fact.

Yeah. You were called a "rape-enabler," I think, by this person.

I believe so.

Because Crumb told an anecdote about where he jumped on a woman's back at a party in the '70s. I say in the comic, the "cloying" thing that he does, where he tries flirtatiously to piggy-back on a woman all cutesy like. I describe it in the comic as invasive, and of a sexual nature, but it's not fucking rape. So when I saw someone saying that they'd been crying in the toilets for two hours because you interviewed Crumb in the '70s and you giggled when he said that he'd jumped on a woman's back at a party, saying that you are a "rape enabler" and that Crumb was a full-on rapist, I saw that as intensely hyperbolic. "Where's this woman now? Is she OK?" Like I wrote in the comic – it was in the '70s, she's probably dead! [*Laughter.*] She's at peace now.

That was genuinely funny.

That was a funny joke. That's a dark joke.

But dark jokes are also frowned upon.

LEFT: From the *Truth Zone* zine *Portrait*, winter 2017.

They are. But again, I thought that was a nuanced comic. I was castigating Crumb. I was saying he was cloying and it *is* invasive and sexual. But I was trying to have a discussion of sexual assault. Because, online, at that time, everyone – still! – is getting really fucking frothed up. #Metoo is happening all around us in all industries. Good! Shitty men suck. Where is the line though? You've got your Weinsteins, your Aziz Ansaris. Where's the middle ground? So that comic was an attempt at a discussion of that. In this case, this person was perhaps overreacting on the internet. I feel bad that I made a comic about someone's genuine distress – someone maybe a bit unbalanced – who had to cry for two hours at work because of an old Crumb interview. At the end of the comic, they put Diesel, the stand-in, into therapy. Not necessarily my opinion that that person might need therapy, but maybe. A lot of people might think that. Therapy is good. These comics throw a lot of different ideas around and readers can make their own conclusions.

[*Laughs*.] I think you're suggesting she might need therapy.

Eh, that's for the reader to decide.

What do you think when someone overreacts, in your view, so disproportionately to something you write and draw? Their position, I think, is that you should have to respect and acknowledge whatever their reaction is. And I think you're saying that, no, you don't, that there is a sense of proportionality that you have to honor.

Yeah. The vile *right-wing* comedian Dave Chappelle [*Laughter*] put it best a few years ago when he said [that people have a] "brittle spirit." That was in reference to Louis C.K. I don't defend Louis C.K.'s actions, that's creepy as fuck. But look, I've had a lot of weird shit happen to me in my life. I've been fingered by people, like weird fucking sexual-assault shit. It's not stopped me from doing my thing and I can't imagine it ever affecting me like that. But that's me. I'm luckily strong-willed enough to put that kind of shit in my art and work through it. I'm going to take this and let it strengthen me. But some people can't do that. And I feel empathy for those people who can't do that. But there's definitely a wrongheaded cultural weakening going on. I think we're being obsequious toward certain people. If you jerked off at me right now, I'd be offended but I'd probably not be looking to quit making comics. I'd just tell you to fuck off and go to a different, less masturbatory publisher.

Are you familiar with Crumb's work?

Yeah. I'm not a huge Crumb fan but I had *The Big Book of R. Crumb*. I had *Mystic Funnies*, you know. I had some Crumb kicking around. Sold 'em for drug money.

Was he an influence? Did he affect your work?

No. I was more into Clowes and Bagge, and Joe Matt. I like Crumb's work, but I don't love Crumb's work. Great cross-hatcher. On Twitter, people say, "All white guys love Crumb. They worship him. Crumb. Crumb.

RIGHT: From *Weirdo* #22 by Robert Crumb, spring 1988.

Crumb." I'm not Noah Van Sciver. You can tell Noah wants to suck Crumb's dick. No, but seriously, I love Noah. He's one of best working today. But I can take Crumb or leave Crumb.

But you know where Crumb's place is in comics history.

Of course. I respect the fuck out of him. He's a brilliant fucking artist and I respect Crumb's craft. Look, he's done some dicey material. People complain about the comic where he assaulted a woman. It's a fucking comic though, it may not have happened like that. Has he actually come out and said that that comic went 100 percent like that? I think the woman somewhat consents in the comic before she falls asleep, anyway. I can't remember. They're seemingly there to fuck. But, still, it's dicey. It's a sexual assault-y comic.

It's dicey.

He says dicey stuff, he's an old fucking man! He says dicey stuff and he grew up in the fucking '60s making pioneering underground comics. And everyone owes him a debt. You don't have to like his work, you can say he's a cunt if you want. You're allowed to be offended by it, but don't stop me from reading it or enjoying it or saying it has value.

That's what I find so offensive. Not that they criticize him – Crumb can be criticized as much as anyone else.

Criticize him, yeah. But it's that puritanical, schoolmarm, "you're not allowed to enjoy this." This is *bad*, categorically. Like, what? Fuck off. [*Laughs.*] Everyone in comics is always shitting on the "awful boy's club," – the Mike Dianas and the Crumbs. These guys are barely even fucking around anymore! When I go to festivals, I see women. I see women of color. I see all sorts of queer people. All the awards are going to queer anthologies and women of

LEFT: From *Late Bloomer* by Carol Tyler, 2005.

color. Shut the fuck up and enjoy the spoils! What do you keep complaining about? You're the zeitgeist now. Raina Telgemeier is ushering legions of new young women into comics. It's so fucking diverse. If you don't like something, just make your thing. No one can stop you. I don't get this victim mentality. Of course, there's sexism, and some people are going to be fucked over by some bad apples. But on the whole, I don't see it. Just stick to your guns and do your thing. Is it that fucking hard, people? I get it with Crumb, you don't like his dicier work. People keep acting like this is a new discussion, but these conversations have been had forever, ad nauseam. Look around the book fairs, people. I see genuine diversity. Focus on the positives! Crumb is too old to attend and needs to stay near a toilet at all times. Joe Matt is thoroughly forgotten. You won!

There is this sense that they're trying to erase him from history.

Oh, definitely. He's supposed to be canceled and not allowed to exist. For Carol Tyler to get booed at the fucking Ignatz Awards because she just mentioned that he gave her her start in comics – "Boooo!" – and then people on Twitter calling her an old woman, and telling her to fuck off. Fuck you. Telling Carol Tyler to fuck off? I'm sorry, no. That's not going to fucking happen, kids.

That was appalling.

It really was. Everyone was clapping and clicking their fingers. I would have vomited if I had been there. I feel like I would've had had to pull a Kanye West and walk up on stage. "No, no, hell no. This ain't happening." There was talk of me hosting the Ignatz Awards last year. I'm not fucking hosting that. I presented one award the year before and I could just tell the crowd of kids was looking at me and going, "You're a bad man. Our favorite Twitter rabble-rousers say that you're a bad man."

Do you think that there is that same attitude about you forming?

Yeah, some people think I'm a cunt. Pockets of super-progressive political kids on

ABOVE: From the *Truth Zone* zine *Portrait*, winter 2017.

Twitter think I'm evil because I did those *Truth Zone* comics. I dared to say that an 18-year-old writing a big 400-page memoir was a bit funny, which it is. And I dared to do a comic exploring Crumb and sexual assault reactions. I also did a comic about me being pinched on the bottom at a festival by someone from the CBLDF [Comic Book Legal Defense Fund]. Owl tried to have the CBLDF represent him and had them suing themselves. But people thought it was about themselves. This one person on Facebook was like, "You're writing about me and my assault!" Bitch, shut up. This was about *me*. How are you arrogantly assuming I'm writing about you? But yeah, it seems that everyone's been fucking assaulted at some point in their life. But people just run with that person's assumptions and think I'm a bad guy who's written about some girl's assault. No one will ever correct it, either. I'm not going to fucking talk to these people anymore and go, "Hang on! You're wrong." They'll just twist everything. I see it all the time. Interaction has become pointless.

Do you feel like you have to be more careful now?

Oh, yeah. I don't tweet overly opinionated things. Why would I? I'm tired of it. There's no point. "Here's my opinion about this comic and this person." Who the fuck am I to talk about anything? I'm just busy making my art and doing my thing and

trying to enjoy my life. I see it as a big waste of time. I talk to friends "IRL."

I don't want to piss people off, it's not what I'm going for. But yeah, I'm scared of the people who will read the comics, misinterpret my aims and then paint me as something different on the internet. I've seen that happen. People are like, "What did Simon Hanselmann do? Should I not buy his books anymore?" That's what I'm scared of. I'm scared of these fucking misguided, "virtuous" people out there actively trying to tank peoples' careers. I think making a very limited zine which makes a fucking joke about someone is not the same as actively, humorlessly going out on Twitter and trying to destroy somebody's career. How dare somebody fuck with my livelihood? You're fucking playing with peoples' lives, housing, medicine, real shit. Fuck them ... And it's not art what you're doing. You're just fucking tweeting. Shut the fuck up. Make some fucking work. Be a part of the industry or fuck off. So, yeah, I'm not going to do another *Truth Zone*. People grossly misinterpret it and it irritates me.

A lot of your work could be considered offensive by a middle-class sensibility. Are there many artists doing that kind of work now in comics?

Not really. Who else is going to put a rape scene in a book now in the contemporary comics scene? I mean, lots of European artists. But not in the current American scene. Julia Gfrörer will have some rapey cocksucking in her comics. She's not afraid. But she's in with the whole "progressive kids" crowd as well now, so maybe she won't do that anymore. She'd probably get in trouble or get called out, or has been already. It's definitely putting a damper on things. There's a sex worker character in *Bad Gateway* and I feel like I could get in trouble for that because it's not presenting sex work in a flattering light at all. It's completely based on a sex worker I knew who was a friend of the family. My mother's done sex work and it broke her fucking heart. It was horrible and squalid. The most depressing thing ever. It works for some people. I've got sex worker friends who are empowered and having a great time, they love it. Other sex worker friends are broken, doing it for drugs. The saddest thing in the world.

It's like every other profession.

I can see people calling this shit out. I was worried, but now I'm like, "Fuck it." I'm just writing about people I've known and what I see. That's always been my go-to thing – you can get offended by it, fine. You don't have to buy any more of my books. Sorry if you're offended, but I'm just writing about things that have happened to me or I have seen happen. I'm trying to process shit. There was a warning on the cover. You didn't see the warning? Going forward, it's difficult. I'm trying not to compromise.

I'm not saying I'm perfect. I'm riddled with self-doubt. There's room for discourse. There's room for back-and-forth. Please, for the love of fucking god, can we just have some calm discourse?

I had this interesting thing happen at Emerald City Comicon. There was this right-wing couple that came up to my table. They were well-dressed, an Amazon-looking couple. Big, expensive North Face coats. The woman, in a hushed tone started telling me, "I'm a Republican, will you hold that against me?" [*Groth laughs.*]

I think she expected me to start screaming at her, like, "Fuck off!" The bulk of young people at festivals now actually would do something like that. "Take a fucking walk! Fuck you!" But I was like, "OK, all right. I'm not gonna go off. You're here to buy a book from me. Let's do this." She started telling me about how she'd read the books and initially found them fucked up, repellant. She was talking about the queer stuff. The trans stuff. All the squalor. The drug stuff. Initially she thought, "This is fucked. These people are fucked." Then she said she saw the humanity in it. She began to empathize with the characters. She was saying that it made her think more openly about different people and different sexualities.

You've touched the heart of a Republican. That's not easy to do.

BELOW: From *Entertainment*, July 2018.

That's beautiful. That's the goal of art. That's what you want. To change minds and make people more tolerant. You won't do that by screaming at them. The first thing I said to her wasn't "fuck off" or "fuck you." I listened to what she said and thought that that was a great story. We need more tolerance like that. We need to grease the language and go in soft sometimes.

Pronouns

All these neo-pronouns and hardcore language that is evolving within these little online sects and scenes is completely alienating the mainstream. People need to meet and find common ground, real interactions. I didn't really like the pronoun stickers at the festivals at first. CAKE [Chicago Alternative Comics Expo] and TCAF [Toronto Comic Arts Festival] now have all the pronoun stickers.

Pronoun stickers? What are these?

You have a sticker for your chosen pronoun. When I turned up to CAKE last year or the year before, I signed up and got my badge. They were like, "Here's your pronoun sticker!" I was like, "What the fuck? What?" It says "My pronoun is —" and then you can choose from he/him, they/there, she, xe, whatever. I said, "I don't want to wear one. I don't feel the need. I don't personally mind if someone misgenders me." Also, a lot of people were wearing all of them, which negated the whole thing and looked silly. But some people were genuinely wearing them.

These are stickers that say things like Mr., Mrs., Ms. …

Yeah, in a wider variety of choices. It says, "Hi, my pronoun is." It's like those, "Hi, my name is," stickers.

OK, OK.

For a while, I thought they were lame. But I was talking through this with someone and I came to the conclusion that they are a good tool when used properly. I went to a roller-skating rink here in Seattle and the young person behind the counter was wearing a pronoun sticker. It said, "My pronouns are he/him." That's a really great thing because it's integrating it into regular blue-collar society. That individual is obviously very tired of being misgendered, they've decided who they want to be and people are misgendering them. It's good that they are wearing the sticker because it's getting it out there. Just by being out in public, different people are seeing the sticker and interacting with it. They may make fun of it initially, but it will slowly work its way into society. People will start respecting the new pronouns. A good, slow rollout. Gentle integration.

Mhmm.

So, yeah, I think pronoun stickers are a good thing for people that need them and don't want to be misgendered. I don't want to have them forced on me personally though. I'm not fucking wearing one. I keep thinking about when it is going to happen when I'll be on a panel … The trend now is, "Hi, my name is blah blah blah. My pronouns are blah blah blah." Everyone goes down the line and says their name and pronouns. I'd be tempted to act the contrarian if I was on one of these panels.

I wouldn't care.

But that's problematic. The ethos is that everyone should put their pronouns in their Twitter profile to help people. We should *all* put our pronouns everywhere, lead with it. Your Twitter bio should say "Gary Groth – he/him." And then it will make non-binary people more legitimized and comfortable.

Seems a little confining. But choosing not to have a pronoun is also a choice.

ABOVE: From *Megg and Mogg in Amsterdam*, 2016.

Yeah, it is. And people can do whatever the fuck they want. But yeah, I don't want to be forced to do it. And not be made to look like a prick if I literally just don't give a shit…Well, but that's me not being offended by it, and you've got to respect—

So, not choosing one is considered bad form?

It'd be a problem me not playing along, because it'd be me disrespecting their system. "I don't believe in your system, I don't believe it's important." The thing to do is politely goose-step along, don't cause any trouble!

It's complicated. I'm queer as fuck. I wrestle with gender stuff daily…Someone called me a "cis-het white male" on Twitter recently. They're a popular trans activist slash "cartoonist." It pissed me off so much, mostly just on principal. It goes against everything they sanctimoniously preach about. They seriously fucking shit on like 37 years of fucking *trauma* in my head. Because they didn't like *Truth Zone* and don't know how to do basic fucking research before they run their mouth off. Fuck them. I'm sorry, like it or hate it, I'm part of your group. I'm part of the gender fluidity, not happy in their body, trans-y, fucking group. I'm part of it. And I'm a contentious prick! It's very complicated, there's a ton of LGBTQI+ people who are not all "rah rah sunshine and lollipops" and that's OK! Some trans people are loathsome cunts like any other type of person!

So how do you see yourself in terms of gender? Simply fluid?

TOP RIGHT : From *Megahex*, 2014.

BOTTOM RIGHT: Hanselmann in 2016.

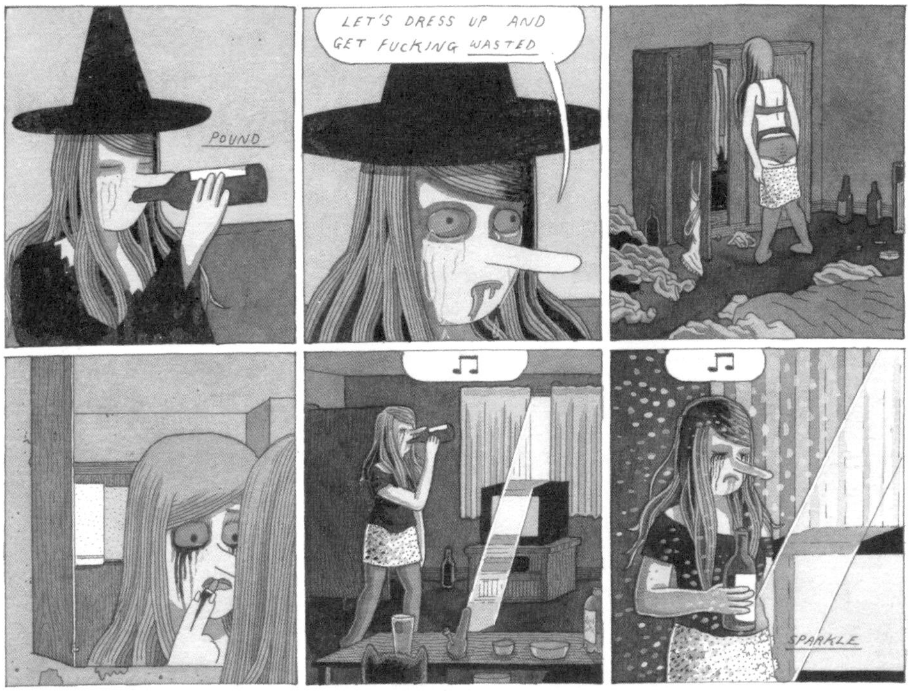

POUND
LET'S DRESS UP AND GET FUCKING WASTED
SPARKLE

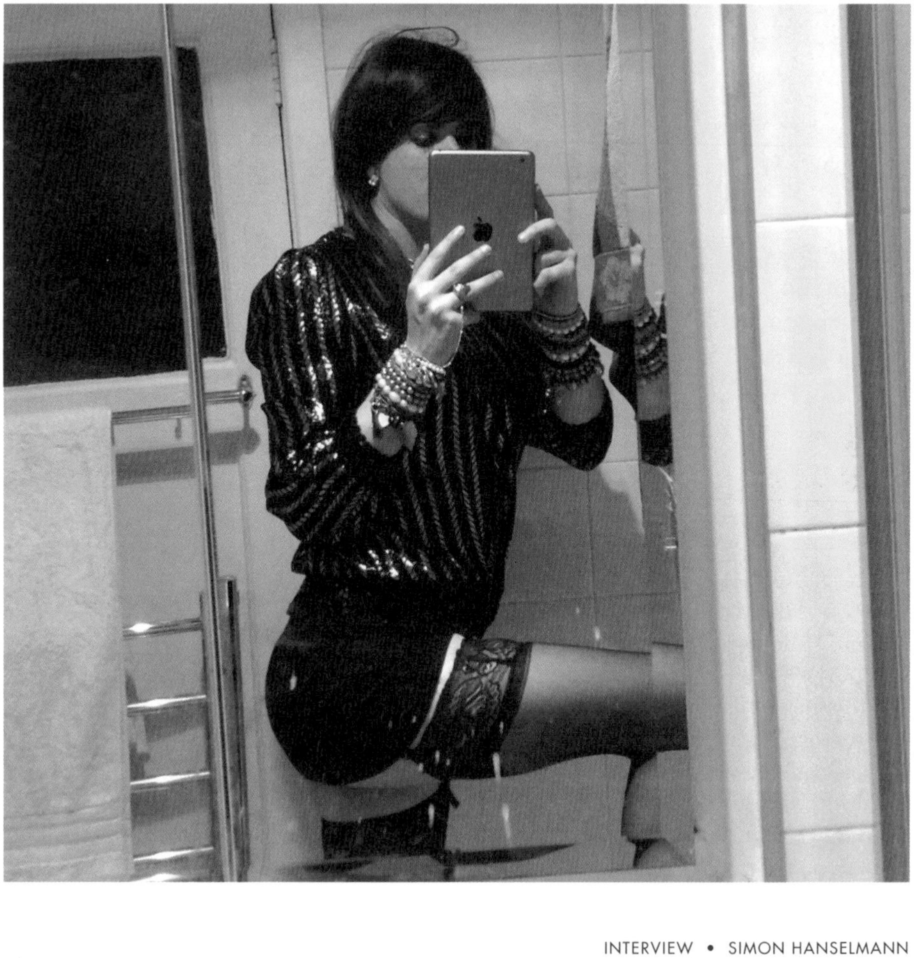

Yeah, I guess I'm gender fluid. I feel feminine, I feel masculine. I try not to think about it. That's the thing, I don't wanna get bogged down overanalyzing it anymore. I don't want to be labeled. People talk about the "queer scene" or whatever. I want to be non-scene. I don't want to join these groups or have a group identity. I'm an individual. I feel fluid about my gender, I don't feel that there's a big difference between men and women, as humans. There are, obviously, biological differences and whatnot but I don't think it's a big deal. I think we can be fluid. If you want to say you're a woman, you can say you're a woman. Live how you want. This is where it gets difficult to talk about though, all these factions are fighting … It's a minefield.

I almost went full-on trans five or six years ago. I was going to a gender clinic and was dressing as a woman 24/7. I broke up with my partner and was feeling really shitty about this stuff. She wouldn't let me wear women's clothes in the house. Catholic upbringing, really uptight about it. I had a few partners like that. But I was free, I had gotten away. I was dressing as a woman a lot more. I was like, "Do I want to do this all the time?" I just decided that I didn't need to. When I'm working, all that melts away. My primary mode of existing is working. I feel like it's a pointless vanity to feel like you need long hair and a dress and makeup all the time. That's a social construct. I don't need that when I'm working. It's kind of fallen by the wayside.

So you don't feel that strongly about what your identity is?

No. I do what I want. I've become more comfortable being male, but I dress femininely when I want. I'm older now, I've figured it out. It's not a big fucking deal. I just need to sit down in pajamas and get to work. It doesn't matter what I look like or what I'm wearing. I'm just me. I just believe on the inside. I'd like if society was a bit more accepting of a tall 6' 1" obvious man dressing as a woman, because it

can be dangerous out there. But I feel like it's all been blown up into this big thing I don't want to be a part of. I don't politically want to be a part of this big trans cabal. I just believe that men and women aren't that different, just wear whatever the fuck you want and leave other people alone. It would be nice if society would let gender be more of a loose spectrum and everyone would be more relaxed. I'm sure you don't give a fuck if men wear dresses or women wear pants. Who gives a shit as long as they aren't pricks to you?

You did say, "I've always kind of wished I was a girl." Didn't you just say a few minutes ago that you were considering being trans?

Yeah, I was going to the clinic, the gender dysphoria clinic, and strongly considering whether I would take hormones or not.

Whether you should actually go through that process.

But I can't help but find it all inherently a bit ridiculous and vain for my life. It's so much money and a lot of physical stress. I just decided that I don't need to do that personally to be happy.

You concluded that you could embody that side of yourself in your current physical manifestation?

Yeah, I can still wear a dress and be feminine enough. Do I have to take it further? I'm used to having a penis and being male and medical stuff terrifies me. I started embracing being male more and fluid change. I don't want to label it, really. I'm confused by all this insane labeling.

I've never quite understood the strict categorization.

No, it divides us further. I think umbrella terms like "gay" and "trans" – that'll do. You've got gay people and people who want

RIGHT: From the *Truth Zone* zine *Landscape*, summer 2016.

... WHY DID YOU UNFOLLOW ME ON TWITTER ?

YOU'RE BORING. IF YOU'RE GOING TO BE POLITICAL, TRY TO BE ENTERTAINING TOO.

to live as a different gender. Won't that do? "Non-binary" too. That's OK. You don't feel like either. I'm non-binary, I guess, but I don't call it that.

It seems obvious to me that we can have it both ways.

I look at nature and see the way it works. Just biology. That's a dirty word these days, biology.

Is it?

Yeah!

Damn.

Apparently, according to some, there's no such thing as a biological man or woman now. It's all very confusing and you're just expected to keep up with it. This small demographic of people, I don't know what they expect to happen. You've got to use a bit of honey to make shit go down. That's just how things work. You have to use a bit of humor and gracefully try to get your ideas across if you want to convince people. You can't go screaming at them and confusing them.

These fucking Southern dumbfucks down in the flyover states are not going be won over by confusing them with fucking 69 different genders. Screaming at them and calling them bigots and Nazis. That's not going to work. It's going to divide things further.

I heard a theory that one of things that might have gotten Trump elected was the fight over gender and bathrooms. Even though I'm perfectly fine with that, I could see that if you're going to be militant about it in the South, you're going to run into resistance.

People are being pushed further to the right. I've heard that as well. I can see that. People are being alienated and screamed at by the "extremists" on either side.

I'm certainly on the side of the left. But on the other hand, I want to be pragmatic about it. If it takes 10 years to accomplish a progressive goal, rather than six months, that's the way it's going to fall.

All this shit just seems to be online. I don't see it out in the real world that much.

No, I don't either.

I don't see that shit at the grocery store, the bar. It's just amplified online.

In the Twitter-verse.

It's very hard to tell. It's so fucked that we have to talk about this constantly because all this Twitter shit has infected comics so deeply. All of this is intrinsically in every art form now.

You can't talk about art without talking about all this political and gender stuff, which I really fucking dislike. I dislike that we've gotten back onto this in this interview. It's fucking frustrating. I don't know. And I'm not immune to fallout, just because I am non-binary or trans or whatever the fuck you want to call it. That doesn't save you anymore. If you say one wrong thing, you're just fucking out. You're one of the bad ones. Everything's so fractured and judgmental.

The orthodoxies seem to get narrower and narrower.

It just seems like these toxic little pools, just getting smaller and smaller, and alienating people, and eating their own, and whittling themselves down. It's not attractive to the mainstream at all, the people who need to be appealed to and sold on this and to be more tolerant. It's so off-putting. It's creating bigger assholes.

It breeds its own intolerance, as we witnessed with Carol Tyler.

Ageism.

It was truly offensive, a tweet about how she was too old to be at SPX, that they should throw her out or not allow her to attend.

Look, my favorite work is always what's happening *now*. Because there's possibilities. Anything can happen, it's free-form, it's kinetic. Old work, it's happened, it's set in stone. The artists are either dead or naturally slowing down a bit. History's not going to change, it's what it is. I'm not going to shit on history, though. It exists. You need to be aware of it. It's like, everyone talks about Stonewall, and gay history. Know your history! Know what people fought for! You need to know what fucking Carol Tyler fought for and what she's *still* fighting for. You need to know what fucking Crumb fought for. You may not like him, but he fucking fought for artists and for freedom of thought.

That people today are reaping the benefits of, like yourself.

It's dismissal of history. But that's fine! Do what you want, kids. They're all wrapped up in their little internet bubble that's probably gonna burst for them real fucking soon. It's ironic, because you have the internet, they have all this fucking information at their fingertips. They have no excuse to be ignorant, not like we did back in the day before all this information was available in our pockets. Everything is nuanced, do your research, listen to different voices, make up your own mind.

Contemporaries

I made a list of artists I think you like and admire. I wanted to know if I could tell you who they are and if you could give me a quick encapsulation about what you like about them.

That sounds like a fun game show.

Exactly.

"Bonus Round."

We could take this on the road if it turns out well.

[*Laughs.*] Gary Groth Speed Round!

How about Christopher Forges? CF?

I love CF. He stopped doing comics so much. I was a big CF biter. I'm man enough to admit it. A lot of people were.

LEFT: From *Powr Mastrs* Vol. 1 by CF, 2007.

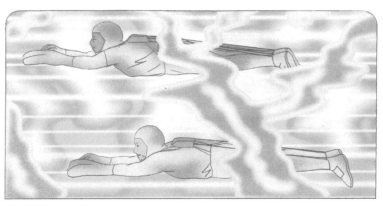

People are hugely influenced by CF. I just found some girl on Instagram. Someone mentioned me and said, "This girl's stuff reminds me of your work. This reminds me of HTML Flowers and Simon Hanselmann." More like fucking CF! I imagine this girl rolling around art school and everyone going, "Wow, what an original style!" But she's just ripping off CF and Aidan Koch. Schrauwen was a CF rip-off for a while. He's indebted to it. He was doing the Winsor McCay thing then you can see when he found CF. A lot of artists, you can see when they discovered CF if you look at their old work and compare it to their new work. He's brilliant. He makes these fucking receipt-roll comics. He hand-made receipt printers and these janky rollers. He prints out 16-foot long comics on these fucking rolls. He makes all these weird paper lampshades. Fanta was going to do *Powr Mstrs* #4 and he just said, "No I don't want to do it," and kept the advance. OK. [*Laughs.*] He's brilliant and does his own thing. He makes noise music. He's fucking amazing.

He's got a big piece in the new *Kramers Ergot* that Fanta is putting out in a couple months. I ordered some receipt rolls. He's famous for not sending out stuff. I didn't send out orders for about two months and my customers got so mad. I've been waiting seven months for some shit from CF. That's just it. That's just him. You've got to just wait. He'll send it eventually.

Where does he live?

He's a Providence guy. He was one of the Fort Thunder dudes. He was like the young tagalong, I think. He was like the young guy. "I really want to be like you guys." And they were like, "All right, Chris," and let him join the gang. He's sort of become one of the main fucking things to come out of that scene.

Alex Schubert.

Fuck Schubert. He's a cunt.

OK. [*Laughs.*]

No, no, no. I like Schubert. He fucked off to TV. We used to have a fake rivalry. I ordered a zine from him and he just sent me a piece of paper that said "U.S.A." on it when I was living in Australia. We had this fake nationalistic beef going. I quite like his comics. They're really fucking dry and stilted, in an interesting way. It's this new visual language sometimes, little effects he does. He had some little tricks. His animation's interesting and I wish him the best. I wish we hadn't lost him. I always hate when people leave comics. You animation cunts. [*Laughs.*]

They can always come back.

They'll come crawling back once the animation bubble bursts. They'll be back.

Bringing us up to date, who are the more contemporary cartoonists that you look at?

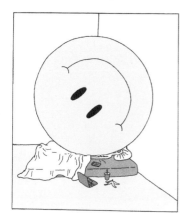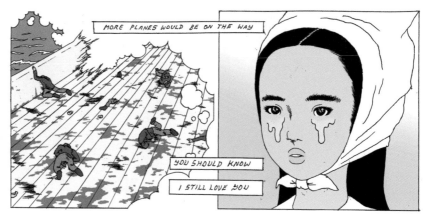

[Olivier] Schrauwen is one of the best cartoonists working today.

What is it about Schrauwen's work that you like? What is it specifically that you admire?

He's just fucking good. I don't know. He doesn't even like sci-fi, but his stuff in *Parallel Lives* was the best fucking sci-fi. Weird, sexy, otherworldly, acid trip … It's the stuff that I can't make. It's the stuff that I can't do as an artist. He conjures up these weird fucking worlds. It's funny, it's dark, it's sexy, it's brutal, it's European. It's good. He's just good.

I love Anna Haifisch, [but she] has been doing too much fucking narration shit, all big single-page illustrations with text recently. That's cool. I like the stories and love the illustrations. I love the binding. But I want more comics!

You love the binding? The binding is good?

Her last one is spiral-bound and printed by Matt Davis, a guy in Chicago who does really good Riso stuff [*"Riso" is short for Risograph, a color photocopying technology that originated in the 1980s*]. Matt's Perfectly Acceptable Press is one of the world's best Riso [printers] currently. There's printing on the spiral spine! There's a flat bit on the spiral. The title is printed on the spiral and I've never seen that. I've never seen a spiral-bound title on a comic like that: attractive spines. I think Anna's

working more on *The Artist,* which is her comic thing. I like her timing. She's dark and funny. There's melancholy and meanness. But tender and mean at the same time. There's cruelty and tenderness in perfect harmony. I think perhaps she's my favorite cartoonist currently.

There's a young guy I love called Nathan Cowdry, in the U.K. He came up to me at Safari, this cool festival that Breakdown Press put on where they have all the stuff I like. All the hip stuff and weirdly designed stuff. I like the heavy design stuff, but it's completely devoid of content. *Lagon Revue* is this fancy French anthology. I was in one of them and did a terrible strip for it. Very embarrassing. But I love that series. The design, impeccable. But it can come off a bit "all style, no substance."

Who published that?

It's self-published. *Lagon Revue.* It's Sammy Stein and Alexis Beauclair and a few others. Alexis and Sammy are two very minimalist cartoonists whose work I really enjoy from an aesthetic standpoint. It'll be literally like 20 pages of pencil drawings of intersecting lines. It's very interesting formally. Kim Jooha – she edited the Beauclair books for 2dcloud – is obsessed with them. She's always writing about this "New Minimalism." It's aesthetically great, but a bit limited really. [*Laughs.*] But Sammy Stein puts out like laser-edged balsa wood comic books. The form, *muah*! In their launch recently, they

ABOVE LEFT: From *The Artist* by Anna Haifisch, 2016.

ABOVE RIGHT: From Nathan Cowdry's contribution to *Now: The New Comics Anthology* #4, 2018.

ABOVE: From Hanselmann's story in the *Lagon Revue* anthology *Gouffre*, 2017.

had all this green velvet and sticks and this big, bubbling pond in the middle of the gallery. It was very inviting and nice looking with candles and everything. All their printing is nice, super slick.

But yeah, I feel like contemporary comics currently is all stylish stuff. Or very simple poetry comics, which is like, cool ... Or it's full-on activism.

BELOW: From *The Lie and How We Told It* by Tommi Parrish, 2017.

What would be an example of that?

Half the comics out there? [*Laughs.*] I don't know. Half of the American comics out there. Not European comics. There's a huge cultural divide between European comics and American comics.

I must have missed most of these. They're just didactic?

Yeah, just TED Talk type stuff. Big blocks of moaning or condescendingly instructive text and maybe a few drawings. Maybe.

And this is mostly self-published?

And regular-published stuff. It's a trend in comics. Helpful activism and stuff, but it's not very entertaining. I feel like there's a dearth of entertaining, challenging series that I can read. I was talking about Nathan Cowdry. It's manga-y in a way. He seems obsessed with Japanese women. It has this weird, creepy, leery, post-Brexit British male vibe. It's exploring "maleness" and the gaze. There's sexuality, and it's dark and weird. I find it really interesting and funny. I think he's got something. He's got some chops.

I really like Tommi Parrish. Fanta did that book [*The Lie and How We Told It*]. Parrish did the cover for *The Best American Non-Required Reading*. Not comics! Reading! Parrish was a colorist on *Megahex* back in 2013 and was terrible at coloring. "Don't start in the middle of a panel. Start on the left and go this way." And 4 or 5 years later, Tommi is a better painter than me and better at lighting. I'm like, "Well, fuck. I've got to step my fucking game up." The whole time I was working on *Bad Gateway*, I was like, "Tommi Parrish is out there showing me up. I've got a Karate Kid here and now I'm old Mr. Miyagi. I've got to step my game up."

You're tough. You are the Charles Bronson of alternative cartoonists.

[*Laughs.*] I'll take that. Yeah. What was his big film series? *Death Wish*. I used to watch them when I was a kid. I loved Charles Bronson when I was a kid.

You did?

I watched action movies. As a kid in a small town, you had to.

I always liked him as a character actor. Then he became this superstar and made endless lousy movies.

Is he dead now?

Yeah.

Rest in peace, Charles.

He cut quite a striking figure. Don't make them like that anymore. Peter Falk. Columbo. Classic. Kids don't appreciate Peter Falk enough these days. Little shits. ☀

LEFT: Megg at Hanselmann's installation at the Bellevue Arts Museum, 2019. Photo courtesy of Eric Reynolds.

Story Minute
by Carol Lay

Shaenon K. Garrity

RIGHT: This sequence is from "Beauty and the Beast with Two Heads," collected in *Goodnight Irene*.

When gravity quit, the world changed significantly.

*The chile relleno concerned him **a lot**.*

Absolutely everyone had two heads.

IT'S ONE OF THE TRUISMS of writing: open strong. Yank the reader in. And if you only have a minute, you have to hook 'em from the first second. A great opening challenges not only the reader but the writer. It demands big ideas. Then the only problem is coming up with an ending.

For 18 years, Carol Lay's *Story Minute* led readers from grabby openings through hairpin plot twists to wicked little endings, all snaking down a 12-panel grid. *Story Minute* is one of the great weekly newspaper strips, standing alongside such titles as *Feiffer*, *Life in Hell* and *Ernie Pook's Comeek*. Flourishing during the 1980s and 1990s, alternative comic strips found a niche in free weekly city newspapers and other print outlets just outside the publishing mainstream. In the 2000s, the internet has gradually replaced weekly papers as an outlet for indy comic-stripping, but in their heyday the weeklies provided an ideal combination of iconoclastic attitude, low editorial oversight and decent (or at least steady) pay perfect for smart, imaginative cartoonists whose *sui generis* work didn't come close to fitting into the stolid daily funny pages.

A stunningly flexible artist with a sharp wit, Carol Lay started her comics career doing a little bit of everything. She lettered for Marvel, inked for Disney, wrote and drew Hanna-Barbera comics, contributed to underground anthologies like *Wimmen's Comix* and *Weirdo* and had her own Fantagraphics series, *Good Girls*. Outside of comics, she was in demand as an advertising illustrator and a storyboard artist for movies and music videos. She even did some lightsaber rotoscoping for *The Empire Strikes Back*. In his introduction to one of the *Story Minute* collections published by Kitchen Sink in the 1990s, Mark Evanier, Lay's editor at Hanna-Barbera, recalls, "Her sketchbook looked like eighteen artists (no two from the same planet) had jammed to fill up pages."

Good Girls, which ran from 1987 to 1991, allowed Lay to show off her range with a loose collection of short comics. By the end of its six-issue run, the series was dominated by its most interesting running storyline – a romance-comic pastiche about an heiress named Irene Van de Kamp who was raised in Africa and has a face altered by elaborate ritual scarification and body modification. (Lay based Irene's appearance on a photo spread of several different tribeswomen in *Hustler*, and thanks to the limited visual reference, Irene's nose plug and lip discs are anatomically impossible.) Irene's tongue-in-cheek adventures whisk her through encounters with handsome men scheming to get her money, a blind paramour who seems like a perfect match until he touches her face, a fetishist with an island of human oddities and other women whose appearances deviate from the Western beauty ideal. Lay's art is detailed, naturalistic and knowingly campy – half 1960s romance comics, half Hernandez Brothers.

Near the end of *Good Girls*, Lay began *Story Minute*, which launched in 1990 in *L.A. Weekly* and soon spread to other publications. The comic-book realism of her *Good Girls* art gave way to a radically different, instantly recognizable style: slender, rubber-limbed cartoon figures with a geometric retro abstraction reminiscent of UPA cartoons or mid-century advertising, inked in strong blocks of black and white. This art style stabilized early in the run of *Story Minute* and changed little over the next two decades. Almost every installment comprised exactly twelve panels of equal size, convenient for papers and magazines that might need to restack them for space.

Within those tight restrictions, Lay could do, and did, anything.

***

ALTHOUGH A FEW *Story Minute* strips link into short storylines, most are self-contained. Each is a snippet of microfiction, usually with an off-kilter premise and a *Twilight Zone* twist. Yet the plotting feels loose, as if Lay starts with an idea, follows it casually and is as surprised as the reader at where it ends up. Sometimes this means the story fizzles out at the end or veers off in unpredictable directions. But the trip is always, well, a trip. Two siblings get the newspaper a day early. A woman becomes a murderer to provide interesting material for her time capsule. A girl is raised by skunks. A woman takes on the lives of people whose laundry she picks up by mistake. A man breaks up with his imaginary friend.

The stories are darkly funny, sometimes warm or sad, but more often harshly ironic, with a nihilistic end-of-the-millennium edge. Some strips touch on the political – Lay is frequently concerned with environmental issues like pollution or overpopulation – but most are as timeless as an O. Henry story. (Then again, one can't always predict what may become topical. A mid-1990s strip in which a TV executive is elected President and turns the U.S. government into ratings-grabbing media circus is so close to current events that, in 2017, Lay couldn't resist rerunning it online with "programming executive" changed to "reality TV star.")

Once in a while an idea provides enough inspiration for multiple strips: there are five strips in a row about a machine that records dreams, for example, and another five on travelers searching the Land of Lost Things. (It's mostly socks.) There are several strips riffing on the concept of a company that removes unwanted memories, one of which encapsulates the exact plot of *Eternal Sunshine*

of the Spotless Mind some ten years early. But most ideas only provide grist for one installment.

Story Minute has only two major recurring characters: Madame Asgar, a sharp-witted and meticulously ethical fortuneteller, and the Devil, whose plans Madame Asgar frequently stops with a coolly plotted intervention. Madame Asgar and the Devil routinely butt heads working through tricky, even paradoxical moral dilemmas, a recurring theme in *Story Minute*. Other common themes that crop up: the meaning of beauty (also a preoccupation of the Irene Van de Kamp comics), the danger of greed, nature vs. nurture, the difficulties of self-discipline and responsibility, and the near-impossibility of humans getting along with each other.

BELOW AND OPPOSITE: All of these Carol Lay strips are circa 1994–1998 and are collected in *Strip Joint*.

But most often of all, Lay's stories are about the power of perspective. In her stories, optimists and pessimists have radically different experiences. Good people and evil see different worlds; art is subjective (but so is everything else); and a swarm of killer bees masquerading as a human is trapped in prison until it remembers it can just dissipate through the bars. One of the most often-reprinted *Story Minute* strips, "The Last Racist," tells the story of a bigot whose worldview becomes so alien to his fellow man that he winds up as a curiosity in a zoo. In another set of strips, Madame Asgar and the Devil sponsor rival positive and negative artists whose paintings change the world for good or evil … only to finally agree that both artists are, aesthetically, terrible.

In this sense, "P.O.V." is the *Story Minute* strip that exemplifies *Story Minute*. A woman who prides herself on noticing interesting details wishes that everyone could see the world through her eyes, and her wish is granted. Seeing literally nothing but what this one woman sees is intolerable for the rest of humanity, so people blindfold themselves to survive. In the last panel, the woman with the wonderful point of view joins them: "In the end, she had to give up all her beautiful insights for the anonymity of darkness."

"I sometimes get email from people who wonder if I'm doing all right," Lay writes in one of the *Story Minute* collections. It's not hard to see why. The strips tend toward the negative – often cynical, sometimes downright misanthropic, seldom afraid to twist

the knife. But darkness is funnier than light. And it'd be a dull world if we saw only the optimist's perspective. At least the slick *Story Minute* Devil, scheming but easily schemed-against, seldom gets his due.

In the new millennium, as the weekly paper market dried up, *Story Minute* moved to Salon.com and continued successfully as an online comic. Eventually, however, Lay brought the strip to an end. In the ten years since, she's diversified again. She published *The Big Skinny*, a graphic novel about her experiences with weight loss. She drew a number of *Simpsons* comics, flawlessly adopting the show's familiar visual style. She began *Murderville*, a comic about a picturesque New England town populated by assassins, publishing installments online and crowdfunding print editions. She continues to draw *Story Minute*-like strips, but in a looser style: mixing up line-work and character design, playing with different page layouts. Much of this work appears, along with *Story Minute* reruns, in her

GoComics-syndicated series *WayLay*. She moves easily from project to project, and no two projects are the same.

Endings are a problem. You have to leave the reader satisfied. You have to bring things back around. Even if the journey was only twelve panels, it has to feel worthwhile. But an ending is always a little artificial, because in the real world there aren't any endings. Just new stories, short and long, grim and happy, usually messy, changing (as when gravity quit) minute by minute.

It would have been a total success, had it not attracted the giant birds.

Upstairs, the doctors were amazed by the janitor's continuing luck in the clinic's death pool.

And true to the impossible nature of fairy tales, everyone lived happily ever after. ☀

BELOW: This Carol Lay strip is circa 1994–1998, collected in *Strip Joint*.

AVAILABLE NOW
from
FANTAGRAPHICS BOOKS

Once a thriving working-class neighborhood on Chicago's South Side, the "Bottomyards" is now the definition of urban blight. When an aspiring fashion designer and her image-obsessed BFF descend upon the hood in search of cheap rent, they discover something far more seductive... and deadly.

Gentrification and body horror collide in this brutal satire from the award-winning creators of *Upgrade Soul* and *Your Black Friend*.

"I fell in love with this comic right about page one, and then just kept falling. Gentrification horror at its finest."
—Victor LaValle, author of *The Changeling*

"A powerful sequential manifesto."
— John Jennings, *NYT* best-selling author/scholar

"A brilliant meteor of a graphic novel ... simultaneously delivering visceral horror, cutting satire, and a nuanced interrogation of urban gentrification."

— Edie Fake, Eisner-winning author of *Gaylord Phoenix*

"I fell in love wth this comic right about page one, and then just kept falling. Gentrification horror at its finest."

— Victor LaValle, author of *The Changeling*

SKETCHBOOK

Sophie Franz

I HAVE MANY SKETCHBOOKS that I use for different purposes. There are big ones with heavy paper for playing around with different media; tiny pocket-sized ones for doodling ideas on the fly; and there are square ones that always end up just floating around awkwardly in my bike bag and poking me in the kidneys. To me, sketchbooks are a hiding place, a security blanket, a collection of thoughts and a place to practice getting good at things without the stress of having to create a final product. And sometimes, it turns out, they *are* the final product that I've tricked myself into making because it "didn't count." ☼

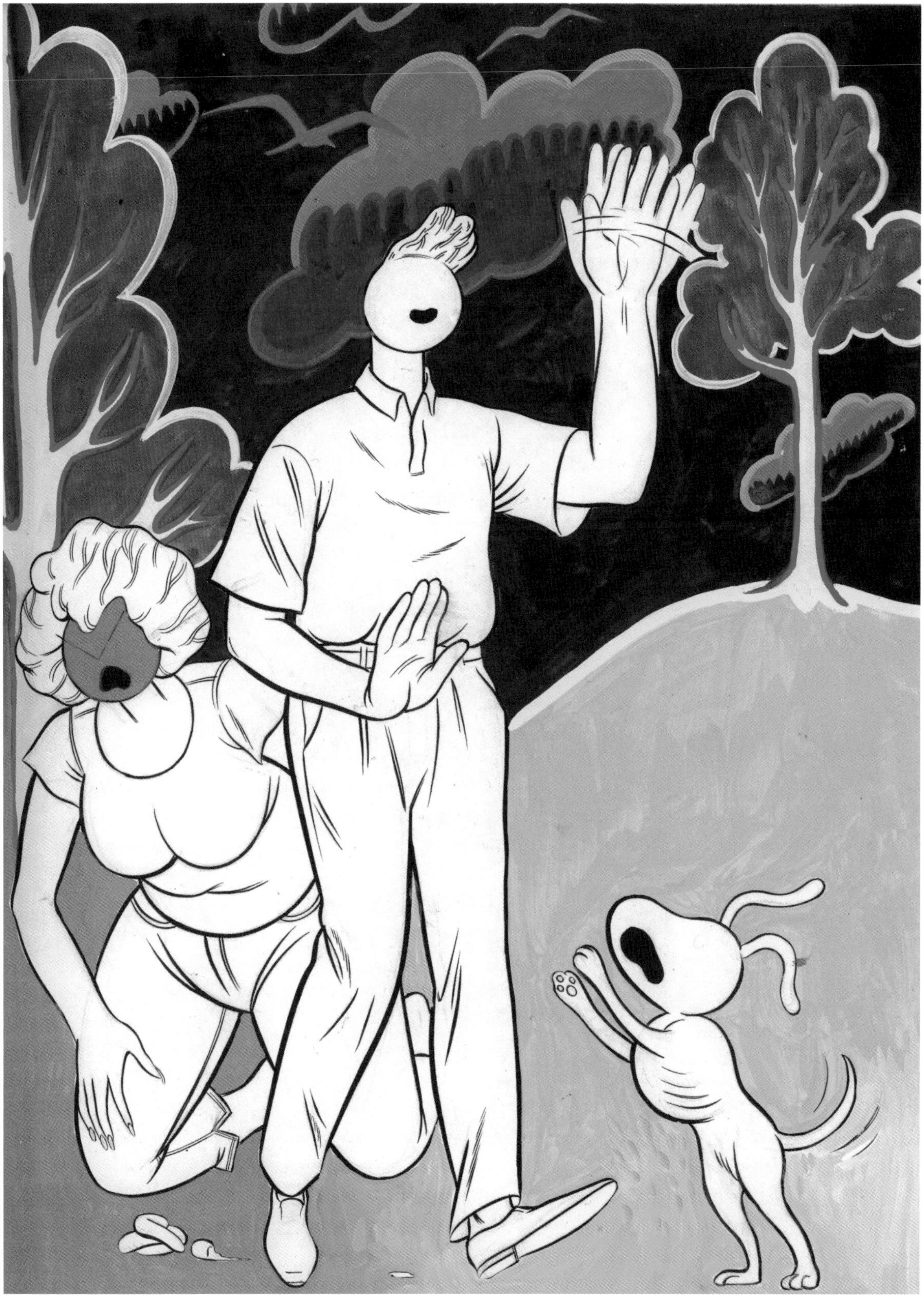

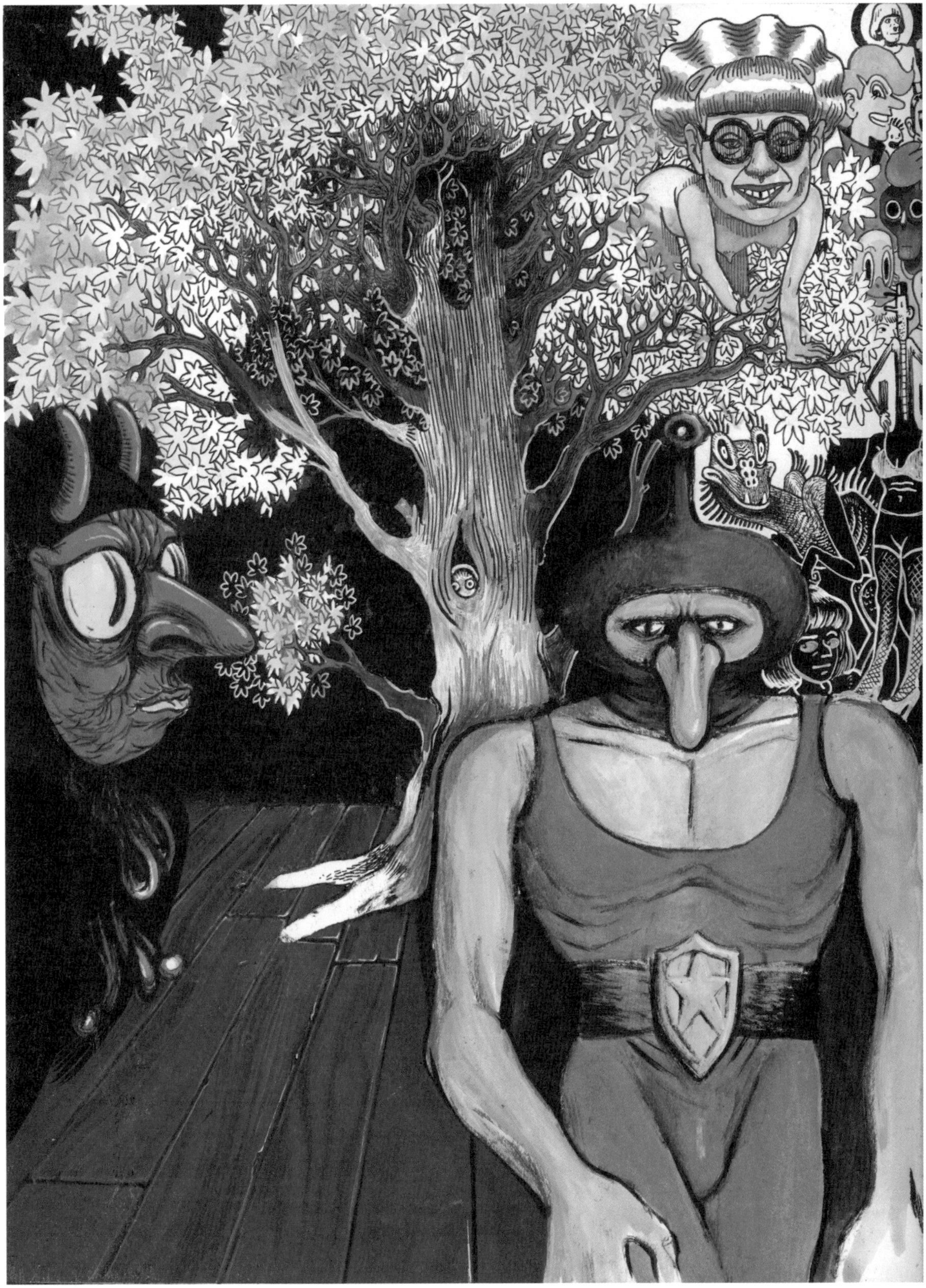

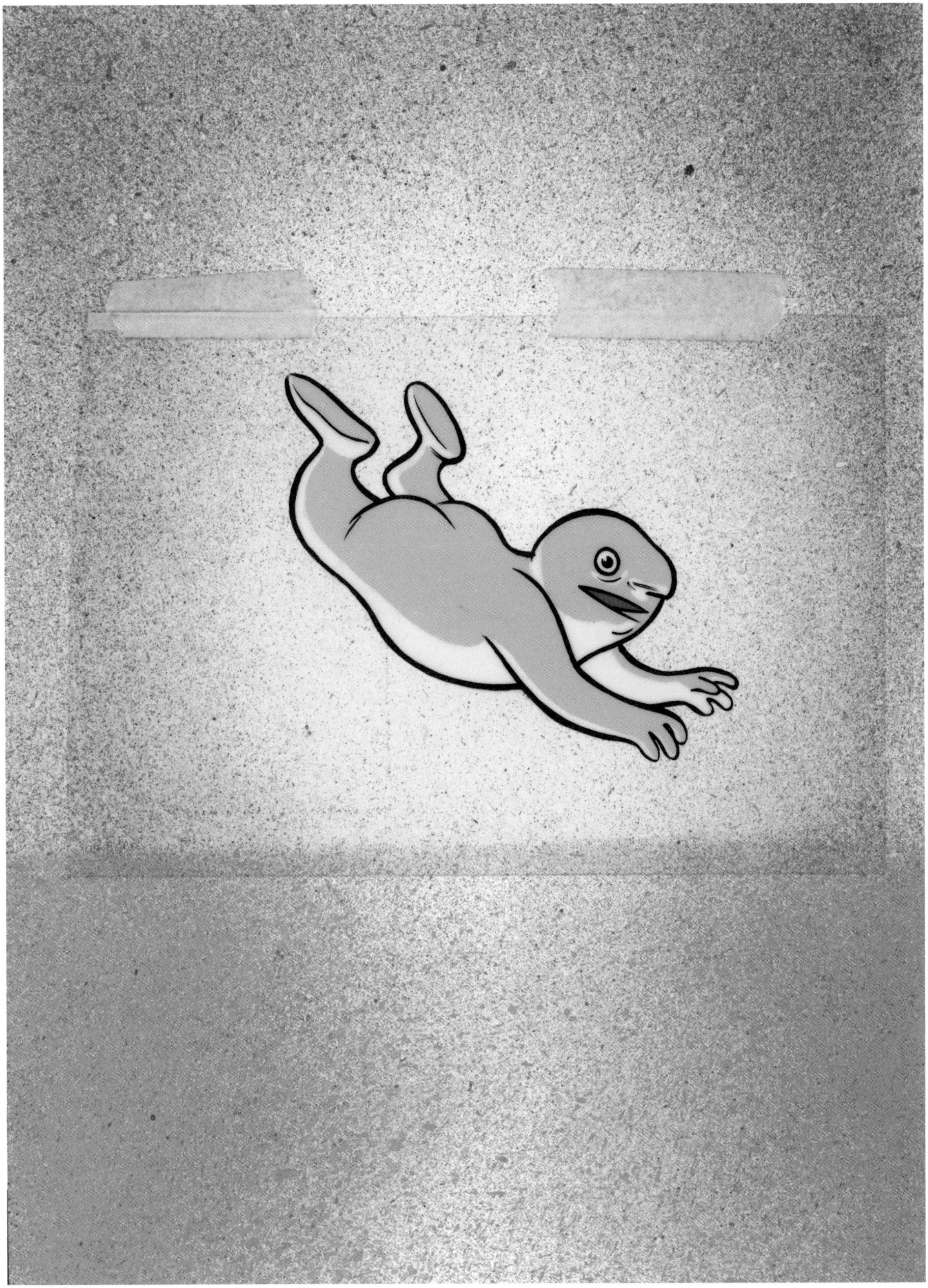

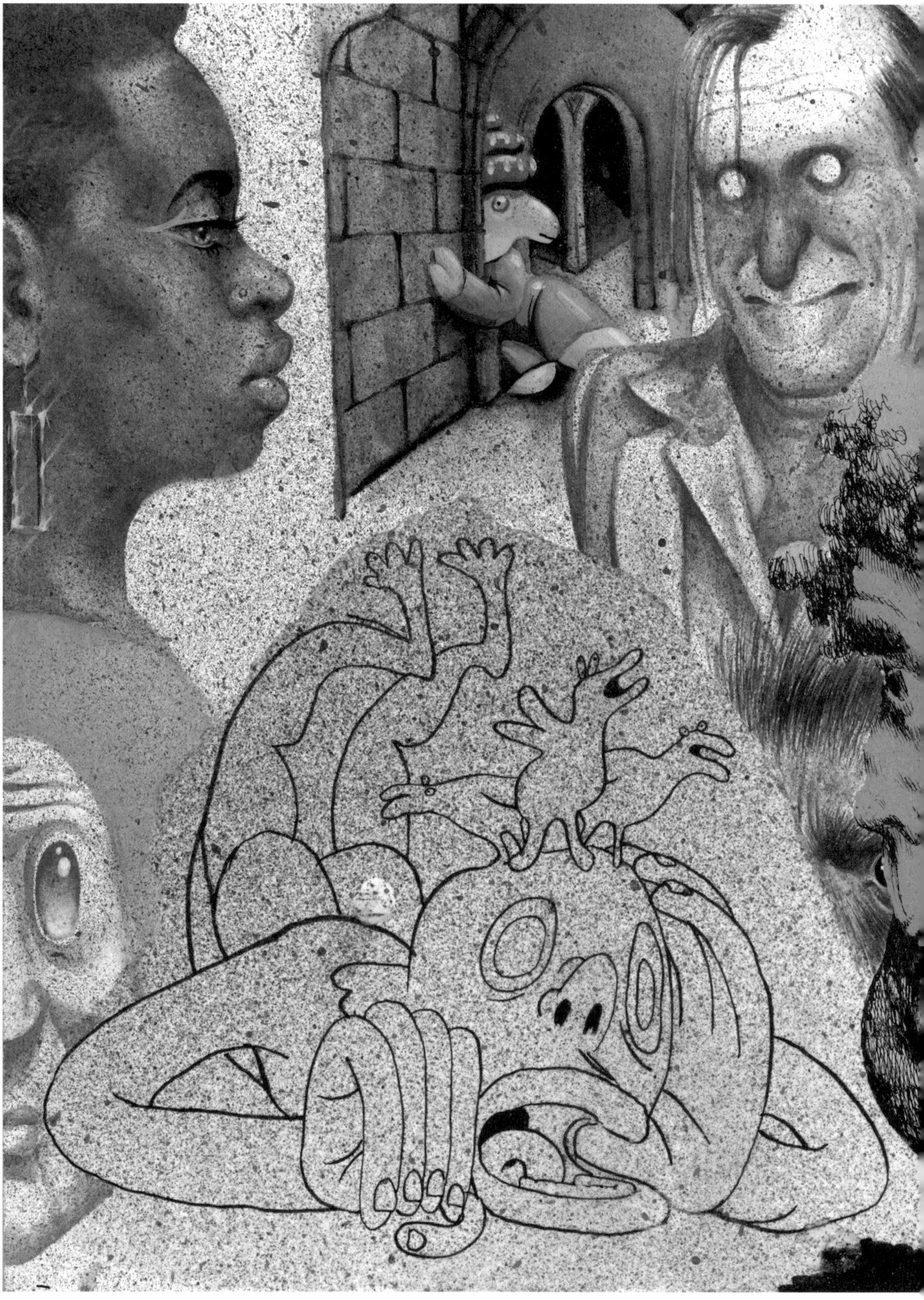

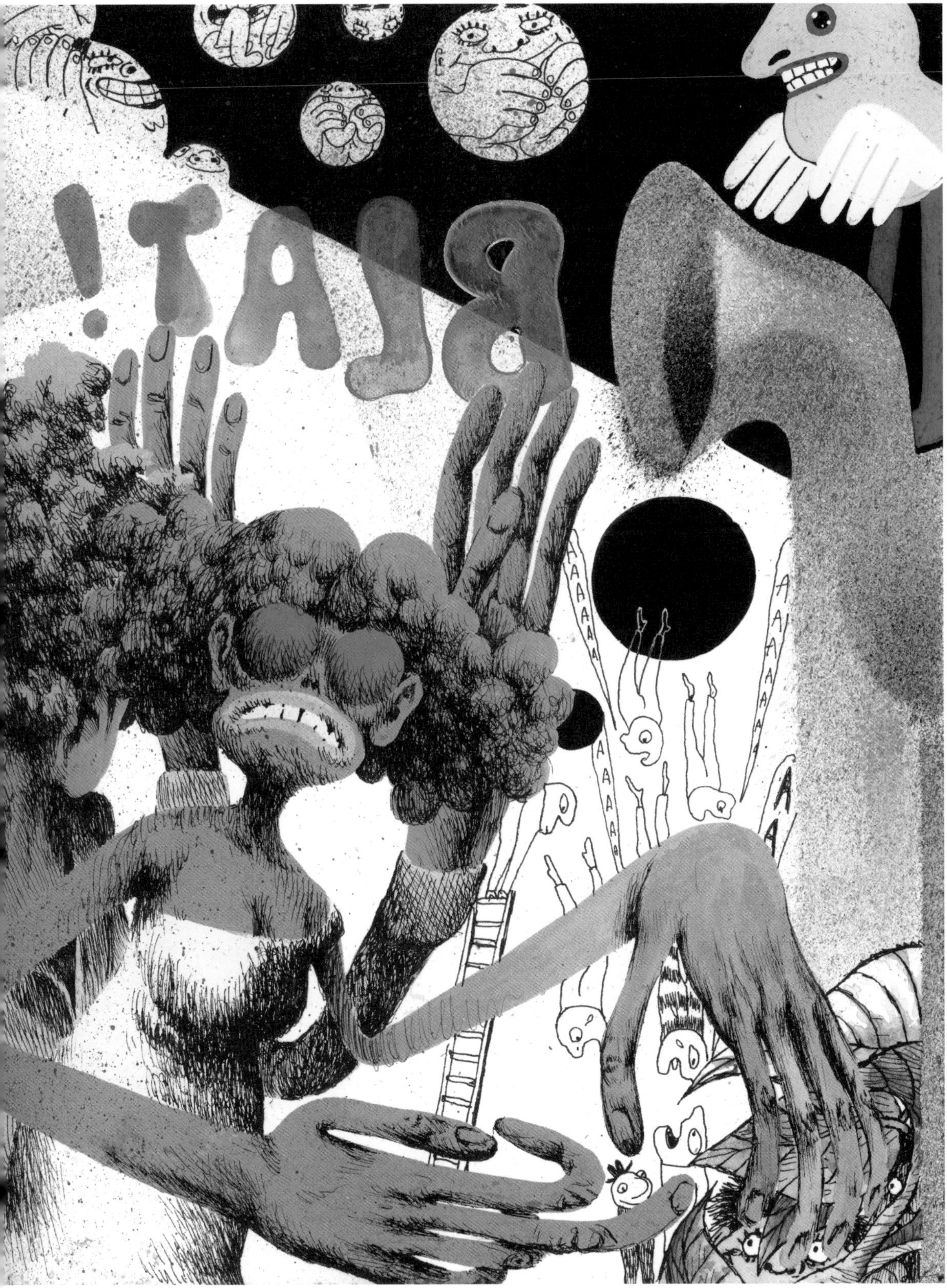

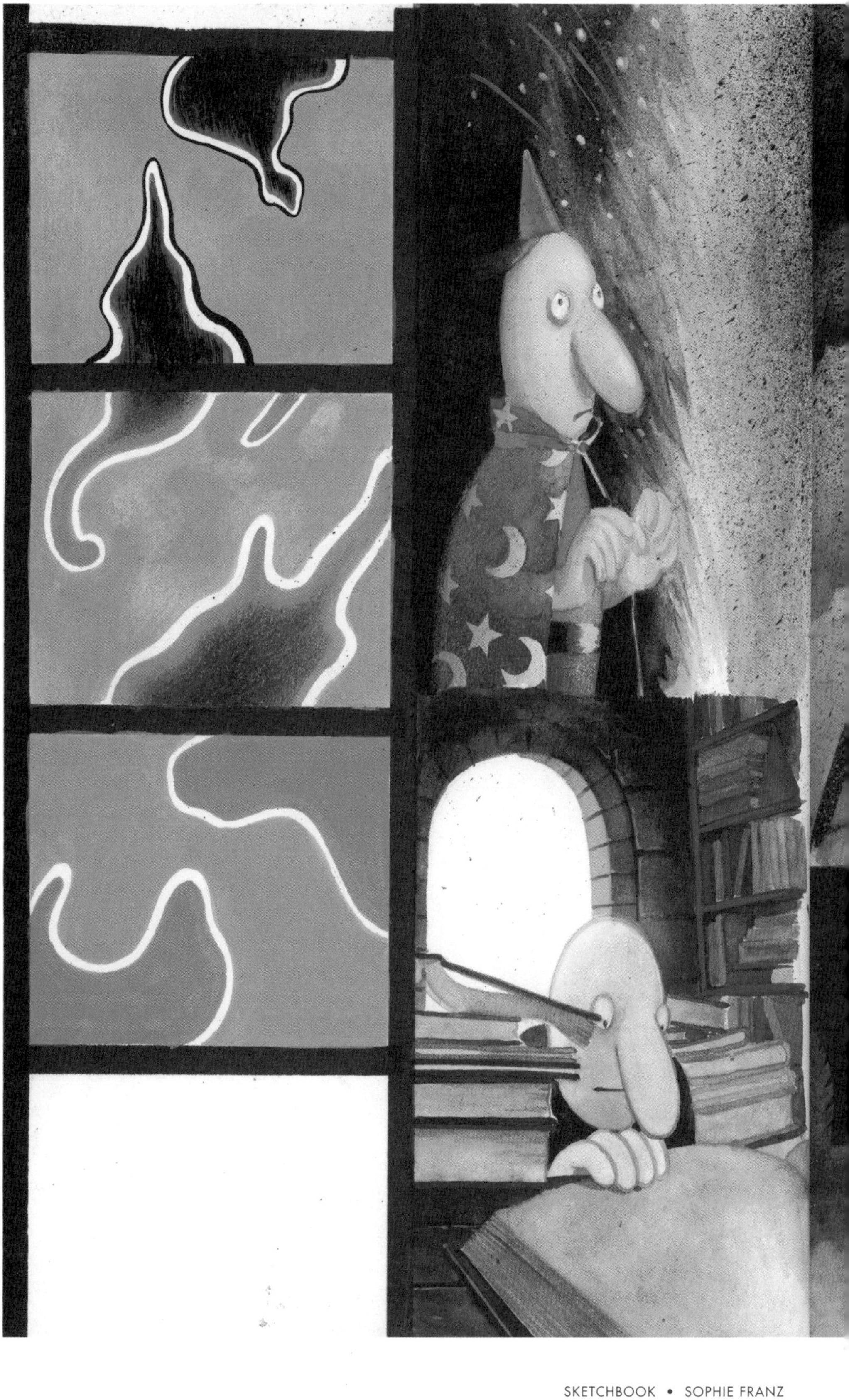

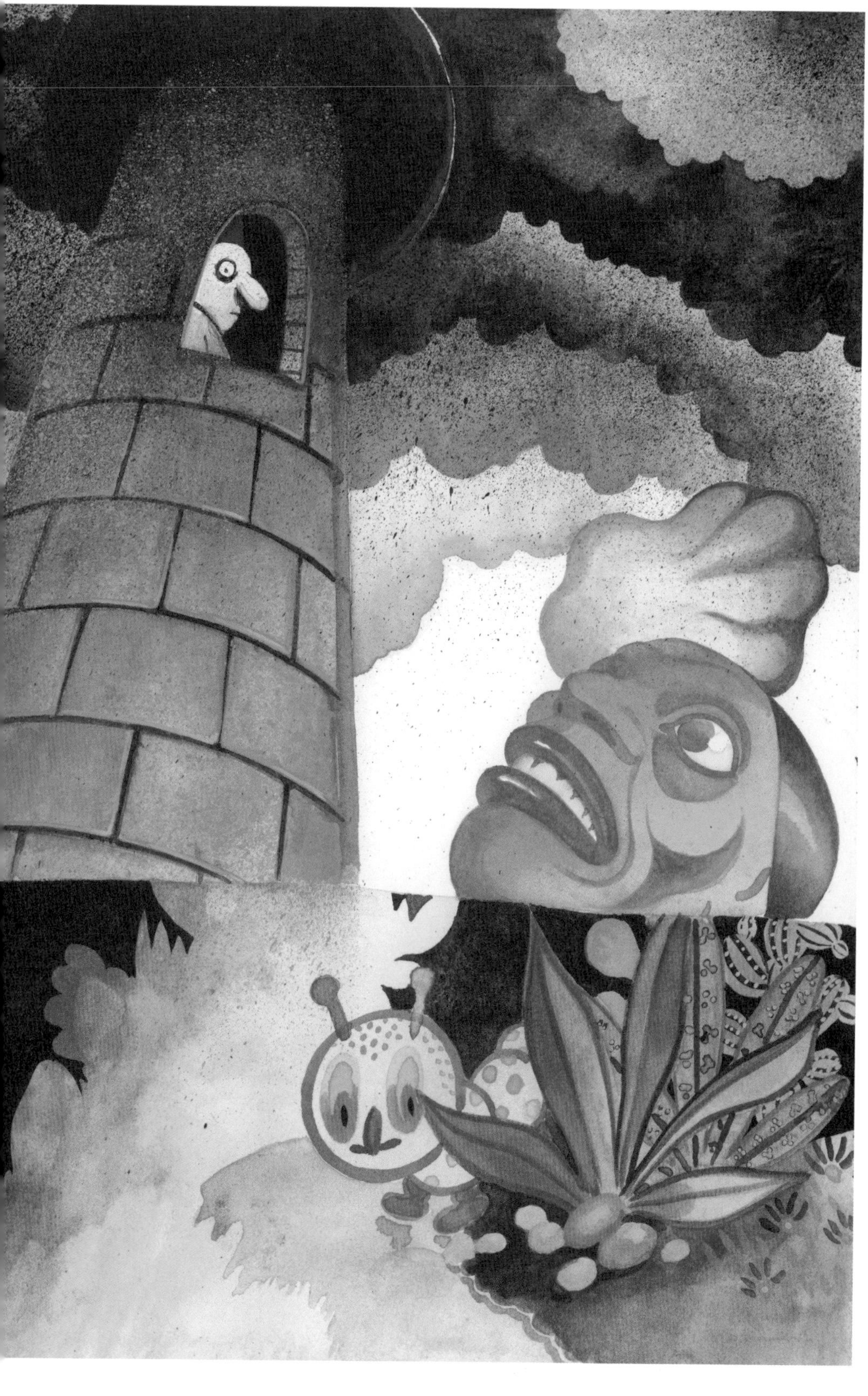

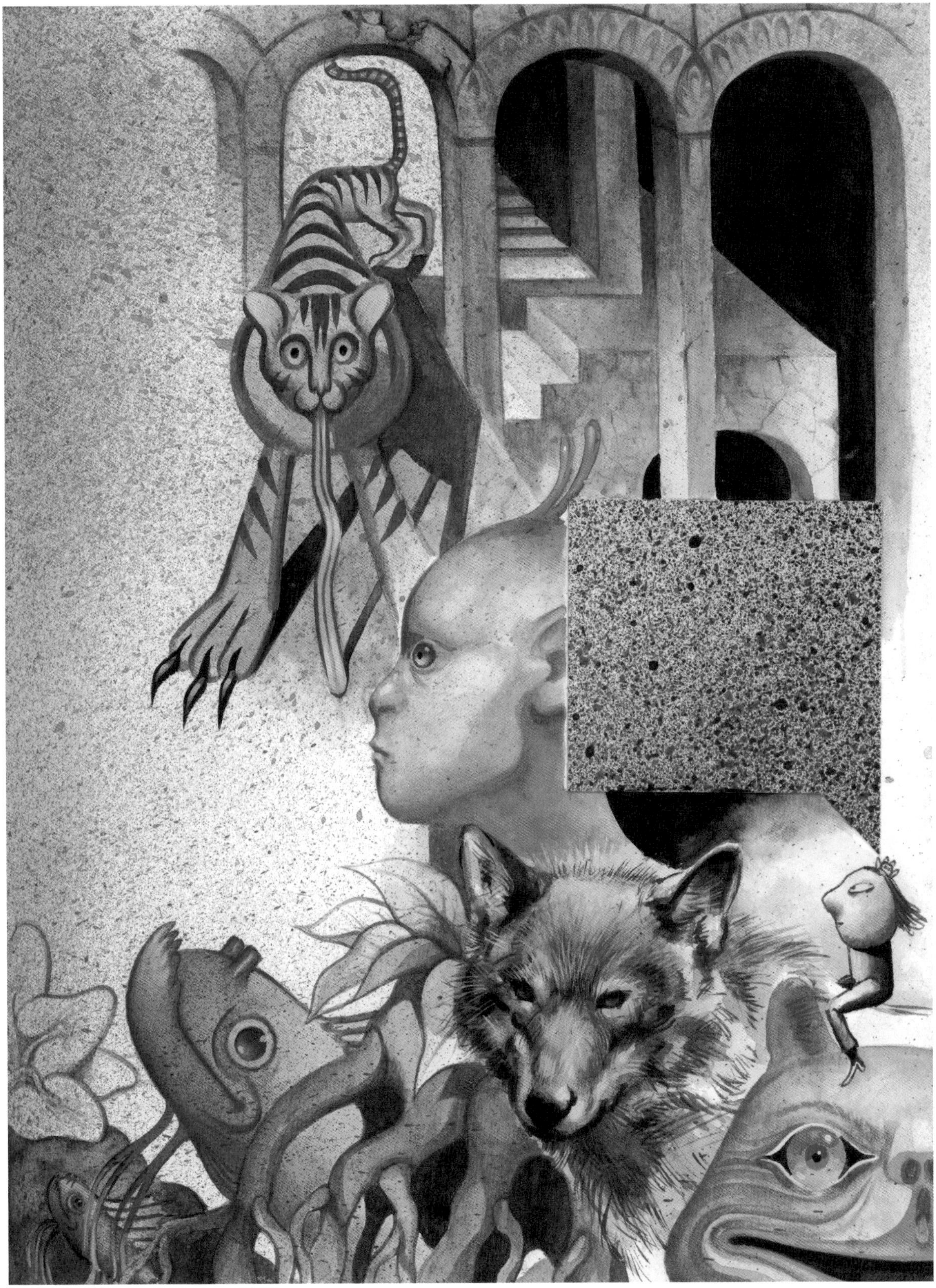

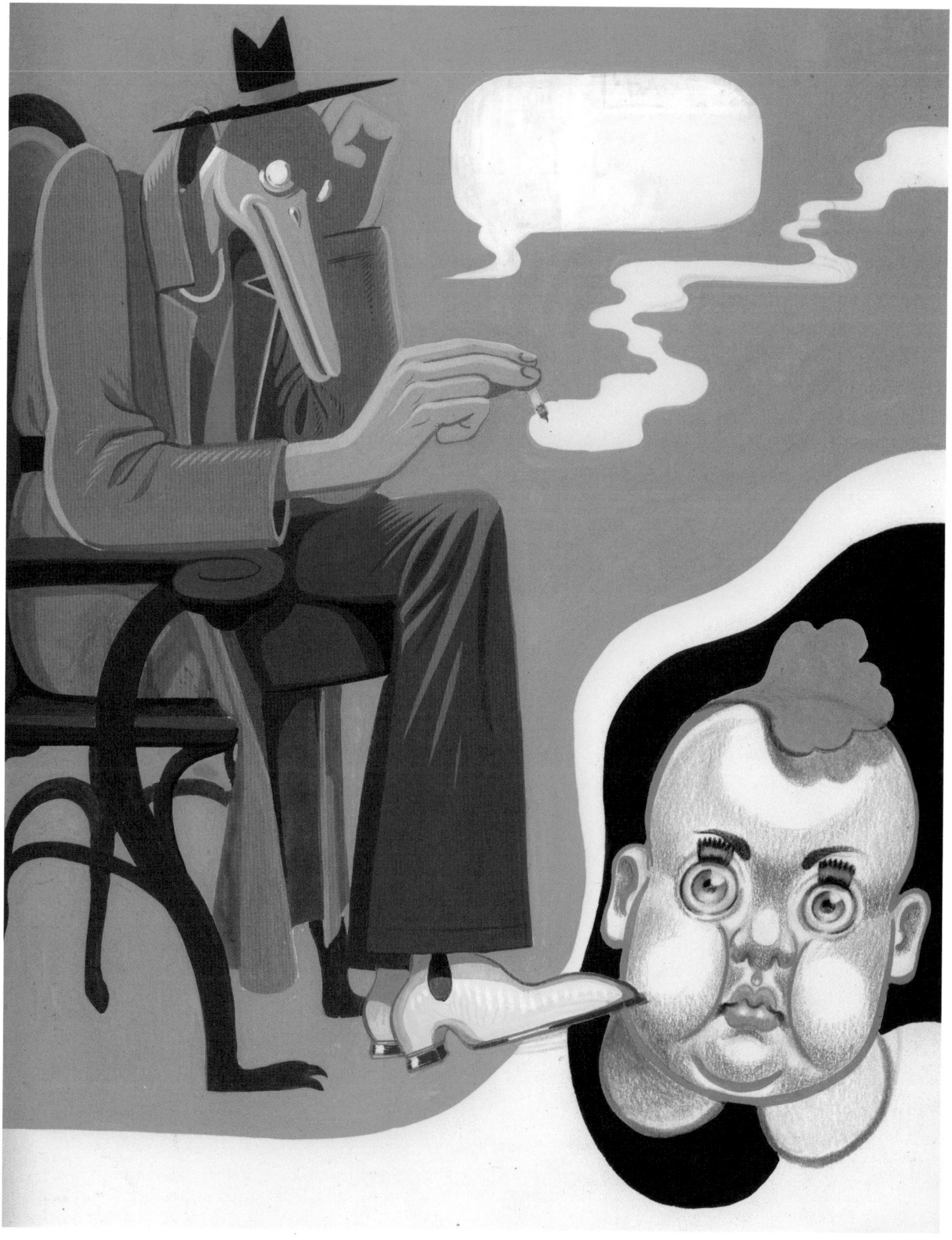

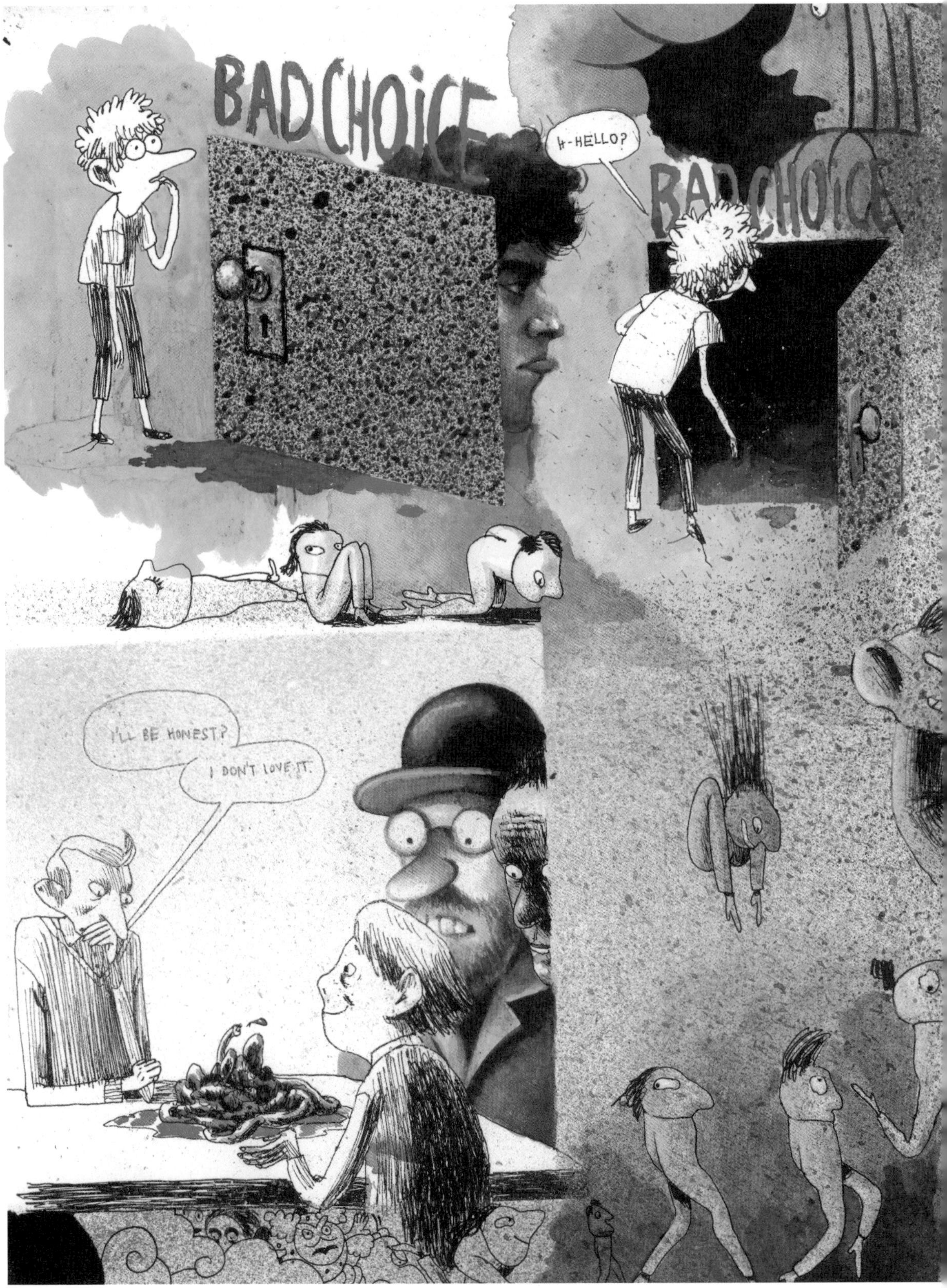
BAD CHOICE
H-HELLO?
BAD CHOICE
I'LL BE HONEST?
I DON'T LOVE IT.

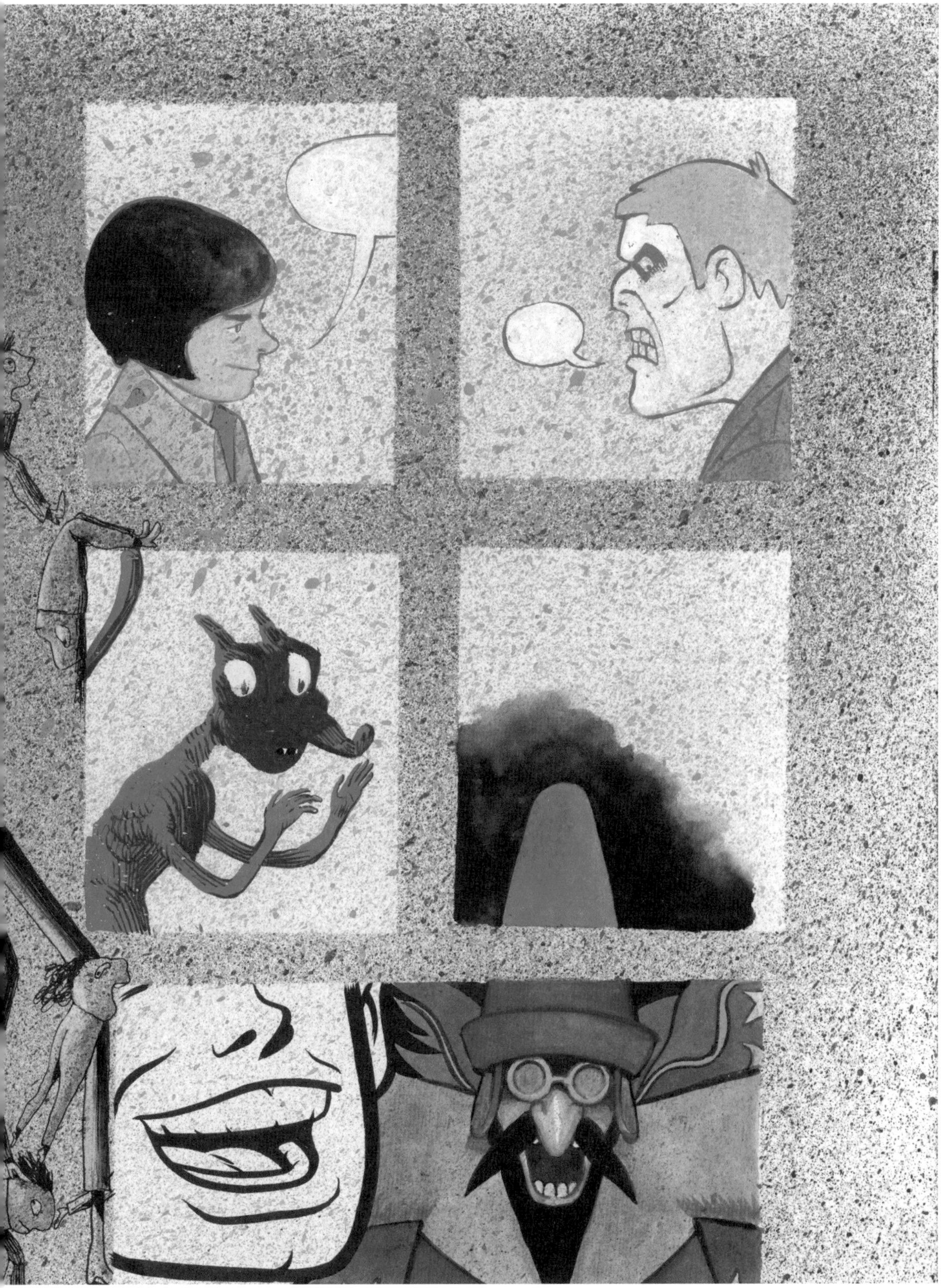

The Conceptual Comics
of Ilan Manouach

Kim Jooha

IN MY LAST ESSAY in *The Comics Journal* #303, I introduced the concept of Expanded Comics: artworks that are not necessarily comics, but they can be read as such – illuminated manuscripts,

BELOW: From *Katz*, 2012.

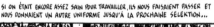

Mesoamerican codices and Charlotte Solomon's *Life? Or Theatre?*, for example. As I wrote, Expanded Comics shows that "comics as we know and read them now consist of a tiny fraction of the comics that are possible."

Greek-Belgian artist Ilan Manouach is one of the most critical contemporary cartoonists and thinkers working today. Manouach critiques the ideologies behind Western comics' popular "mainstream" and "alternative/comics as art" sets, as well as their respective surrounding cultures. In *Katz* (2012), Manouach changed each and every animal character in Art Spiegelman's *Maus* (1991) to cats. He published this "pirated" edition – which looked exactly like the original except for the crucial animal switch – at the Angoulême International Comics Festival, the same year that Spiegelman was serving as its president. In his Pulitzer Prize-winning *Maus*, Spiegelman recounts his father's memories of the Holocaust and the events that led up to it by depicting Poles as pigs, Jews as mice and Germans as cats. Spiegelman's use of animal characters, while acknowledging the "funny animal" history of comics, reinforces ethnic stereotypes and a simplistic, teleological and fatalistic reading of history. Spiegelman's French publisher, Flammarion, sued Manouach for copyright violation and Manouach was forced to burn all of the remaining copies. This ordeal was described in *MetaKatz* (2013), whose title

LEFT: From *Katz*, 2012.

refers to Spiegelman's *MetaMaus* (2011) and was published with ink created from the ashes of the pulped copies of *Katz*. *MetaKatz* is a collection of essays regarding the "*Katz* affair," and includes thoughts on copyright, fear of lawsuits, creative rights, appropriation and collage in comics (coined *détournement* by the Marxist art group Situationist International) and more.

These writings show that Manouach's artistic goal is not just a winking game of trolling but a critical endeavor, which is incredibly lacking in the graphic novel movement which Spiegelman and *Maus* surely represent.

Noir (2014) is Manouach's comment on *Les Schtroumpfs noirs* [*The Black Smurfs*] from 1963. *Les Schtroumpfs noirs* was

published as *The Purple Smurfs* in North America due to the racist implication of a black Smurf being inherently pathological and evil. However, *Les Schtroumpfs noirs* is still sold to children in Europe. Manouach's *Noir* prints *Les Schtroumpfs noirs* using four shades of cyan, instead of the usual four colors of CMYK (cyan, magenta, yellow and black) that is used for offset printing. This printing effect leaves the reader unable not only to recognize the "black" Smurfs from the "normal" Smurfs, but also the foreground from the background. Onomatopoeias, captions and contextual panel boundaries are meshed together and undistinguishable. We assume that some things as basic as the printing technique and color are neutral and apolitical. But what Manouach shows is that even the most impartial technology conceals an ideology.

Manouach's "pirated" translation of Hergé's *Tintin in the Congo* (1931), *Tintin akei Kongo* (2015), is in Lingala, the language spoken in much of the Democratic Republic of the Congo. Hergé's *Tintin in the Congo* is not sold in some parts of the world due to its racist, imperialist depictions, but is still sold in France as a well as Francophone Africa. The fact that it has not been translated into a Congolese national and indigenous language before shows that something is definitely amiss in discussions of the current "postcolonial" world. The matter of translating multinational intellectual properties, which sounds just as mechanical as printing techniques, serves as Manouach's commentary on colonialism.

Lastly, *Un monde un peu meilleur* [*A World a Little Better*] is Manouach's stretched, square version of Lewis Trondheim's original title by the same name. Trondheim is one of the founders of the publishing house L'Association, who collectively openly ridiculed "48CC" – the standard 48-page French hardcover album format. They were not merely against the format, however. French mainstream publishers are mostly owned by large corporate conglomerates that kowtow to editorial and sales pressures, while L'Association,

in contrast, was formed as a co-op. But as Trondheim and L'Association became more critically and commercially successful, they too began to create "48CC" like *Un monde un peu meilleur*. Manouach's reformatting of the work transfigures the format that Trondheim and his publishing house argued is politically biased – but later submitted to – and questions what is so "alternative" about alternative comics.

Manouach pulls the veil off of ideologies behind matters that are assumed to be apolitical in the medium – formats, colors, printings, translation, character design – and demonstrates how indifferent comics discourse has been toward these matters.

Ilan Manouach's comics don't have to be read panel by panel to understand them. It is the very act of making them that manifests the artist's message. Some critics argue whether these works should be regarded as comics or not, which I find unproductive nitpicking. It is more constructive to regard them as Conceptual Comics – or Expanded Comics – and start asking questions that actually matter.

* * *

ILAN MANOUACH'S own research project "Conceptual Comics (CoCo)" inspired my ideas on Conceptual Comics. My definition is more general in that it applies to any comics work employing the method of creating conceptual art. See: http://ilanmanouach.com/project/coco/

ABOVE LEFT: From *Un monde un peu meilleur*, reformatted by Manouach, 2018.

ABOVE RIGHT: From *Un monde un peu meilleur*, by Lewis Trondheim, 2018.

Unionize Comics!
The Comics Guild and the Possibility of Collective Action

Austin Lanari

BELOW: Cover to *The Comics Journal* #42, Oct. 1978. Art by John Byrne and Joe Rubinstein.

IN THE OCTOBER 1978 ISSUE of *The Comics Journal*, Gary Groth published a multi-part report titled "The Comics Guild: A Professional Guild to Protect the Rights of Visual Creators." The first part of the report was dedicated to an overview of what the

Comics Guild was, why it was being formed and the problems that it was already facing in its infant stages. The second part of the report consisted of brief asides with various creators and people either involved with or very close to the Guild's initial proceedings and what they thought about the Guild. The final part, titled "Birth of the Guild," was Groth's transcription of the first (and really only) major meeting of the Comics Guild on May 7, 1978. The report had almost-top-billing on the front cover of the issue, only being beaten out in prominence by the words "STAN LEE INTERVIEWED!" over an image of Stan sitting with all of the characters he didn't draw.

The next mention of the Comics Guild in *The Comics Journal* was in issue #48, 10 months later in August of 1979. There was no mention of it on the cover. It managed to fit into a stream of small news blurbs in the opening pages, just before the letters to the editor but about nine pages after a report about the fact that Howard the Duck was going to start wearing pants.

The trajectory of the Comics Guild coverage in the *Journal* from 1978 to 1979 is not an indictment of *TCJ* journalism: It is an accurate cross-section of the trajectory of the Comics Guild itself. Other than the eight-page newsletter published in January of 1979 and the various new priorities mentioned by Neal Adams within the August 1979 *TCJ* coverage, the Comics Guild had done nothing. While a mishap with a

lawyer is mentioned, even once things were on the right track, the Comics Guild more or less folded before it even began. Since there was never even a proper committee elected, nor an official set of agreed-upon positions for contracts or anything else, there was nothing to even dissolve.

What went wrong?

On one level, this is an extremely naive question. Independent of Groth's transcripts of the May 7 meeting – which reveals a room that was a boringly toxic mix of apathetic, confused and angry about weirdly specific things – Groth is explicit at the outset about the problems with the Guild stemming from a lack of organization, unity and vision. Major figures in the proceedings, including Adams, were dismissive of letterers and essentially anyone not contributing to line art or scripting. The initial page rates that were requested were so high that eventually the Guild itself would reject them.

Though the question has been asked a few times over the course of coverage as to "What went wrong?," very little, if anything, has been said about what it would have taken for things to go *right*. The fundamental questions that never got asked – but needed to be – were tripartite and inextricable. The first is: What balance of compensation and rights forfeiture provide fair

recompense to creators, both immediately and over time? The second is: What is an effective vehicle for creator consensus on these needs? The third and most foundational question is: How do creators get a seat at the table along with publishers in establishing and normalizing these agreed-upon standards of fairness?

The fact of the matter is that, in this country, without a labor union, you cannot answer any of these questions. There is no labor autonomy without a union because any group, no matter how disciplined, cannot and will not stick to a set of standards if they all have to negotiate with the boss privately. People will sell out. People will be taken advantage of. Loosely agreeing on terms is not collective action: It is distributed folly. All autonomy – especially that which is intra-creator – flows from having a collective bargaining unit. Once you have someone settling your rates and rights, then you can go about internally

LEFT: From the cover to *Howard the Duck* #32, Jan. 1986. Penciled by Jack Abel and inked by Vince Colletta.

BELOW: Neal Adams, circa mid-1970s.

resolving disputes along a set of internally agreed upon procedures.

The reason that no comic labor movement – least of all the Comics Guild – has gotten off the ground is because they have often acted from a position that mourns the loss of independent contractor status. Rather, comic labor needs to embrace its work-made-for-hire contracts and accept their status as outright employees: employees who can unionize.

✳✳✳

I CANNOT THINK of a more apt title for an essay about the history of attempts to organize labor in comics than Jean-Paul Gabilliet's choice of "The Impossibility of Collective Action" in his 2009 overview of American comics entitled *Of Comics and Men: A Cultural History of American Comic Books* (which, as of this writing, has a review of 3.5 stars on Amazon because of one guy who gave it 1 star for having

no pretty pictures in it). In any profession, collective action is not a foregone conclusion, but all historical evidence in comics suggests some such level of both disorganization and apathy that is hard to ignore.

Since the 1950s, there has been a Society of Comic Book Illustrators (SOCBI), an Academy of Comic Book Arts (ACBA), a United Cartoon Workers of America (UCWA) and a Comic Creators Guild (the Guild or CCG). None of these remain, arguably only two of them (SOCBI and ACBA) were ever even something resembling solvent and I would wager the majority of comic creators working today have not heard much, if anything, about a single one.

Despite their failures in executing or even organizing a lasting plan, the demands remained notably similar to the chattering in 1951 that led to the birth of SOCBI in the following year to the final time the Guild was heard from in the pages of *The Comics Journal* 28 years on, in the latter half of 1979. In 1951, when Bernard Krigstein, Edd Ashe,

George Evans and Arthur Petty started discussing what an organization representing the interests of comic book artists might want to fight for, the big three goals were publishers paying for health care, return of original pages and a minimum page rate. Almost three decades later, although mentions of health care took a back seat to outright copyright dealings with publishers, Adams still explicitly mentioned minimum payment for freelancers and the return of artwork as key parts of the platform just before the Guild faded into obscurity. From post-War to pre-Reagan, very little of the comic creators' enduring platform had been achieved, with the exception of the return of artwork.

In *TCJ* #42, Groth listed off the problems that were already apparent with the Guild:

1. "The very concept of a Guild is based on a collective voice, but even members of the Ad Hoc Committee don't seem to talk with one another, or to even know what the Guild's progress is."

Independent of the committee, the number of people asked about the Guild in the pages of *TCJ* itself who don't seem to know what's going on is alarming. Steve Ditko called it "too ill-defined to talk about at this stage." Alex Toth said, "I don't know anything about [the Guild]." Jack Kirby replied, "I can't make a statement on it – I know so little about it." These are just a few examples of folks expressing their complete lack of knowledge about the Guild, but they don't exactly seem like people who should be left out of a conversation about creators' rights issues.

2. "The Ad Hoc Committee members do not appear to be thoroughly aware of the issues."

Here Groth expounds on the fact that Marshall Rogers, chair of the Committee, never read "the new copyright law." Groth then goes on to explain how a statement of intent

LEFT: Panels from *Astonishing* #16, Aug. 1952. Penciled and inked by Bernie Krigstein, recolored by Greg Sadowski.

given out for the only Guild meeting mentioned the Guild as the "sole bargaining agent" for those who joined, an ability it would plainly lack. The rest of the present article is dedicated to exploring this misunderstanding and how to better frame the comic creatives' labor situation. Groth, at the time, opted to try and lean into the Authors' Guild as a model. Unfortunately, a model similar to that of a novelist makes little sense for companies who have a heavily vested interest in maintaining authorship over their intellectual property. Later, we will closely inspect another Guild that provides a better analog.

3. "The Guild's Ad Hoc Committee is inefficient and ineffective."

Given the above, this goes without saying, and hardly needs to be put under a microscope. Walt Simonson said, "I've applied for membership, but I haven't heard from them." And he's Walt Simonson.

ABOVE: Jim Shooter, 1982.

responsible and wise enough not to destroy the basis for all our livelihoods. I've seen a lot of newspapers go under because of union demands."

To be candid, this is the most passive-aggressive, thinly veiled, milquetoast-manipulative shit you will ever hear. It is textbook union busting by a middle manager. All employees in their lives in any of their workplaces have received a memo that sounds exactly like this from someone in charge once they've gotten wind of unionization. And somehow, all of the managers with real salaries, titles and benefits bestowed unto them by corporate think that unionizing is a bad idea.

Go figure.

Shooter's presence at the Guild meeting is questionable at best and absurd at worst. If you were organizing your workplace, you wouldn't go to your boss until you had the votes to unionize for sure. Otherwise, you and everyone you work with might get fired (whether or not that's illegal). And yet here was the newly minted editor in chief of Marvel at a labor organizing meeting. Not only was it inappropriate, but Groth reported that Shooter was actively disruptive and literally went out of his way to sow discord at the meeting:

> Adams: It's about time that we think of ourselves differently.
> Shooter: Neal, you keep saying "we" and you mean "I."
> Adams: No, I don't mean "I."
> Shooter: [...] The biggest benefiters [sic] here are the pencillers and the writers.
> Adams: Unfortunately, yes.
> Shooter: You're saying, "Hey, guys, it will be great for us, if you tag along we'll get you better rates."

4. "Finally, [...] most of the Committee members earn only a small portion of their income from comic book work."

A lack of skin in the game worried some rank-and-file members because the loudest folks – Adams being the poster child for this – could be banned from comics and still make a solid living. While lack of knowledge and organization are at the heart of the Guild's woes, there was another problem in the room that Groth fails to mention: Jim Shooter.

✳ ✳ ✳

"IT COULD BE a very, very good Guild or a very, very bad Guild." So began Jim Shooter with a Trump-esque eloquence in his response to Groth's Guild status outreach to people around the industry. Shooter continued: "[A Guild] could destroy the industry. It should be obvious to everybody that a Guild represents potential harm as well as good. I would hope people in the Guild are

Groth's transcript then says, "Pandemonium erupted, with everyone talking at the same time." Shooter was attempting to rake Adams over the coals for allegedly leading on letterers and colorists who would not make out well under Adams's independent-contractor model of negotiating

LEFT: From *Green Lantern* #76, April 1970. Written by Dennis O'Neil, penciled and inked by Neal Adams, colored by Cory Adams, lettered by John Costanza.

with Marvel. Although Shooter is right in this instance, Adams is very much not the person creating the troubling labor circumstances. The bureaucrats at Marvel, including Jim Shooter, were responsible for that state of affairs. Couple this uncomfortable lack of irony with the tone and timing of Shooter's comments, and his cute derailment reads as malicious.

Including Shooter's mentions of "economics" and "the company's point of view" at least one time each, it's clear that Shooter's presence was an intensely toxic one to the discussion. While you might argue that he is merely being pragmatic in discussing the concerns of the company, there are ways to discuss the optics and strategy of labor organizing that don't just serve to derail constructive labor-forward discussion. At several points herein, I will mention something being untenable from Marvel's or DC's point of view but at no point do I take that to be in conflict with creators getting their fair share.

* * *

"SUCH AS IT IS. It is nothing." These are the words of the late Dick Giordano when asked in a 1980 interview (published in

ABOVE: Dick Giordano, 1971.

2. Lack of motivation on behalf of key parties: "The people who put the Guild into operation are the people who need the Guild least. Motivation simply isn't there."

3. Low ceiling for improved conditions within the current consumer-facing corporate structure: "There are very few people who will face up to the fact that there really isn't a whole lot that can be done to improve the lot of the comic book artist or writer until you change the entire package and method of merchandising comic books, that a 50-cent item simply doesn't provide enough cash in order for artists to do what they say they'd like to do."

* * *

March 1981 in *TCJ* #62) to talk about "the [Comics] Guild, such as it is."

Groth follows, "I assume it would be correct to say that it failed," to which Giordano responds, "I can't argue with that."

Now, I have a confession to make: when I first came across this Giordano interview (available online), having started on Part Two, I did not see any dates and assumed that this interview had been conducted as late as the early 2000s. I thought this because Giordano's words about the Guild were so final. A man after my own heart, Giordano was known for his candidness; still, it is jarring to see someone involved in a project that was being written about just a year before this interview as if it was a specter from the past that he can shrug at. This does not register as a fresh wound, let alone as a wound at all.

Why?

Giordano provides three main reasons for the Guild's short life:

1. Lack of time: "The people who can make the Guild work are perhaps the busiest people in the industry."

BEFORE EXAMINING THESE POINTS, let's first consider why it's worth dissecting Giordano's take on the Guild. First, there's the freshness of this perspective: The Guild had collapsed not just a year before this interview had taken place. Second, there's the perspective itself: the way that Giordano is thinking about what could be done, who could do it and why it was worth doing is the viewpoint of a key historical figure in comics from within the Guild. The opinions he's expressing aren't just hand-wavy hot takes (even when his candidness might make them sound a little less thoughtful than they are); rather, they are an archetypal case of the thoughts and feelings that would drive the kind of apathy that killed the Guild before it was really even born.

In terms of the issues facing organization, we can usually just throw out "too busy" since it's true for everybody who works full time (and even a lot of people who don't). That's not to say it's not an issue facing organizing more generally, but it is certainly an issue facing everyone equally in nearly any labor organizing circumstance. The following two reasons – that there was a lack of motivation from key figures and a limit on material improvement within the existing frame-work – dovetail in that any material improvement for non-"key figures" (i.e. the rank-and-file) are welcome. Of course, the rank-and-file often have the most unfavorable free-time-to-resource ratio, and so in addition to having the most to gain from small improvements, they also have the most to lose as they are the least secure and lack the flexibility afforded by their resources at any given time. Still, this also makes them the most effective organizers because the stakes are highest and they have the greatest strength in numbers to affect positive change.

It is Giordano's third point on its own that causes the most concern while simultaneously being perhaps most emblematic of the issue within the Guild. The thought that the corporation would have to make untenable changes to its customer-facing business model in order to accommodate artists is in parallel with a rather more typical union-busting line. We saw an example of that in the transcripts of the original Guild meeting where Jim Shooter insists several times that Marvel isn't making as much money as everyone thinks. He continuously insists – both there and elsewhere, even to the present day – that bringing the Guild demands to Marvel and arriving at an impasse would blow up the whole kit and caboodle for everyone involved.

If we accept this as pretty typical anti-union fear mongering, we can see Giordano's comments in a similar light. Giordano's comments are obviously not as malicious since he's speaking candidly in an interview and not using them to bully lower-middle-class artists into signing contracts, but it's apparent how they're in the same vein. The fact of the matter is that the corporations that own Marvel and DC in the present day and age (Disney and Warner Media, respectively) have the resources and wherewithal to restructure internally and more justly compensate their artists without ever having to charge customers

another dime. I don't have to do a lick of math to tell you that the profits on a single Marvel film could subsidize the print runs of every single Marvel comic that's come out in the last year and then some.

To be clear, this isn't a slight to Giordano. The Marvel of today is very much not the Marvel of 1980, independent of whatever half-truths he and other creators may have heard about their past financial situation. What's important is that this corporate-centric viewpoint is only pragmatic in a capitalist sense and hardly has a place among the organizing principles and concepts of a guild trying to get rank-and-file members their fair share.

✳✳✳

THE RETURN OF ARTWORK – one of the few Guild platforms to have seen a resolution completely in spite of the Guild itself – is a historically tenuous and semi-codified practice. Since each publisher handles this differently and on a contract-to-contract

ABOVE: A panel from a promotional flyer for Adams's and Giordano's own Continuity Studios, 1971.

RIGHT: From *X-Men* #23, Aug. 1966. Written by Roy Thomas, penciled by Werner Roth, inked by Dick Ayers, lettered by Artie Simek.

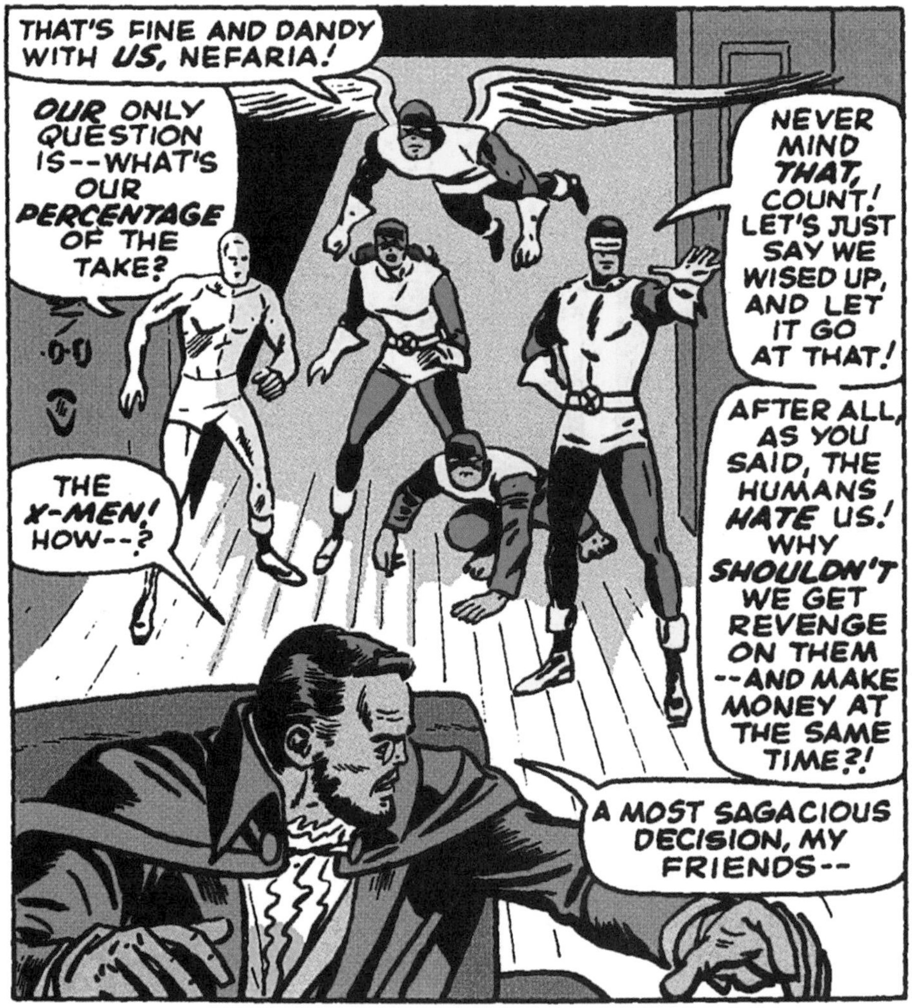
THAT'S FINE AND DANDY WITH *US*, NEFARIA!
OUR ONLY QUESTION IS--WHAT'S OUR *PERCENTAGE* OF THE TAKE?
NEVER MIND *THAT*, COUNT! LET'S JUST SAY WE WISED UP, AND LET IT GO AT THAT!
AFTER ALL, AS YOU SAID, THE HUMANS *HATE* US! WHY *SHOULDN'T* WE GET REVENGE ON THEM --AND MAKE MONEY AT THE SAME TIME?!
THE *X-MEN!* HOW--?
A MOST SAGACIOUS DECISION, MY FRIENDS--

basis, there is no such thing as an "industry standard," and the concept of fairness within which each publisher operates is itself an amorphous appeasement. Inspecting this practice, its history and the way various bureaucrats and creators have talked about it is instructive of the need for normalization and thus a unified bargaining unit to achieve it.

As early as 1974, the return of artwork became a fairly normal practice at Marvel Comics, carried out at its "sole discretion" according to the whims of Editor-in-Chief Roy Thomas. As Jim Shooter has pointed out on his own website, this was very much a matter of whim, and these pages were tantamount to gifts being given out by the publisher. The artists and writers, according to their contracts at the time, had no legal right to those pages. Even if it had been a "policy" (which Shooter considered it when he took over as EiC in 1978), there is no real legal status to a policy unless it is challenged in such a context as to establish it as such. In the case of work made for hire, there was no such precedent waiting around the corner: in that situation, your work belongs to the employer as if you were an employee (an employee's work is itself "work made for hire" by virtue of their employment). The only exceptions to that rule are ones spelled out in the contracts as individually signed.

It was this state of affairs that moved Neal Adams to start the Comic Creators

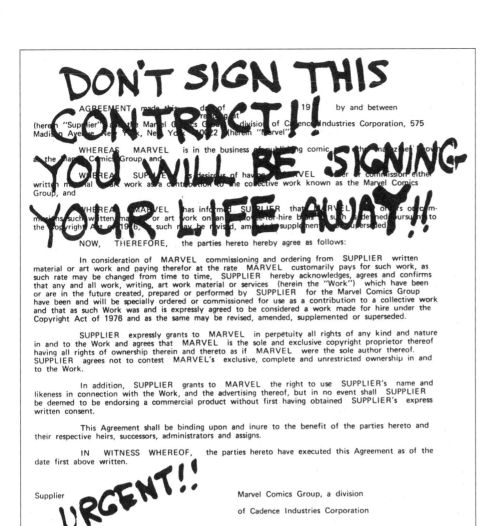

DON'T SIGN THIS CONTRACT!! YOU WILL BE SIGNING YOUR LIFE AWAY!!

AGREEMENT, made this ___ day of ___ 19___ by and between _____ residing at _____ (herein "Supplier") and the Marvel Comics Group, a division of Cadence Industries Corporation, 575 Madison Avenue, New York, New York 10022 (herein "Marvel")

WHEREAS MARVEL is in the business of publishing comic magazines known as the Marvel Comics Group, and

WHEREAS SUPPLIER is desirous of having MARVEL order or commission either written material or art work as a contribution to the collective work known as the Marvel Comics Group, and

WHEREAS MARVEL has informed SUPPLIER that MARVEL orders or commissions such written material or art work on an employee-for-hire basis as such is defined pursuant to the Copyright Act of 1976, as such may be revised, amended, supplemented or superseded;

NOW, THEREFORE, the parties hereto hereby agree as follows:

In consideration of MARVEL commissioning and ordering from SUPPLIER written material or art work and paying therefor at the rate MARVEL customarily pays for such work, as such rate may be changed from time to time, SUPPLIER hereby acknowledges, agrees and confirms that any and all work, writing, art work material or services (herein the "Work") which have been or are in the future created, prepared or performed by SUPPLIER for the Marvel Comics Group have been and will be specially ordered or commissioned for use as a contribution to a collective work and that as such Work was and is expressly agreed to be considered a work made for hire under the Copyright Act of 1976 and as the same may be revised, amended, supplemented or superseded.

SUPPLIER expressly grants to MARVEL in perpetuity all rights of any kind and nature in and to the Work and agrees that MARVEL is the sole and exclusive copyright proprietor thereof having all rights of ownership therein and thereto as if MARVEL were the sole author thereof. SUPPLIER agrees not to contest MARVEL's exclusive, complete and unrestricted ownership in and to the Work.

In addition, SUPPLIER grants to MARVEL the right to use SUPPLIER's name and likeness in connection with the Work, and the advertising thereof, but in no event shall SUPPLIER be deemed to be endorsing a commercial product without first having obtained SUPPLIER's express written consent.

This Agreement shall be binding upon and inure to the benefit of the parties hereto and their respective heirs, successors, administrators and assigns.

IN WITNESS WHEREOF, the parties hereto have executed this Agreement as of the date first above written.

Supplier   URGENT!!   Marvel Comics Group, a division
                                              of Cadence Industries Corporation

by _____   by _____

COMICS CONTRACT MEETING SUNDAY MAY 7, 9 E. 48½ ST THIRD FLOOR 4:00 P:M

LEFT: Adams's flyer for the first Guild meeting, written on top of a Marvel work-made-for-hire contract, 1978.

Guild in the first place. While "work made for hire" was largely put in place to protect businesses hiring freelancers, the manner in which it positioned contractors themselves was, loosely speaking, not completely unfavorable. Adams's thinking was that if a creator does not "have" to sign an agreement – if they are not legally obligated to sign away all their rights in a work-made-for-hire agreement – then they ought not to.

He is correct about this, and one can find pretty lucid legal scholarship about corporations-as-authors (the basis of the idea of work made for hire) as a legal fiction (i.e. there's no real substantive moral claim underwriting it outside of the context of courts). Still, it's a legal fiction with over 100 years of precedent backing it up, whether or not Adams had the moral and ethical high ground. But the legal approach was always shaky because of a simple fact: It was not

ABOVE: Bill Mantlo, 1970.

clear what the Guild was really fighting for when it was fighting for "the return of artwork," especially in the context of a business where one major employer was already doing so. In fact, by 1980, most of the discussion about the return of artwork was not whether to return it but rather to whom the pages should be returned and in what proportion.

According (again) to his own site, in September of 1980, Jim Shooter changed Marvel's *de facto* policy of returning artwork such that writers – who had been receiving a not-insubstantial cut of original pages, even though they got last pick of them – would no longer get a cut of the pages, while also adjusting the proportion among the other artists (who also would now have the option to break it down among themselves). While the decision to allow artists to decide how to break things up among themselves seems fair, it's worth

noting that this was only because Marvel allowed for that discussion to take place within the scope of their broader, more definitive concept of fairness which explicitly did not include writers.

Part of Shooter's decision process was to poll Marvel contributors. It's assumed Shooter's thinking is that, before he makes a decision as to how to best edit Thomas's policy, he should get the lay of the land and see how different contributors – artists, pencilers, inkers, etc. – as different groups feel about the prospective changes. The result of the poll favored the return of all artwork to the artists.

Bill Mantlo wasn't happy about this: "Of course a vote amongst artists and writers (there are more of the former than the latter, you know) would produce a poll favoring the return of all artwork to the artists." So began a memo Bill Mantlo wrote to Jim Shooter. Its title?

"ANGRY MEMO!"

Mantlo continued, frustrated by the fact that some writers also voted in favor of the position which favored the artists, noting that the poll did not weight writers based on the relative volume of their contributions to Marvel. He went on to state that "the main point […] is money," explaining that he made a substantial amount of money in the previous year from sale of original pages and that, since the previously lucrative policy was "company policy," that "legally, a challenge could be mounted for a unilateral changing of that policy now."

In the folly of Mantlo's agitated threat lies a key to understanding where things went wrong for the Guild and the most vocal of comics labor advocates. The changing of Marvel's policy was not, in fact, best characterized as a unilateral change in some kind of established company policy. Rather, Shooter's policy of how, when and to whom to return original artwork is a semi-arbitrary, only partially philosophical, almost wholly bureaucratic decision that could be changed at Marvel's "sole discretion" both any time it wants and with any employee it wants. While they may state an interest in fairness and act as if they have a broad company policy, without a collective bargaining unit flowing through one point to negotiate contracts, any given contract for any given creative team could have a more or less favorable artwork return policy at any given time. One could say that the legal fiction of corporations-as-authors in the realm of works made for hire gives corporations the leeway to create corporate fictions such as ephemeral concepts of fairness that change when the wind (read: money) changes.

* * *

BEING ONLY ONE ASPECT among many, return of original art is not the rallying cry around which comic creators can focus their quest for material gains. While sale of original pages is lucrative, there is a hard cap on the number of pages that any line artists can take part in producing in a given calendar year. This is a physical and temporal limit that is in stark contrast with the unlimited social capital that any given bit of intellectual property is worth when it's generated for a multi-billion-dollar corporation. To this day, however, the way in which return of original art is handled by major publishers is instructive of the continued problems with how much control creators lack over how they can capitalize on the one small piece of their work that is allotted to them.

Presently, if a team signs a contract to work on a project with DC, there is a provision which states that original artwork will be returned according to their "current policy," unless the team would like to share it in a different way, in which case they have to notify DC in writing. Original art is returned "1 year after the initial publication," or, if the series is canceled, "within 1 year after the cancelation." The signee cannot reproduce, publish or license the use of the art in any way other than what is allowed by copyright law (i.e. literally selling the art itself, transferring the physical ownership of it along with the license

restrictions). And, even then, the signee can't actually sell or even publicly display the art or a reproduction of the art before whichever comes first out of the art's initial publication *or* the second anniversary of the delivery of the art.

For those keeping score at home, that means that artists working for a title for which everything goes off without a hitch might have to wait up to a year to get their artwork back. Assuming this is after publication in this case, they would be able to do as they please with the artwork. However, for a project that experiences substantial delays, or, notably, for an artist whose project gets canceled, the signee cannot sell or publicly display the original artwork until two years have lapsed since its delivery. There are artists creating pages for a job that falls through and because the pages are no longer attached to a project with an initial publication date, they cannot sell these pages for two years!

I do not think there is any ambiguity to the message this kind of policy sends, and it does not even operate under the guise of any reasonable concept of "fairness." It is clear that this kind of policy serves to protect DC from having too much interest in the artwork split between what's on the shelves and what's for private sale. In the case of canceled titles, this protective stance further extends to guarding what could possibly be more novel intellectual property from the light of day so that it could be used in another fashion before getting too much attention.

While a company certainly has a right to protect its IP, it is undeniable that it is at the cost of the creators. There can be no question about how the scales are tipped. The attention that Marvel and DC receive as brands is fed by a massive nerd culture funnel unrivaled in the history of free marketing, and it is dubious at best to have boilerplate policy founded on the assumption that the timelier presence of original artwork on the market would harm that. The sale of original artwork in itself is a niche industry, especially now that many

NEXT THREE PAGES:
DC Comics's current work-made-for-hire contract in full.

DC COMICS

SERVICES AGREEMENT

Date [redacted]   Contract No. [redacted]

Talent [redacted]

(Full name or, if Talent is a loan-out company or other separate legal entity that will be providing the services of an individual hereunder, full name of company)

Employee [redacted]

(Name of individual whose services will be furnished by the loan-out company or other contracting entity, if applicable)

Address Line1 [redacted]

Art & Editorial Payments								Additional Compensation Rates* (Percentage of Net Revenue)	
Title	Issue	Service	Pages	Pg. Rate	Cont %	Flat Fee	Totals	DC Publication %	Licensed Reprint %
[redacted]	[redacted]	[redacted]	[redacted]	[redacted]	100	[redacted]			

*Subject to the terms and conditions of this Agreement

This agreement (Agreement) is made as of the Date set forth above, by and between Talent and DC Comics (DC), with respect to the Services as more fully described herein.

1. DEFINITIONS: The following terms as used in this Agreement have the following respective meanings:

(a) Additional Compensation means the sums due to the Talent hereunder from DC's reproduction and use of the Work.

(b) DC Publication means any book or magazine published by DC in any print or digital format.

(c) Licensed Reprint means any publication by a third party under license from DC in any language in any print or digital format.

(d) Net Revenue for DC Publications in print format means the cover price, less any distributor fees, trade discounts, and retailer incentives, multiplied by Net Sales; for DC Publications in digital format means all monies actually received by DC from Net Sales less any digital conversion costs and third-party platform, hosting, or distributor fees, or any other costs or fees attendant to such digital distribution; and for Licensed Reprints means all monies actually received by DC from actual sales or licenses to consumers of Licensed Reprints less third-party agency commissions, any applicable foreign taxes, currency exchange charges, and the direct cost of providing proofs, negatives, or color separations to such licensees if not reimbursed by the licensees.

(e) Net Sales means, for print format DC Publications, the number of copies of a DC Publication sold by DC less the number of copies that are returned, damaged, lost, subject to a reserve for returns, sold to uncollectible accounts, or for use as premiums (as such term is commonly understood in the publishing industry), given away at no charge for promotional or other purposes, or sold at discounts in excess of 70% off of cover price. For digital format DC Publications, Net Sales means the number of copies of a DC Publication accessed by end users through sale, license, rental, or other provision of access thereto.

(f) Page means a page of text or artwork produced and intended for use on an interior page of a DC Publication.

(g) Results and Proceeds means all results and proceeds of Talent's engagement under this Agreement or otherwise relating to the Work, including all themes, plots, characters, formats, ideas, and stories contained therein, and all other materials of any kind created or developed by Talent hereunder.

(h) Work means all of the Pages produced by Talent hereunder, and the Results and Proceeds.

2. ENGAGEMENT: DC engages Talent to produce the Work. Talent accepts such engagement and agrees to produce and deliver the Work in accordance with this Agreement.

3. FIXED COMPENSATION: DC will pay Talent the Per Page Rate for any Pages delivered to and accepted by DC, in DC's sole discretion, consistent with DC's then-current editorial standards.

4. DELIVERY: Talent will perform the Services in accordance with DC's instructions and editorial standards and will deliver the completed Work to DC by the date(s) DC specifies or, in the absence of any specified delivery date(s), no later than 30 days after the Date of this Agreement, after which DC will no longer be obligated to accept or pay for any Page(s) not previously accepted by DC.

5. REVISIONS: After Talent delivers any Page(s) to DC, Talent will make any revisions of such Page(s) that DC requests, within the time frame DC specifies for such revisions, at no additional cost to DC.

6. COPYRIGHT AND OTHER RIGHTS: (a) DC specially commissioned the Work for use as a contribution to a collective work and, for this reason, among others, the Work constitutes work made for hire, as such term is used in the United States Copyright Act of 1976. DC may alter, and may engage others to alter, the Work in any way, including by adding or deleting Pages, in DC's sole discretion.

(b) If DC is deemed not to be the author and owner of the Work, then Talent irrevocably assigns to DC, for no additional consideration, all right, title, and interest in and to the Work, effective as of its creation, including copyright and any extensions, or revivals thereof, trademark rights and any attendant goodwill, and all other rights to exploit the Work in all media now known or hereafter devised, throughout the universe, in perpetuity.

(c) Talent irrevocably waives all rights of droit morale or moral rights of authors or any similar rights or principles of law that Talent may now have or later acquire in the Work (whether now existing or hereinafter enacted) that may not be assigned under applicable law, and agrees that Talent will not seek to enforce such rights against DC in any location.

(d) If Talent may not assign or waive any rights in the Work under applicable law, Talent grants to DC an exclusive, worldwide, irrevocable, perpetual, fully paid, freely transferable license to use, reproduce, distribute, create derivative works of, publicly perform, and publicly display the Work for any purpose in all media now known or hereafter devised, to the extent permitted under applicable law.

(e) Talent grants DC the right to use and to permit others to use Talent's (and, if Talent is a loan-out company or other separate legal entity providing the services of Employee, Employee's) name, likeness, and biographical information in connection with the Work, and the advertising, publicity, and promotion thereof, and in connection with DC.

(f) Talent acknowledges that: (i) Talent has entered into this Agreement before commencing any Services hereunder; (ii) the Work will be derivative of preexisting material, including the names, pictorial, and literary representations of fictional characters, companies, places, and things (Preexisting Material);

(iii) DC owns or otherwise has rights in the Preexisting Material; (iv) Talent would be unable to produce the Work without the Preexisting Material; and (v) Talent does not have, and Talent will not acquire, any right whatsoever in or to any of the Preexisting Material or the Work, and Talent does not have the right or privilege to use any of the Preexisting Material or the Work, except as provided herein or as DC otherwise expressly consents in writing.

7. ADDITIONAL COMPENSATION:

(a) DC Publications and Licensed Reprints: Subject to ¶7(b) and ¶7(e) below, for any DC Publication that includes the Work as the entire story content and any Licensed Reprint that includes the Work as the entire story content, DC will pay Talent Additional Compensation based on the applicable Additional Compensation Rate.

(b) Adjustments and Reprint Formats: Additional Compensation calculations under ¶7(a) above are subject to the following: (i) for DC Publications in periodical format, the Additional Compensation Rate will be payable only on Net Sales in excess of 60,000 copies; (ii) if the Work does not constitute the entire story content of a DC Publication or a Licensed Reprint, DC will pay Talent Additional Compensation prorated by the total number of pages of such publication; (iii) if the Work consists of Text, Sketches, Pinup Pencils and/or Pinup Inks only, no Additional Compensation will be due or payable to Talent except as may be otherwise provided in ¶7(c) below; (iv) if a DC Publication or Licensed Reprint containing the Work also includes pages of work for which another contributor performed the same Services independently of Talent, or if a DC Publication or Licensed Reprint contains Work for which another contributor performed the Services together with Talent, DC will prorate the Additional Compensation payable to Talent by the number of Pages or contributors, respectively; (v) for any full Page included as less than a full page of a book or magazine, DC may prorate the Additional Compensation in its good faith discretion; and (vi) Net Sales of additional printings of any DC Publication containing the Work will be counted as Net Sales of DC's initial publication of such DC Publication, and in calculating the 60,000-copy threshold above, print and digital format copies of a DC Publication will be counted in the aggregate. As used herein, the publication of a DC Publication will be considered an additional printing if it is substantially unchanged from the first printing, as determined by DC, in its sole, good faith discretion. If a DC Publication including the Work is initially published or reprinted in any format, such as a collected edition (i.e., a DC Publication comprised of two or more previously published DC Publications that may include new original material) that has an additional compensation structure that differs from the structure contained in this Agreement, DC will pay Talent additional compensation for such use of the Work in accordance with DC's then-current additional compensation structure for such other format in which the Work is published.

(c) New Uses of Non-Eligible Pages and Preliminary Materials: If DC reprints, or licenses third parties the right to reprint, any Page previously published by DC that is not otherwise eligible for Additional Compensation pursuant to ¶7(a) or ¶7(b) above, or any preliminary materials such as sketches produced by Talent as a result of Talent's performance of the Services, DC will pay Talent additional compensation in accordance with DC's then-standard practices.

(d) Accountings: DC will pay Additional Compensation due to Talent hereunder on a quarterly basis within 90 days of the close of each calendar quarter following the quarter in which Publisher received the applicable Net Revenues. If any payments due to Talent hereunder are less than $100.00, DC may delay such payments until a total of at least $100.00 is due to Talent. If DC fails to make any payment due to Talent hereunder, Talent's sole remedy for any such failure, in lieu of all other remedies at law or in equity, will be an action at law to obtain such payment, and under no circumstances will any such failure entitle Talent to any reversion or termination of DC's rights under this Agreement.

(e) Additional Compensation Term: DC's Additional Compensation payment obligations to Talent hereunder will expire and be of no further force or effect as of the tenth anniversary of Talent's or, if applicable, Employee's death.

8. REPRESENTATIONS: Talent represents and warrants that: (i) Talent has the right, authority, and power to execute and fully perform this Agreement and to grant all of the rights herein granted; and (ii) except to the extent the Work is based on material provided by DC to be used as the basis thereof, the Work and any publication thereof: (A) is or will be wholly original with Talent; (B) will not be unlawful and does not and will not defame or infringe or violate any personal, proprietary, or other rights (including copyright, trademark, contract rights, moral rights, or rights of privacy or publicity) of any person or entity; and (C) is not and will not be the subject of any litigation or other proceeding or claim that might give rise to litigation or any other proceeding. Talent will indemnify and hold harmless DC, its successors and assigns, and its and their employees, officers, directors, and agents from and against any and all liabilities, suits, judgments, costs, or expenses (including counsel fees and court costs, whether or not in connection with litigation) arising from any breach of any of the representations or warranties made by Talent herein. Talent's warranties, representations, and indemnifications herein will survive the expiration or termination of this Agreement. DC will have the sole and exclusive right to undertake the defense and settlement of any such claim.

9. TERMINATION: If Talent fails to complete Talent's obligations hereunder other than by reason of incapacity (of Employee, if applicable) or force majeure or takes any action inconsistent with any of the terms of this Agreement, DC may terminate Talent's engagement without further compensation to Talent by giving written notice to Talent.

10. ADDITIONAL DOCUMENTS: Talent shall execute any document(s) and perform any other acts that DC or its assignees or licensees may require to further evidence or effectuate DC's rights as set forth in this Agreement. If Talent fails to do so promptly, Talent appoints DC as Talent's attorney-in-fact for such purposes (it being acknowledged that such appointment is irrevocable and coupled with an interest) with full power of substitution and delegation.

11. ORIGINAL ARTWORK: DC will return to Talent any original artwork delivered by Talent hereunder (the Original Art) in accordance with DC's current policy. If Talent wishes to share the Original Art in a different way, Talent must notify DC in writing, before the initial publication of the Work. Except as otherwise provided below, DC will return the Original Art within 1 year after the initial publication of the Work or, if the applicable DC Publication(s) is cancelled before the initial publication of the Work, within 1 year after such cancellation. Notwithstanding the foregoing, DC may retain, destroy, or otherwise dispose of the Original Art without any liability to Talent if, after reasonable diligence, DC is unable to locate Talent or if Talent refuses delivery for any reason. If DC delivers the Original Art to Talent's last known address, DC will not be liable if the Original Art becomes lost or damaged after delivery. If the Original Art is lost or substantially damaged (in excess of the normal wear and tear sustained in publishing a comic publication), DC will reimburse Talent an amount equal to the Per Page Rate actually paid to Talent for the lost or damaged Original Art. Talent will not have any right to reproduce, publish, or otherwise use or license the use of any of the Original Art except that Talent may assign, sell, or transfer possession of the Original Art only, subject to the United States Copyright Act of 1976 (particularly §106 and §109) and to all of the terms and conditions of this Agreement, and provided that Talent may not sell or publicly display any Original Art or any reproduction thereof before the earlier of: (a) the initial publication of the DC Publication in which the Original Art is reproduced; or (b) the second anniversary of Talent's delivery of the Original Art or any reproduction thereof to DC. Talent shall take all necessary steps to protect copyright in the Original Art and must affix any copyright and trademark notices required by DC permanently and in such manner and location as to give reasonable notice to viewers. DC has no obligation to return any Original Art delivered to it in any electronic, digital, magnetic, mechanical, or similar data format.

12. MISCELLANEOUS:

(a) The parties expressly intend and agree that Talent is an independent contractor. Without limiting the generality of the foregoing, Talent is solely responsible for payment of Talent's own federal, state, and local income and Social Security taxes, where applicable; provided, however, that DC may withhold applicable United States taxes from foreign persons or entities, based upon then-current statutory rates. Talent does not have the right to receive any of the benefits that DC offers its own employees.

(b) Talent shall not disclose, in whole or in part, the financial terms of this Agreement other than to professional advisors or as required by law. Talent shall not make public statements or issue any press releases regarding this Agreement or Talent's services hereunder (other than publicity that relates primarily to Talent and only incidentally refers to DC, Talent's services, or the existence of this Agreement), without DC's prior written consent. Talent acknowledges that in connection with Talent's rendition of Services hereunder, DC will be sharing with Talent and Talent will be preparing and sharing with DC ideas, information, plots, storylines, artwork, promotion strategies, and other materials for one or more DC Publications (Confidential Information). Talent agrees that the Confidential Information is highly confidential in nature, that Talent will use the Confidential Information only in the manner requested or directed by DC, and that the unauthorized disclosure or use of any Confidential Information by Talent will cause DC irreparable and immediate harm. Among other damages, such disclosure will: (i) damage DC's carefully planned advertising and promotion strategies; (ii) reduce interest in undisclosed aspects of the DC Publications; (iii) make unique or novel elements of the DC Publications susceptible to imitation or copying in entertainment projects of third parties; and (iv) provide unauthorized third parties with materials capable of being used to create counterfeit and unauthorized DC Publication–related merchandise. Talent shall not disclose any Confidential Information in whole or in part, in its original or any other form, to any third party before DC has published the applicable DC Publication or publicly released the pertinent information in promotional materials for the applicable DC Publication. If Talent, in breach of this ¶12(b), discloses any of the financial terms of this Agreement or any Confidential Information, DC's obligation to make any additional compensation payments to Talent under ¶7 above shall immediately and permanently cease effective as of the date that Talent made the unauthorized disclosure.

(c) Nothing herein contained shall in any way obligate DC to publish the Work. If DC decides not to publish the Work, DC shall inform Talent and DC shall pay Talent in full for all portions of the Work delivered to and accepted by DC before the date it notifies Talent of its decision not to publish the Work, such acceptance not to be unreasonably withheld.

(d) In the event of any breach of this Agreement or any portion thereof by DC, Talent's sole remedy shall be an action at law for damages, if any. In no event shall Talent have the right to injunctive relief or to enjoin or restrain or otherwise interfere with the publication or distribution of any materials prepared hereunder or the exercise of any rights granted to DC herein and under no circumstances shall any such breach entitle Talent to any reversion or termination of DC's rights under this Agreement.

(e) This Agreement will be governed by and construed in accordance with the laws of the State of New York applicable to agreements executed and to be fully performed therein. New York courts (state and federal) only will have exclusive jurisdiction over the parties and any controversies regarding this Agreement. Any action or proceeding that involves such a controversy will be brought only in those courts in New York County.

(f) This Agreement contains the entire agreement between the parties with respect to its subject matter. In the event of any conflict between a provision of this Agreement and any statute, law, ordinance, or regulation, this Agreement will be deemed modified, but only to the extent required to comply with such statute, law, ordinance, or regulation. A waiver of any provision of this Agreement in any instance shall not be deemed a waiver of such provision for the future, nor of any subsequent breach thereof.

(g) This Agreement may be executed in any number of counterparts, each of which shall be deemed to be an original and all of which together shall be deemed to be the same agreement.

Facsimile, JPG, TIFF, PDF, and other digital copies hereof and electronic signatures thereon shall be valid and binding.

13. TALENT INCORPORATION: If Talent is a loan-out company or other separate legal entity that will be providing the services of an individual hereunder, the following terms and provisions apply: (i) Talent will produce the Work by providing Employee's services, and Talent will cause Employee to perform all of Talent's obligations under this Agreement, including, without limitation, Talent's obligations under paragraphs 2, 4, and 5 hereof; and (ii) Talent represents and warrants that: (A) it is a duly authorized and validly existing legal entity separate from Employee; (B) Talent has entered into an employment agreement with Employee that provides, among other things, the following: (1) Employee is engaged by Talent to prepare and deliver the Work to Talent; (2) Employee will prepare the Work within the regular scope of Employee's employment by Talent and the Work will constitute work made for hire as that Term is used in the United States Copyright Act of 1976; (3) if the Work is deemed not to be work made for hire, then Employee assigns to Talent all rights in the Work, effective as of the creation thereof, including copyright and any renewals, extensions, or revivals thereof, trademark rights and any attendant goodwill, and all other rights to exploit the Work in all media now known or hereafter devised, throughout the universe, in perpetuity; (4) Employee irrevocably waives all rights of droit morale or moral rights of authors or any similar rights or principles of law that Employee may now have or later acquire in the Work (whether now existing or hereinafter enacted) that may not be assigned under applicable law, and agrees that Employee will not seek to enforce such rights against DC in any location; (5) if Employee may not assign or waive any rights in the Work under applicable law, Employee grants to Talent an exclusive, worldwide, irrevocable, perpetual, fully paid, freely transferable license to use, reproduce, distribute, create derivative works of, publicly perform, and publicly display the Work for any purpose in any and all media now known or hereafter devised, to the extent permitted under applicable law; and (6) Talent will have the right, but not the obligation, to use, and to permit others to use, Employee's name, likeness, and biographical information in connection with the Work, and the advertising, publicity, and promotion thereof, and in connection with DC; (C) such agreement with Employee will be in full force and effect as of the execution of this Agreement, and Talent will not alter, permit alteration, terminate, or permit the termination of such agreement until Talent has performed all of its obligations hereunder to DC's satisfaction; and (D) Talent will provide DC with a copy of such agreement upon DC's request.

ACCEPTED AND AGREED

By:_____

Talent's Signature (If Talent is a loan-out company or other separate legal entity providing the services of Employee, Authorized Officer's Signature)

DC Comics

Company Name_____ and Authorized Officer's Title _____

EMPLOYEE ACKNOWLEDGEMENT

In order to induce DC to enter into the foregoing Agreement and in consideration of DC's execution of the Agreement, I acknowledge that I am familiar with and approve of the terms of the Agreement, and I consent to the execution and delivery of the Agreement by Talent. I further agree to render all of the Services to be rendered by Talent and to be bound by and duly perform and observe each and all of the terms and conditions of the Agreement requiring performance or compliance by Talent, and I join in all warranties, representations, agreements, and indemnities made by Talent in the Agreement. I agree that if Talent is dissolved or otherwise ceases to exist or for any reason fails, refuses, or is otherwise unable to duly perform and observe each and all of the terms and conditions of the Agreement requiring performance or compliance by Talent, I shall, at DC's election, be deemed substituted as a direct party to the Agreement in place of Talent. I further agree that if Talent breaches the Agreement, DC shall be entitled to seek legal and equitable relief by way of injunction or otherwise against Talent, or against me, or against both Talent and me, in DC's discretion, and, in any event, without first resorting to or exhausting any rights or remedies that DC may have against Talent; all of the foregoing to be to the same extent and with the same force and effect as if I had entered into the Agreement directly with DC. I will look solely to Talent for any and all compensation that I may become entitled to receive in connection with the Agreement.

(Employee's Signature if Talent is a loan-out company or other separate legal entity providing services of Employee) artists work mostly or exclusively in digital and can never even profit from the sale of original art in these cases.

It may seem like a small victory to be allowed to sell original artwork one year after your book never got published rather than two years. But having a say in this type of decision represents something much larger. Self-determination is not just about being able to make a lot of small decisions that may or may not add up to real material benefits in the long run (although it does mean this and may very well have some measurable impact where no determination would, at best, gain you nothing). Rather, it's about having a say in shaping industry standards. And, importantly, it's about making the artist's place at the table a standard in and of itself.

The fact of the matter is that it doesn't make any sense for each individual publisher to make a decision about what it thinks is "fair" compensation for the reuse of a work in any context: these are goal posts that could very easily be moved. And, as a matter of fact, all of the publishers already have many of these goal posts in different places on too many compensatory issues for one person to keep track of. If publishers are the only ones allowed to set these standards, and the manner in which each publisher sets its standards is largely arbitrary, then when we talk about artists organizing to embrace self-determination, we're not talking about them picking up a butter knife and trying to "death-by-a-thousand-cuts" the publishers: we are talking about the fact that publishers have made the concept of fair compensation a moving target. The minute that creatives force publishers to come to the table for this mundane stuff, they can no longer pull the rug out from the creatives who form the foundation of the industry.

* * *

IN FULL, here are the demands which Neal Adams put forward to all other creators with respect to taking their work seriously

ABOVE: Cover of *Wonder Woman #73*, April 1993. Written by William Messner-Loebs, penciled and inked by Brian Bolland.

and embracing the updates to Copyright Law in the 1970s:

1. Refuse to sign any "work for hire" contracts.

2. Cross out "work for hire" on a contract, initial it and say you're a free-lancer, and request that the rights being purchased are specifically laid out for you.

3. Talk to a lawyer. Be active in the drafting of the contract which you sign.

4. Solidarity: every time you sign a contract as work for hire, you're allowing it to become the norm and are complicit in "outrageous thievery" from publishers.

5. "This, above all, remember: a lot of people fought for this new copyright law for us. If it doesn't help us we'll know who to blame."

Adams's position is clear: if a creative individual is not legally obligated to forfeit the whole of the copyright to the work that they produce, then they are conversely obligated not to uncritically forfeit that copyright. One of his main arguments is that the properties to which comic book creatives contribute were being licensed left and right, and the originators of those characters, plots, designs and ideas were receiving very little, if anything. More importantly, not only were they not receiving anything, but there was no clear possibility of them ever receiving anything from their own creation. They were forfeiting all of the normal rights of authorship with respect to the work they created and receiving disproportionate recompense (unfavorably so) for the surrender of these rights.

A key question in this discussion – especially as Adams frames it – is whether comic artists and writers are independent contractors or "work made for hire" employees. When thinking of an independent contractor, consider the artist doing sketches at a comic convention. When you approach the artist, they either have a set fee or you negotiate one in order for them to produce a work to your specifications. If that artist has their shit together, they're also going to be upfront with you in the early stages about two important things: they won't redo the art endlessly to your satisfaction (they might be nice enough to allow a few small edits), and you need to specify whether or not this is an exclusive work or one that the artist can use elsewhere.

Both of those things are incredibly important distinctions, especially with respect to work-made-for-hire product. The two defining characteristics of an independent contractor are that they maintain editorial control over what they produce (perhaps not completely, but to a very major extent) and they can buy and sell the rights to their work at their own discretion. I can charge you more for a sketch of your favorite animal if you'd like it to be exclusively for you than if you simply commissioned it and I later sold the image elsewhere.

I can't do that if I'm drawing the latest *X-Men* book. I can't sell my stories, character designs or even original characters elsewhere under any circumstance if I'm under a work-made-for-hire contract for Marvel. It's just never even a possibility. In addition, I do not maintain editorial control in a work-made-for-hire scenario. Like a full employee, I am not only forfeiting the copyright and authorship of my work to the business for which I perform the labor, but I also agree that the employer has final say over what I produce.

You might now wonder what the difference is between agreeing to do "work made for hire" and being a proper employee of a business. In the state of California, there is none. California Labor Code 3351.5c states that the legal definition of "Employee" includes "Any person while engaged by contract for the creation of a specially ordered or commissioned work of authorship in which the parties expressly agree [...] that the work shall be considered a work made for hire." This means that anyone signed on to a work-made-for-hire contract by a company in the state of California (which now includes Boom! Studios, DC, IDW, amongst others) ought to have their business – at the bare minimum – covering unemployment insurance and workers comp.

[I've reached out to DC, IDW and BOOM! and asked for them to confirm whether or not they pay into unemployment and disability on behalf of their work-made-for-hire contractors. As of publication date, none of them responded. If they are not, they are breaking state law.] The fact is, in the majority of the U.S., this policy is not the case. But there is a very good reason that it is the case in California: there is essentially no functional difference for a worker in terms of rights forfeited between being an employee and being a work-made-for-hire contractor.

Oh, I guess except for the whole "employees have benefits and are legally allowed to unionize and collectively bargain" thing.

Adams is right that the work-made-for-hire path is one of exploitation, and that there must be a better way. Work-made-for-hire employees forfeit all the rights of a full-time employee and get none of the benefits thereof unless otherwise specified, and even then, these added benefits are arbitrary, tenuous and pit colleagues against each other.

Where Adams and the Comics Guild failed was in putting their eggs in the "independent contractor" basket. As independent contractors, each and every comic creator would have to go to the comic publisher themselves with their demands. Solidarity would be completely federated, since independent contractors cannot have their contract collectively bargained by a single entity. Could they all ask for the same thing? Sure. But if The Man gets you alone in a room and me alone in a room to talk dollars and cents and each of our livelihoods is on the line, dividing and conquering is a lot easier. We're talking about dozens upon dozens of short-to-long-term contracts.

Rather than embracing their status as artists as Adams encouraged the Guild to do, the group ought to have embraced its status as labor similar to another group of creatives who have spent eight decades winning hard-fought battles and reaping the benefits of their work as employees under a collective bargaining agreement: The Writers' Guild.

* * *

"ON JUNE 11, 1937, The Screen Writers' Guild of the Authors' League of America, Inc., herein called the Guild, filed [...] 21 separate petitions alleging that questions affecting commerce had arisen concerning the representation of screen writers." So begins the Statement of the Case in the matter of Metro-Goldwyn-Mayer Studios and Motion Picture Producers Assn., et al. and Screen Writers' Guild, Inc., the landmark National Labor Relations Board (NLRB) ruling decided on June 4, 1938, which upheld that Hollywood screenwriters working for major studios were, in fact, employees, and would as such be represented by the Screen Writers' Guild (the forerunner to the present day Writers' Guild).

When the screenwriters that organized under the banner of the SWG came to the producers saying that the SWG would collectively bargain on their behalf — i.e., that a majority of working screenwriters wanted union representation — the Hollywood studios scoffed. "The Companies [MGM et al.] contend that the screenwriters are not employees," the ruling continues, saying in support of this that screenwriters are "creative" and receive "high salaries" and that unions are meant for "mechanical" employments and "lower income brackets"; screenwriters also "perform their services free from the control of the Companies and must be considered as independent contractors," adding in favor of this that "screenwriters are not required to observe regular office hours or to maintain office discipline" and that "they are free to develop screen material in accordance with their own ideas."

With respect to "being free to develop" material, the NLRB pointed out that "screenwriters work under the direction of a producer or an associate producer." Further, they "may be given the result of another writer's work in developing a story and be required to write a screenplay" in accordance with that prior work. The NLRB also noted that it was "customary to consult with the producer with respect to the different sequences." As was concluded, "it is clear that the writer's work is subject to the critical examination and close scrutiny of the producer and that the producer's word is usually final as to the contents and ultimate form of the script."

Working on a comic book with at least one editor, in addition to a series editor, at the discretion of the publisher, with direction as to where your story fits in the canon and what you are and are not allowed to do with that character sounds an awful lot like the above description. Of course, the lack

of freedom with respect to executing one's creative work is merely a necessary and not a sufficient condition for counting as an employee; however, it is almost certainly a box that gets ticked for the majority of comic artists and writers working for major publishers, and is as close to a singularly sufficient condition for status as employee as any other.

And the boxes don't stop checking themselves there. Consider also the comment about having to "maintain office discipline." Since office hours are also mentioned, one ought to assume that what is meant here is decorum, in some sense. The Hollywood studios were essentially claiming that the writers were free to gallivant. We can thus assume that the opposite situation – censuring an employee for their behavior – would be holding them to a public standard of decorum such that the employer has a necessary degree of control to deem this person an employee.

On September 11, 2017, Aubrey Sitterson made a prickly tweet about the way in which some people in America choose to memorialize the anniversary of the September 11 attacks. In late November, IDW's *Scarlett's Strike Force* G.I. Joe comic, for which Sitterson was the writer, was canceled before both its final order cutoff and the completion of its final issue. While IDW claimed this was due to low sales, Sitterson mentioned in a late November interview that that he had been actively banned from doing any interviews during the intervening period.

If Sitterson's claims that he was prevented from conducting interviews about his work by IDW are true (IDW has not disputed this part of the story), then this is a prime example of the kind of control even Hollywood studios didn't often exercise over their writers. In other words, the office decorum point was not even one that Hollywood writers fought, and yet even they were considered employees. If anything, this kind of activity is indicative of the fact that comics publishers sometimes outstrip the kind of control that other employers exercise in ways that are essential to being employers.

BELOW: Cover of *Scarlett's Strike Force* #1, Dec. 2017. Written by Aubrey Sitterson; penciled and inked by Nelson Daniel and Harvey Tolibao; colored by Ryan Hill.

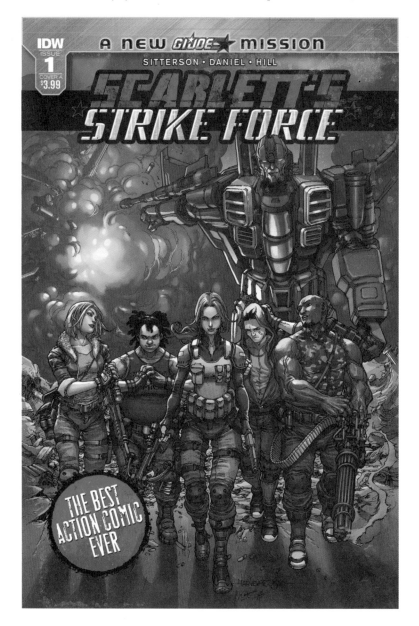

While we're on the topic of IDW, it is worth mentioning that at least one revision of their work-made-for-hire agreement that the *Journal* obtained contains the following clause: "The parties expressly intend and agree that I am an independent contractor and not an employee of IDW." It then goes on to say that the contract is bound by the laws of the state of California, in which IDW is headquartered. If this is true, then according to the labor laws of California which clearly state that contractors signed to work-made-for-hire agreements *are* employees, IDW's work-made-for-hire agreement has at least one illegal clause and is in direct and unambiguous conflict with California law. One must wonder whether IDW has been leaning on this clause to avoid paying unemployment insurance for its employees.

Further, IDW contractors agree that their work must be "satisfactory to IDW," or else IDW retains the right to terminate the relevant agreement. Though IDW's enforcement of decorum is itself of interest and adds to an increasingly sufficient pile of conditions for legal employee status, this type of editorial control is an exact analog of that which the NLRB found relevant in the case of affirming the employee status of screenwriters. It is also very typical of other comic publishers' contracts.

To confirm my take on the control exercised by the employer being a (if not the) key factor in assessing whether or not a worker is an employee (as opposed to merely an independent contractor), I reached out to Professor Catherine Fisk, Barbara Nachtrieb Armstrong Professor of Law at UC Berkeley. "It doesn't matter whether someone works on a series of short-term contracts or is labeled a freelance writer," writes Professor Fisk. "What matters is the degree of control exercised by the putative employer."

Professor Fisk is unfamiliar with the employment terms of comics, but is a studied writer on the history of work made for hire and the Writers' Guild. Her insights on the topic extend directly into comics

and into their more extreme cousin, the gig economy at large. Her 2018 paper "Hollywood Writers and the Gig Economy" for the University of Chicago Legal Forum begins, "The notion that large numbers of workers are independent contractors not entitled to unionize or to the protections of employment law is a product of twentieth-century legal categories that are a poor fit for twenty-first-century companies and labor markets." Despite this fact, she argues that rather than amending our labor laws to cover independent contractors – a large legal step that some might think to be necessary in the case of comic creatives – we can and should look to the Writers' Guild for guidance. As Professor Fisk remarks in response to interviewing dozens of writers and showrunners involved in the Writers' Guild, "collective bargaining by independent workers today is an important and effective way of accommodating employer flexibility with employee protection."

If it is in the best interest of comic book publishers to employ creatives on a work-made-for-hire basis, then they lose nothing in terms of authorship by acknowledging that the creatives they hire are employees, since all employee work is, *de facto*, work made for hire. DC Comics has, in the past, hired creatives working on major titles as employees. And, as mentioned earlier, in the state of California, landing anywhere on the spectrum of "work made for hire" makes you an employee.

That comic book creatives signing any length of work-made-for-hire contract for publishers are employees is not only not beyond the pale; it is a matter of precedent waiting to be acknowledged by the employees who could seize it any day now to form a union.

***

THE PATH THAT Neal Adams wanted to take in 1978 is still open. Comic creators can refuse to sign work-made-for-hire contracts and instead exclusively sign contracts that painstakingly enumerate the rights being forfeited by the contractor at the time of signing. If the price isn't suitable for those rights, then everybody should refuse to sign.

But beyond a very disciplined and distributed solidarity, the comic creator will have no legal recourse. The closest thing to this kind of arrangement is The Dramatists' Guild. Though similar in name to the Writers' Guild, the Dramatists' Guild is not a labor union; it is just an affiliation of playwrights who share resources and have a *de facto* agreement as to what constitutes acceptable labor standards. One important issue for playwrights, for instance, is that they want to be able to have ownership over their script if it gets made into a movie. Dramatists only license their scripts to producers and retain that level of creative and financial autonomy, something Adams would dream of. The issue, though, is that it stops there: as a dream. Marvel and DC would never, ever, in a million years, merely license an *X-Men* story and all the intellectual property therein.

It will never happen.

And why the fuck would it happen? Marvel owns the X-Men! Whether or not you think that's right, that's where they are as a business: they are the corporate authors of the X-Men. Marvel has no reason to cede that point and fundamentally change the relationship between their property and the people who generate more of it, especially in a way that warps Marvel's business model and makes future IP questions even more of a nightmare than they already are. That comic creators writing scripts and drawing pages for established intellectual property at major publishers are hired "work made for hire" on the basis that they are "contributing to a collective work" is the exact spirit and intent of the "work made for hire" clause, at least in terms of how it was meant to protect corporations as authors.

While creators should not be happy in principle with forfeiting the rights to their work in abstract, and while corporations-as-authors is itself a legal fiction worth poking at, it is not the foundational issue with which comic writers and artists should be concerned. Rather, comics creators should first and foremost be concerned with the fact that many find themselves in a limbo in which almost no other creative or creative-adjacent employee finds themselves.

Your editor gets paid. She probably has benefits. She is an employee.

Your friend does regular illustration work. The pay is not great, his taxes suck, he's fucked for health insurance, but it's at least a possibility that he could make something that he wholly owns and could take to the bank in the right circumstance. He's an independent contractor.

You draw dozens of pages for a major comic publisher per year. You don't get health care or normal employment taxes, nor do you get creative autonomy. The quickest route to improving the material conditions of a work-made-for-hire contract is to quit squabbling over rights and embrace their forfeiture (to a degree) by fighting for benefits as a union employee.

* * *

COLLECTIVE BARGAINING MEANS you have a representative going into the room for all of you, rather than all of you individually trying to figure out what works for each of you while you're implicitly pitted against each other in silence. Collective bargaining means someone who knows what they're doing (a lawyer, not you and 18 Google tabs) can help hash out meaningful improvements to your contracts. A concrete example is something that Howard Chaykin suggested offhand at the first Guild meeting in 1978, and something that the Writers' Guild does in a specific form: a committee of peers meant to allocate credit. In the Writers' Guild, for instance, there can be disputes over who receives credit for a screenplay in a film. If this happens, three writers from the guild get together and hash it out, and their decision is binding. The alternative is that the studio gets to decide, and if the studio decides credit, then the thought is (correctly) that the studio then essentially has real power over the authorship of the film: power they aren't supposed to have.

The advantage of being employees is that, though ceding authorship in some ways, collective bargaining restores the possibility of retaining authorship in ways that are important for a comic creator's career and livelihood. At the moment, authorship is more or less forfeited completely, except where publishers have made some form of concession here or there. But these gains are fleeting, vary from creator to creator and are sometimes – similar to the old Hollywood method – at the discretion of the employer.

For instance, in *Mad* magazine's work-made-for-hire agreement (which is owned and published by DC Comics), creators receive a flat cut of money (50 percent) for the sale of any media rights to material involving the undisputed creation of an original character. But how the funds should be divided up if the publisher uses this character with other original material, or how much the creator is due if the publisher explicitly creates any kind of spin-off character, or, the determination as to whether the character actually even counts as "original" is wholly at the discretion of the publisher itself!

It's true that at least one other publisher, BOOM! Studios, doesn't offer any cut for any reuse of any character at all. According to a contract obtained by the *Journal*, "Talent *irrevocably* assigns to the corporation all rights *of every kind and nature* in the Work, including *without limitation* copyright and trademark rights and *all other rights to exploit the Work in all media now or hereafter existing throughout the world in perpetuity*" [emphasis mine]. In the gulf between fuzzy flat cuts and the absolutely dire language of BOOM!'s contract, media rights vary wildly. When each individual publisher is the arbiter of what counts as fair, the concept of fairness itself is so nebulous that there isn't actually, in practice, any such thing.

ABOVE: Howard Chaykin, 1982.

This is exactly the kind of rights question that can and should be answered by an organized comics labor force. Not only is there precedent, but the current state of comics and its cultural capital is begging for this kind of intervention on the part of those people generating the intellectual-property-driven billion-dollar franchises. When the Guild met in 1978, it was at least a question as to how Marvel was doing. Even if we grant Jim Shooter's dubious claim that Marvel wasn't doing as well as everyone seemed to think, the fact of the matter is that there's no question how Marvel is doing now. The only question is where its priorities lie, and it's not much of a question with respect to Marvel's talent if they aren't getting any meaningful proportion of the riches being generated at the top.

* * *

IT SEEMS COMPLETELY REASONABLE to argue that anybody working on a comic book whose plot or character designs are explicitly borrowed for use in a film deserves some type of real remuneration. Anybody designing a character whose likeness is licensed across the country for comic book conventions deserves remuneration.

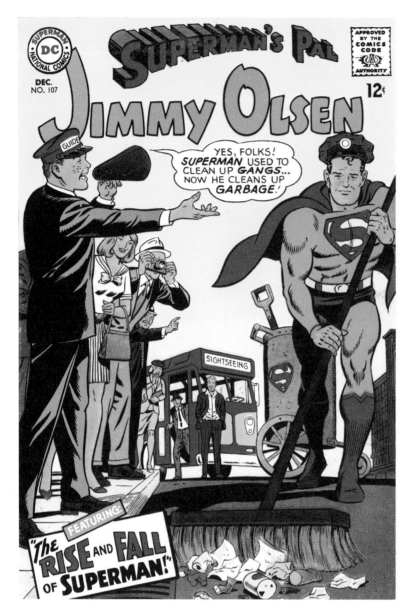

ABOVE: Cover of *Superman's Pal, Jimmy Olsen* #107, Dec. 1967. Penciled by Curt Swan and inked by George Klein.

around everywhere, and it is extremely obvious that they do not funnel back down in any meaningful proportion to the point at which the intellectual property was generated. Allowing comic creators a degree of democratic self-determination over how best to compensate them for their collateral impact on "nerd culture" is a small price for parent companies making billions of dollars to pay.

At Marvel and DC at the very least it would be disingenuous to suggest that unionization would hurt the workplace and its bottom line. If anything, it is clearly in the best interest of any major IP farm to retain its creators as employees to ensure the maximum amount of control over their output and contributions to their collective works. On the flip side, it also doesn't make much sense to seek independent-contractor status in order to work on a property you can never realistically monetize yourself.

✳✳✳

SINCE THE RELEASE of *Man of Steel* in 2013, box office movies licensing DC comics material have grossed over $3.75 billion worldwide. Marvel-licensed movies starting with *Iron Man* in 2008 have grossed $17.45 billion. The budgets alone for both sets of films averages $120 million, while the revenue from each averages between $750–850 million dollars, meaning net revenue is at least $600 million, more or less, for a movie released in the "cinematic universe" of either of the Big Two comic book publishers.

The financial numbers that were obfuscated and bickered over in the late 1970s are a far cry from the financial status of things now. Comics is no longer a niche newsstand phenomenon. They are now part of a cycle of unprecedented cultural capital. Tell a comic fan or a movie producer twenty years ago that you found a way to bank half a billion without breaking a sweat and they'd laugh in your face. Publicly being a fan of something is almost as bankable in terms of social capital, a

While this currently seems like money that major publishers would never be willing to pay, the disparity of resources in comics culture is one that speaks for itself, and the economically weak position of comic artists and writers is a strong one from a bargaining standpoint.

Comic creators have been doing labor for decades that has now generated several industries, at least one of which is entirely dedicated to merely talking about the work that they do (I'm making money writing this right now). Resources are flying triumph of geekdom that both feeds and is fed by its corporate counterparts happy to clean up on licensing. It's staggering to think the box office is just the beginning of the profits for these corporations and the adjacent performative nerd industry.

So why isn't every creator signing a contract for DC or Marvel compensated competitively for the very real, very valuable cultural capital that rests almost entirely on the IP that the creator's work has generated? Why don't all of these people have health benefits for the duration of the time that they are helping pour more ideas into the pot and invent characters and settings and plots? Why don't creators have any say or role in the concrete value of their abstract IP when their plot inevitably gets mined for the next billion-dollar hit?

Why was William Mesner-Loebs homeless? Why did Jerry Siegel and Joe Shuster have to settle for being bought off for a pittance of a stipend? Why will Shuster's heirs have to settle for DC covering his relatively small outstanding debts at the cost of never contesting ownership over their most iconic character? Why does Bill Mantlo, co-creator of Rocket Raccoon, have to rely on private charity to afford his hospital bills while Bradley Cooper likely gets tens of millions of dollars just to do some line readings for the very same character?

The answer is not nuanced. It is two-fold, and the first part is easy: corporate greed. Jim Shooter was not a champion of creators' rights. He was a bureaucrat, like every editor in chief that followed him and will continue to follow him. But the second part is what we've been talking about all along: creators have failed – not "not tried," not "avoided" – failed, outright, wholly and completely, to put their collective feet down and ask for a fair slice of an unprecedentedly massive pie. The money is there. The legal precedents are there. The evidence of failure, the tragedy of men like Mesner-Loebs and others – it's all there.

The only things that are missing are the creators themselves. Unionization is the best legal path to just compensation, but

ABOVE: The first appearance of Rocket Raccoon from *Marvel Preview #7*, Jan. 1976. Written by Bill Mantlo, penciled and inked by Keith Giffen, lettered by Karen Mantly.

anything short of demanding a major renegotiation of acceptable standards – however temporary – is a continued failure on the part of every creator who signs a work-made-for-hire contract from a comic publisher. Bill Mantlo said it best in issue #42 of *The Comics Journal*, 40 years ago.

"A Guild isn't strong enough. We need a union." ☀

I PUT IN SO MUCH WORK

BY LAURA LANNES

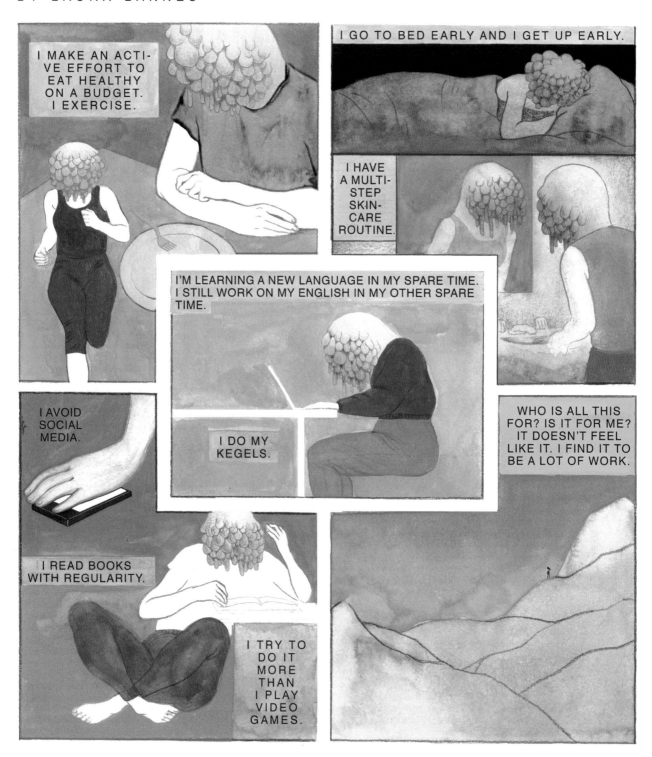

IT DOESN'T MATTER. IT STILL COMES, ALWAYS.

EVEN IF I CAN MOST OFTEN KEEP IT AT BAY -

IT COMES, AND I FEEL LIKE TRASH.

IT COMES, AND I BINGE EAT OR FAST. I SLEEP TOO MUCH OR TOO LITTLE. MAKING FOOD BECOMES SO MUCH EFFORT. SHOWERING. CLEANING ANYTHING. I CAN'T MOVE. I DON'T WANT TO SEE ANYONE, I DON'T WANT TO BE SEEN. I'M REPULSED BY MYSELF, REPULSED BY HOW FAR DOWN I'VE COME. TAKING CARE OF MYSELF IS TOO HARD, TOO MUCH WORK. I "SHOULD" BE DOING IT. BUT IT DOESN'T FEEL LIKE THERE'S A PAYOFF. THE SELF-CARE DOESN'T TAKE. SO I DON'T WANT TO PUT IN THE WORK.

DURING THESE PERIODS, I FEEL LIKE TAKING A BREAK FROM MY WORK. BUT I CAN'T.

I HAVE TO KEEP GOING, EVEN WHEN I DON'T WANT TO. I HAVE COME TO HATE MY WORK. I'M EXHAUSTED BY IT. I DON'T WANT TO LOOK AT ANY DRAWING. I JUST WANT TO BE ABLE TO STOP.

I STARTED DRAWING BECAUSE I LIKED IT. I PURSUED IT AS A CAREER BECAUSE I WASN'T INTERESTED IN ANYTHING ELSE. THIS WAS THE ONLY THING I ENJOYED DOING. THAT'S BEEN DESTROYED SOMEWHERE ALONG THE WAY. I TURNED MY ONLY PASSION INTO A MONEYMAKING SKILL AND TIED IT ETERNALLY TO MY LIVELIHOOD.

ME

MY FEARS OF FAILURE AS AN ARTIST

BECAME ENMESHED WITH

MY FEARS OF FAILURE TO MAKE A LIVING

NOW

I HATE DRAWING

BECAUSE

IT'S TOO STRESSFUL

IT'S NOT FUN ANYMORE.

BUT, IF I DON'T DO IT,

I CAN'T PAY RENT,

SO I DO IT.

I WILL NOW QUOTE MARX (AND WIKIPEDIA). MARX WROTE THAT, "ALIENATION FROM THE SELF IS A CONSEQUENCE OF BEING A MECHANISTIC PART" OF SOCIETY. THE WORKER SUFFERS FOUR KINDS OF ALIENATION:

1. THE WORKER IS ALIENATED FROM THEIR HUMANITY BECAUSE THEY "CAN ONLY EXPRESS LABOR - A FUNDAMENTAL SOCIAL ASPECT OF PERSONAL INDIVIDUALITY - THROUGH A PRIVATE SYSTEM OF INDUSTRIAL PRODUCTION IN WHICH EACH WORKER IS AN INSTRUMENT, A THING, NOT A PERSON."

2. THE WORKER IS ALIENATED FROM THE PRODUCT BECAUSE EVERYTHING ABOUT ITS MAKING AND DESIGN IS DETERMINED BY THE BOSS CLASS, IN SEARCH OF MAXIMUM PROFIT - WHICH IN TURN GOES ONLY TO THE BOSS, NOT TO THE WORKER.

I DON'T KNOW WHAT I WANT ANYMORE. I DON'T KNOW WHAT I LIKE. I CAN'T MAKE ANY PROGRESS WITH MY WORK BECAUSE I DON'T KNOW WHAT WAY IS PROGRESS.

WHICH WAY
IS ME?

WHAT DO
I WANT?

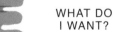

WHAT DO
I LIKE?

3. THE WORKER IS ALIENATED FROM THE ACT OF PRODUCTION BECAUSE THEY ARE ONLY RESPONSIBLE FOR ONE PIECE OF IT. THE LABOR POWER IS COMMODIFIED AND CATEGORIZED. NO SENSE OF ACCOMPLISHMENT; NOTHING TO ADMIRE AT THE END. THE WORK IS NEVER DONE. IT IS PERFORMED FOR WAGES, NOT FOR SELF-SATISFACTION OR USEFULNESS. THE WAGES THEMSELVES ARE AS LOW AS POSSIBLE, MEANT ONLY TO ALLOW SURVIVAL - SOMETIMES BARELY.

I'VE DEDICATED SO MUCH OF MY TIME AND ENERGY TO DRAWING, AND THIS MESS IS ALL I HAVE, AFTER ALL THAT.

WHO ARE THESE PEOPLE WHO DID THESE DRAWINGS? NONE OF THEM ARE ME.

SEVERAL DIFFERENT CLIENTS, SEVERAL DIFFERENT STYLES AND APPROACHES. I FEEL NO CONNECTION TO THIS WORK.

I FEEL LIKE I HAVE NOTHING TO SHOW FOR ALL MY EFFORT - NOTHING THAT IS "ME."

4. THE WORKER IS ALIENATED FROM OTHER WORKERS. THIS IS BECAUSE OF WAGE COMPULSION. THE WORKER IS BOUND TO UNWANTED LABOR AS A MEANS OF SURVIVAL. LABOR IS "NOT VOLUNTARY, BUT COERCED." THE WORKER IS UNABLE TO REJECT WAGE COMPULSION AT THE EXPENSE OF THEIR LIFE AND THAT OF THEIR FAMILY. WORKERS ARE PITTED AGAINST EACH OTHER IN A COMPETITION FOR JOBS AND HIGHER WAGES.

MY VISA TO LIVE IN THE U.S. ONLY ALLOWS ME TO WORK IN JOBS IN MY FIELD (ARTS). I AM DOING MY BEST TO MAKE MONEY WHILE THE ENTIRE FIELD UNDERGOES MASSIVE DEVALUATION OF LABOR, WITH NO UNIONS OR FULL-TIME EMPLOYMENT.

ME →

I USED TO MAKE ART FOR FUN AND SELF-EXPRESSION, BUT NOW I AM A

DEPLETED ART WORKER

CREATIVE WORK MEANS THEY WANT TO TAKE A LITTLE BIT OF ME IN THE PROCESS.

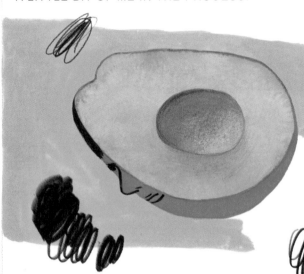

WHATEVER UNIQUENESS THERE IS ABOUT ME,

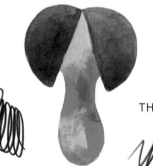

WHATEVER I HAVE THAT COMES THROUGH AND IS SOLELY MINE,

THAT IS WHAT THEY WANT.

MY UNIQUENESS IS ASSIMILATED BY THE BRAND. IT BECOMES THEIRS, NO LONGER MINE.

I GIVE A BODY AND PERSONALITY TO INCORPOREAL THINGS, SO THAT YOU WILL BUY THEM. THAT'S WHAT I DO, AS AN ART WORKER. I HELP MAKE "HIP" OR "FEMINIST" OR "MILLENNIAL" A REGULAR CORPORATION SEEKING TO FOOL YOU INTO GIVING THEM MONEY.

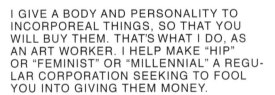

HAVING MADE MY ART SUCH A HUGE PART OF MY IDENTITY, I BROUGHT MY WHOLE SELF TO WORK, AND AS A RESULT I NOW FEEL THAT I HAVE LOST MY WHOLE SELF.

THEY MAY CALL IT A CREATIVE JOB, BUT I HAVE THE SAME FUNCTION AS EVERYONE ELSE IN THE COMPANY: MAKE IT AS PROFITABLE AS POSSIBLE. WORK IS NOT CREATIVE, OR INNOVATIVE OR AT ALL NEW, IF IT SERVES THE ETERNAL PURPOSE OF MAINTAINING THE STATUS QUO. IT IS THE OPPOSITE OF CREATIVE: IT IS REGULATORY.

CAPITALISM IS ELASTIC AND ENGULFS ALL NEW MANNERS OF SELF-EXPRESSION, ALL NEW CULTURE, ALL NEW ART, AND MAKES IT TURN A PROFIT.

I AM A PERSON DOING A JOB, SAME AS THE MANAGER OR THE ACCOUNTANT, ONLY THEIR JOB IS TO PAY ME AS LITTLE AS THEY CAN GET AWAY WITH.

I'M ALIENATED FROM MY WORK. ITS PRODUCT, ITS MEANS OF PRODUCTION — I CAN'T AFFORD ADOBE PRODUCTS, AND MY PIRATED COPIES CRASH EVERY FEW MONTHS.

BECAUSE I AM A FREELANCER, I DON'T HAVE A CLEAR DIVISION OF WORK AND HOME. I AM ALWAYS AT HOME AND I AM ALWAYS AT WORK.

BOSS MAKES A DOLLAR, I MAKE A DIME, EVERY SINGLE TIME I POOP IS ON COMPANY TIME.

I WORK FROM MY BEDROOM. I AM QUITE LITERALLY ALIENATED FROM OTHER PEOPLE.

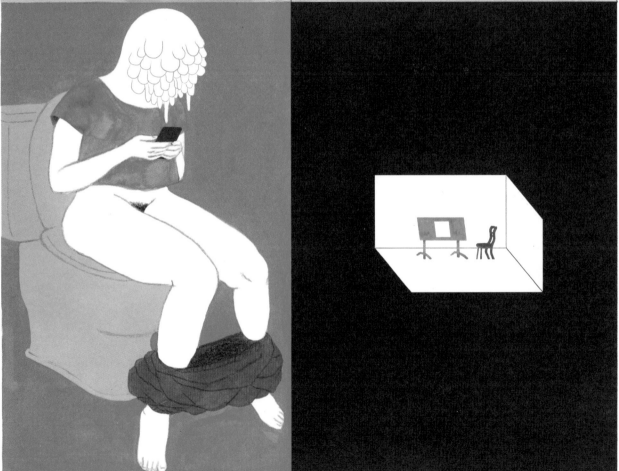

CAPITALISM PUSHED ME INTO WORKAHOLISM, AND I TWISTED IT INTO A PERSONALITY TRAIT. HAVE I FOOLED MYSELF INTO BELIEVING THIS IS JUST HOW I AM, INDEPENDENTLY OF ANY OPPRESSIVE EXTERIOR CONDITIONS? I AM ALWAYS BURIED IN WORK AND TOO EXHAUSTED AND DEPRESSED TO LEAVE THE HOUSE (OFFICE). *IN WHOSE INTEREST IS IT THAT I LIVE THIS WAY?*

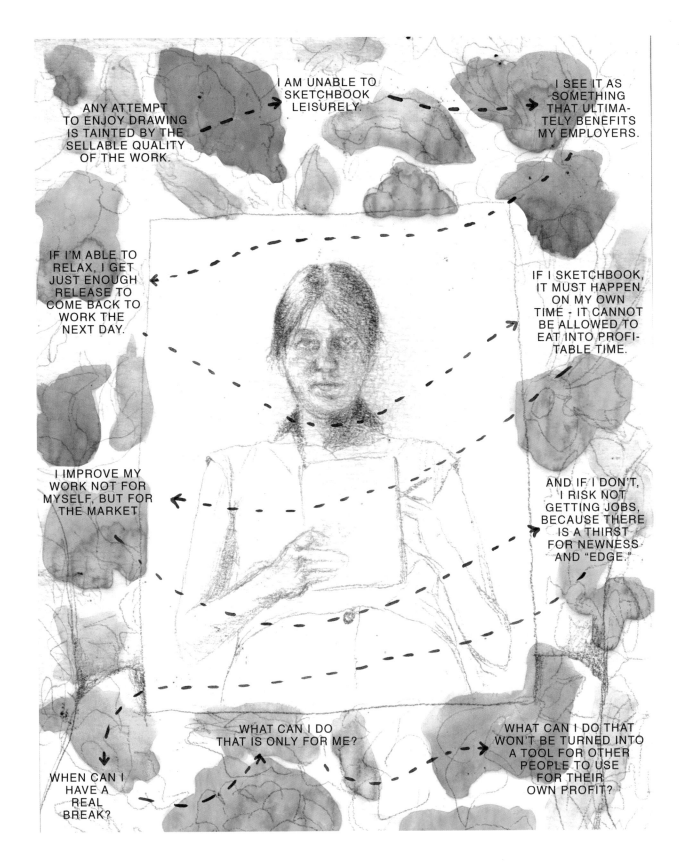

ANY ATTEMPT TO ENJOY DRAWING IS TAINTED BY THE SELLABLE QUALITY OF THE WORK.

I AM UNABLE TO SKETCHBOOK LEISURELY.

I SEE IT AS SOMETHING THAT ULTIMATELY BENEFITS MY EMPLOYERS.

IF I'M ABLE TO RELAX, I GET JUST ENOUGH RELEASE TO COME BACK TO WORK THE NEXT DAY.

IF I SKETCHBOOK, IT MUST HAPPEN ON MY OWN TIME - IT CANNOT BE ALLOWED TO EAT INTO PROFITABLE TIME.

I IMPROVE MY WORK NOT FOR MYSELF, BUT FOR THE MARKET

AND IF I DON'T, I RISK NOT GETTING JOBS, BECAUSE THERE IS A THIRST FOR NEWNESS AND "EDGE."

WHAT CAN I DO THAT IS ONLY FOR ME?

WHAT CAN I DO THAT WON'T BE TURNED INTO A TOOL FOR OTHER PEOPLE TO USE FOR THEIR OWN PROFIT?

WHEN CAN I HAVE A REAL BREAK?

I THINK CRAFTS AND HANDMADE STUFF ARE "IN" WITH MILLENNIALS LIKE ME

BECAUSE EACH PIECE IS UNIQUE, AND CAN BE CREATED WITH A PROCESS THAT IS ENTIRELY UNDER OUR CONTROL.

WE ARE ALIENATED FROM OUR LABOR, SO WE START DOING CERAMICS

OR MAKING OUR OWN BREAD, WHICH GIVES US A SENSE OF ACCOMPLISHMENT.

WE CREATE A PHYSICAL ITEM WITH OUR HANDS, AND SHARE IT WITH OUR COMMUNITY.

BUT WE ARE SO POISONED, WE TRY TO MONETI-ZE OUR SHITTY MUGS AND HOMEMADE BREAD.

FEMINIST MUG
$30

THE ANSWER DOES NOT LIE WITHIN THE UGLY MUG. THE ANSWER IS MUTUAL SUPPORT. CAPI-TALISM TAUGHT US TO SELF-OPTIMIZE RATHER THAN LOOK AROUND AND NOTICE THE SYSTEM DESTROYING US.

DON'T TALK TO ME UNTIL I'VE HAD MY MUTUAL SUPPORT

THE TRUTH IS IN COMMUNITY BUILDING AND COLLECTIVE PROSPERITY. IT'S IN INVESTING IN WHAT'S OVERLOOKED BECAUSE IT'S UNPROFI-TABLE.

CAPITALISM MADE ME DEPRESSED, AND I MONE-TIZED MY DEPRESSION FOR THIS COMIC.

IT FEEDS INTO THE CYCLE, OF COURSE. IT MAKES ME UNHAPPY. BUT I HAVE TO STAY IN COMICS -

THE MONEY IS JUST SO GOOD.

Adam Griffiths

RJ Casey

RIGHT: Adam Griffiths, 2019.
Photo by Alexandra Silverthorne.

ADAM GRIFFITHS CREATES deeply knotty comics. To read them is to unwind a bundle of block letters, bumpy, billowy artwork and sweeping invectives on society's ills. Through *Washington White*, an in-progress opus inspired by his grandmother's civil-rights lawsuit, a small collection of mini and webcomics, as well his gallery exhibitions, Griffiths has fearlessly tackled the Big Stuff — sex, politics, gender, race — through circuitous and speculative science fiction. Needless to say, Griffiths's work is complicated and dense and us comics readers are better off for it.

RJ CASEY: You've written that you like to play with "mutabilities" when creating comics. What does that mean?

ADAM GRIFFITHS: The internet has altered our connection to information; this has been a drastic change over a very short period of time. For illustrators, a shared canon of symbolism is what turns narrative drawing into a communication medium. Part of the argument in lots of my work is about the breakdown of institutional symbolism as a result of technology, the rise of the knowledge economy and its limits. Symbols now all have a hobo's stick and bag that will only steadily get heavier. The scale of magnitude for drawing is the weight of the symbolism. Through manual work, I can unleash a ton of a symbol's original contents or throw them to the wind, cherry pick and mix or add more to them, so long as it's comics.

That term "mutabilities" seems to apply to your drawings and layouts too.

Yeah, I like the specific and peculiar — everything that skin can't show.

That explains your unconventional character design. What do you use to create your spindly line?

I work in either pencil or ballpoint pen.

LEFT: From *The Permanent Night*, 2017.

All of your comics have a large cast of characters and a lot of moving parts. Have you always been interested in this type of ambitious storytelling? Do you like working within a narrative puzzle?

"Puzzle" is correct. The symbolism is in a constant play of mattering and not mattering. I believe readers are sophisticated, so I deliberately engineer references and manipulate the suspension of disbelief constantly. When a reader can begin to play these kinds of games with a story, they're given a sort of freedom. Imbibing the reader with the tools for critical thinking is one of my aims. For instance, in my comic *The Permanent Night*, a character from one storyline is guided out of his story and completely inappropriately plopped into another story – where he nevertheless interacts with the storyline. Characters come as an ensemble for me. With lots of them, more interesting things can happen that still illuminate each character deeply.

Your lettering immediately stands out when reading your comics. Usually a cartoonist will use exaggerated lettering

ABOVE: From *The Hanging at Linestone Road,* 2018.

for sounds effects and stuff like that, but you do it for *every* word. When did that practice start?

The hand-lettering was immediate. I wanted to do something different. Hand-writing can pull a reader into your mindset and the mood of the story – in the same way that a doctor with terrible handwriting forces you to understand the tightly looped, barely legible cursive that she's scrawled on a prescription slip. The stories I write are brutal and confrontational, so that goofy lettering provides a tension and lightness.

Do you worry that it makes your comics harder to digest?

No. I always like to play with typography and sometimes the clarity disappears when I'm switching between writing and drawing. Words get crazy unintelligible between two people or in a crowd, purposefully.

You've taken classes at The Center for Cartoon Studies (CCS), the Sequential Artists Workshop (SAW) and with the Comics Workbook. What's prompted you to continue your education so aggressively?

There's always something new to learn. I can do a lot of research and training by myself, but there's good in the guidance received from other people who practice and study comics.

Is there a big difference in the teaching methods between all those schools?

Each school has something unique to offer. With the Comics Workbook, I did the Rowhouse Residency where Frank Santoro works closely with you one-on-one, giving you lots of input with the expectation of self-direction. At SAW, it's a classroom environment with lots of lectures and demonstrations. At CCS, the courses tend to be project-focused and the lectures are more scholarly. The instructors there help you get a handle on your project. With all these places, I've observed the hardest part is getting students to forget about their drawing skills and embrace the language.

You've also taught comics classes, right?

Yes, and lectured to some college students, here in D.C. at American University and also at two art schools in Rome: the Accademia di Belle Arti di Roma and Rome University of Fine Arts. Also in my past life as an arts administrator, there were so many studio visits with both professional and student artists. I was giving feedback to creative people about their work.

What have you taken away from teaching and providing that sort of feedback? Has it impacted your art-making at all?

You have to give everything away to be a good teacher. When you're assessing someone's art to their face, telling them what you think about how they've executed something – whether they're a child or adult – you learn very quickly that cruelty is useless. So, learning to be constructive when dealing with people who are trying to understand their own art has definitely attached a few morals to the making of my own work.

I didn't draw much in art school. I did Community Arts with ongoing art classes in Baltimore City after-school programs in public elementary schools. The idea was to pair art school students with non-artist students in order to recognize their shared community. The art created was the relationship between the artists and their collaborators, making things like video art, neighborhood murals and puppets.

When I'm in my studio alone working now, I'll occasionally think that I'm not practicing the kind of "useful art" that could make a finite impact on others. But then I think, "I'm just one person." I can't carry comics plus the baggage of "relational aesthetics" too. What I took away from my experience in education is that big-picture thinking can teeter on a line. On one side, it can empower you to be experimental and freewheeling, or it can be nearly debilitating to self-expression. But then again, I've never been a salaried teacher in a segregated school system explaining to students every day that they're going to get less of everything.

Is your next project the continuation of your *Washington White* series? I read that you're planning on that being a total of 600 pages or something like that.

Washington White will have three chapters. Part one was self-published and released as a tabloid newspaper in November 2017. This seemed appropriate as the central subject matter of the story is a black-owned newspaper and the machinations of the people who control its headlines. It is indeed going to be 600 pages. I'm very excited about it. I'm editing, redesigning pages and coloring it right now.

I have a hard time fathoming working on something that is 600 pages. Are you worried about biting off more than you can chew or straight-up burnout?

Been there, done that! Before devoting myself to comics, I worked three jobs over the course of a decade. The final one, as an arts administrator, was that high-pressure environment that some people crave to work in. My lovely husband had been encouraging me to quit each of those jobs – I was certainly worried then about not being able to make my own way. Consequentially, I got very passionate about the local arts scene in D.C. All of this time, I was making art, but I didn't think I should do art full-time, no matter how much art I was making, no matter how much I saved, no matter that my husband was definitely egging me on to forget about the "suitable work-life" and be an artist.

What got me to finally move on was a brusque gesture that resulted in a burn-out on fine art institutions. In late 2010, I stood outside the National Portrait Gallery in handcuffs to protest the censorship of David Wojnarowicz's *Fire in My Belly* video artwork. That incident of censorship went on to become a little infamous. I didn't show up at any of the subsequent protests – I felt like collateral damage in a scenario that actually had too much to do with politics and very little to do with making art – but something had broken. Because of the incident, I was able to observe the dissonance I was living between making art versus working for artists. All the non-profit work of trying to get artists things like healthcare, studio space, exhibitions and employment opportunities became this murky reflection of the fact that I myself was not being an artist. I realized I had never really made a decision about how I could best serve others through the arts. I quit my job shortly after that and it was like, "Finally!" So, having had such a complete experience of burning out on something, I now know the difference between healthy engagement versus flying too close to the sun. I'm comics-hungry forever.

Circling back to politics, *Washington White* deals with conspiracies, constitutional scandals and national intrigue. Are those difficult subjects to tackle during this very particular time we're living in?

Those who would own the world have been with us since the beginning. There's always something juicy to write about them, and a writer can introduce the timeless concepts of those swift and wealthy within the space of a book – that sort of convenience can be very specific, and as cutting as the writer would prefer it to be. But within art, there's the danger in the power of diverging interpretations, which to me mirrors the new reality of mass media. I remember when our president was running, and there was just this giant glut of editorial cartooning. As I'd scroll through my feed seeing caricature after caricature, I was thinking to myself, "This is not a person whose inner reserves are toppled by grotesque representation." Weaponized cartooning felt perhaps in his favor. Conspiracy is a storytelling medium for people who feel they need access to reality from within their own twisted fantasies about how the world works. With fiction, I try to point out the sources of oppression as specifically as possible, couched within characters. Readers get more out of stories that are small and tight. With *Washington White*, one of the challenges is to be really thorough about despicable characters' motivations. I'm grateful to not write nonfiction. That gets the nutsos showing up at your door in the middle of the night.

Is it correct that *Washington White* is loosely based on your family history?

Yes! My grandmother, Peggy Sue Griffiths, sued the U.S. Civil Service Commission in 1974 for not receiving a promotion on the basis of her race and gender. She was passed over for the position twice, which was allegedly a violation of the merit promotion plan that the CSC prescribed for the entire government. So, the government body that had been designated to police discrimination amongst its workers was now being accused of discrimination themselves. The Title VII case was filed under the Civil Rights Act of 1964. The ludicrous concept of race and gender superiority existing in any advanced civilization is demonstrated within this redundancy. The villains in *Washington White* are the all-male, all-white chairmen of the commission who are trying to block her from getting the job.

Originally, I had hoped to do a straight-forward account of the case that was going to be very dignified and solemn. After searching for documents related to the lawsuit and coming up with nothing, I decided to fictionalize the story, and with that came all the speculative sci-fi and mes-merism elements. They seemed necessary to capture the mood of someone who had worked hard for most of their life, only to find another closed door when trying to further advance their profession.

Speaking of doors, your social-media accounts are filled with photographs of them. Where does your interest in door-ways come from?

Sometimes I get up and leave my studio to take a walk. Then suddenly I'm somewhere random in D.C., snapping source photos for *Washington White* and also a lot of doors. So many that I stopped counting!

What's the appeal?

Doors are practice for storytelling. Doors from all backgrounds and origins. Precious doors, dilapidated doors, who-knows doors.

What does the future of comics look like for you?

I already know what stories I want to get to next. When I think about the future of comics, I think about my brother's comic collection — all late '80s and '90s stuff — which sits in a trunk underneath my porch. I look at the stuff that's being made today, and the foundations are still there. We both still read comics because the medium hasn't changed: composition, story, art. There's enough to explore in that to keep life messy. An artist gleans something from putting out a comic. It gets etched in you. For me, that best represents the value that other people put into comics. Someone made a leap to bring a fully

realized story about — that person willfully changed — converted not by another person, not by some pervading ideology and not by circumstance, but from within, from a place of generosity. Comics will be the same, but I won't and there's nothing I can do about that. ☼

ABOVE: From *Washington White Part 1: Algorithm*, 2017.

Lovo and The Firewolf
Geoffrey Hayes's Final Comic

Eric Reynolds

IN 2008, I became a father. This was also the year that gave us Toon Books, the publishing house of early-reader comics, founded by editor/art director extraordinaire Françoise Mouly. Mouly, drawing on decades of experience collaborating with cartoonists on *Raw* and the *New Yorker* magazine – and raising two children – quickly turned Toon Books into a wonderful, prestige line, showcasing a head-spinning, murderer's row of international talent, including Art Spiegelman, Jeff Smith, Harry Bliss, Eleanor Davis and many more.

As a self-respecting comics dad with a child firmly in Toon's prime early-reader demographic, we collected all of them. I probably would have collected them whether she liked them or not, but like them she did. They were surprisingly unlike anything else out there: comics created to be read to toddlers and kindergarteners! As a result, the Toon line was in heavy rotation during my daughter's early reading years. (There are still several Toon Books I can recite entire pages of from memory.)

But all Toon Books were not equal in my daughter's eyes. She had her favorites, ones we would return to more frequently than others. The most popular titles were, hands down, Geoffrey Hayes's series of *Benny and Penny* books. Hayes, a veteran children's book illustrator and author, seemed invigorated by Toon Books' mission and released six *Benny and Penny* books between 2013 and 2016: *Benny and Penny in Just Pretend*, *Benny and Penny in the Big No-No!*, *Benny and Penny in the Toy Breaker*, *Benny and Penny in Lights Out!*, *Benny and Penny in Lost and Found!* and *Benny and Penny in How to Say Goodbye*.

Each book is a mini-masterpiece of characterization, economy and structure – helping children navigate a panoply of emotions and experiences that life has

BELOW: From *Benny and Penny in Lights Out!*, 2012.

only just begun to unveil to them. Benny and Penny are two sibling mice who play, fight, pretend, explore, get scared, get hurt, etc. They laugh, they cry and they emote and playact in ways that my daughter lived vicariously through – and would demand endless re-readings of. (To the point, frankly, where I'd often try to unsuccessfully cajole her into *anything* else, for sheer variety.) They are deceptively simple in their mastery, but the proof is in the way these characters lived and breathed in my daughter's eyes. Benny and Penny became such an ongoing concern in our lives that in 2011, I reached out to Mouly to see if she could put me in touch with Hayes so I could possibly acquire a piece of Benny and Penny artwork to hang in my kid's bedroom.

It's here I should mention that Geoffrey Hayes was the younger brother of the late underground cartoonist Rory Hayes, whose work Fantagraphics published a retrospective of in 2008: *Where Demented Wented: The Art and Comics of Rory Hayes*, edited by Glenn Bray and Dan Nadel. Geoffrey was fond of this collection, and as a result, when I wrote to him from my Fantagraphics email address, he responded generously and favorably and we struck up an ongoing correspondence. He sent my daughter a wonderful illustration (which still hangs in her bedroom), and we struck up a modest internet friendship.

Hayes was very enthusiastic about the medium of comics and had a genuine curiosity about the form beyond just the young reader applications he was primarily focused on. The *Benny and Penny* books had afforded him some success (including a Geisel Award and an Eisner Award). At one point, he mentioned to me that he harbored a desire to do a full-length graphic novel. Something that was still all ages, but would be entirely his own and not explicitly a "children's book." It didn't take long for me to tell him that I thought this was a great idea, and that I wanted to publish it. He had already been sketching out roughs on the side before he ever mentioned it to me, but he seemed

buoyed by my desire to publish it, and one thing led to another.

On September 21, 2016, with the help of Hayes's longtime agent, Edite Kroll, we signed a contract to publish what was to be Hayes's first graphic novel, *Lovo and the Firewolf*. Hayes had some other projects that he needed to finish first, but over the next year he would occasionally send me sketches, panels or ideas that he wanted feedback on. He was especially concerned about getting the lettering just right (he told me that his favorite letterer was Dick Moores, of *Gasoline Alley* fame), using a font in a way that would look like a part of a page's organic whole, and we experimented with a few different options created from his hand-lettering.

On June 2, 2017 – I remember it was a Friday – Hayes emailed me a PDF of the finished first chapter of *Lovo and the Firewolf*. He was excited to share it; it felt like a milestone towards making the book a reality. He was also excited to report

ABOVE: Hayes drew this illustration for Reynolds's daughter.

that he'd cleared his deck of other projects and expected to work exclusively on *Lovo* for the rest of the year – so we could schedule the book for a Fall 2018 release. He was headed to a doctor's appointment (a routine checkup) but looked forward to hearing what I thought of the pages next week. I printed out the PDF to review at home over the weekend. The next morning, I woke up, checked my email and found an email from Kroll, telling me that Hayes had apparently died in his sleep. Details were vague. Hayes lived modestly, by himself, with no immediate family.

Until Hayes's death, I'd never known an author who passed away in the middle of a project like this. Aside from the obvious tragedy when anyone dies too young (Hayes was 69, seemingly in decent health and enjoying a creative renaissance), knowing that *Lovo and the Firewolf* will never exist is almost as frustrating and heartbreaking as the death itself. The cartoonist Kim Deitch once told me that because he wasn't a religious man, his books were his only true hope for some kind of life after death. This is a notion that has stuck with me for more than 20 years now, and I can't help but think of it when I think about *Lovo and the Firewolf*.

Thanks to Edite Kroll, a true friend of Hayes's in addition to acting as his agent for over 30 years, we are able to share the finished first chapter of *Lovo and the Firewolf* here. Though we considered a few options after Hayes passed, it became quite clear very quickly that there simply wasn't enough of *Lovo* completed to ever publish it as its own book. When I floated the possibility of running these pages as a feature in *The Comics Journal*, Kroll was able to retrieve the high-resolution files from Hayes's hard drive and saw the value in sharing them with *TCJ* readers. Though merely a stage-setter for what was supposed to come, *Lovo and the Firewolf* has all the markings of a classic Geoffrey Hayes book. Lovo, a sweet-natured innocent – "Quit being so windy, wind!" – is instantly relatable to young readers, grounding the otherwise fantastic fairy tale trappings, while Hayes's deceptively simple illustrations and intuitive panel-to-panel storytelling further immerse readers in Lovo's world.

Geoffrey Hayes has left us with an incredible body of work that will continue to inform the worlds of young readers for generations to come, for which we as comics fans, and as parents, can be grateful. I hope you'll view these pages and think less about what could have been, and more about Hayes's remarkable body of work that exists and has enriched the lives of so many children. There's a strange alchemy to making kid's books, and for the life of me, I have no idea how Hayes – a man with no children himself – could speak so directly and meaningfully to young readers, but I have a 10-year-old who is living proof that he did, and I will be forever grateful. ✺

ONCE UPON A TIME, IN THE VALLEY OF THE CHIMNEYS

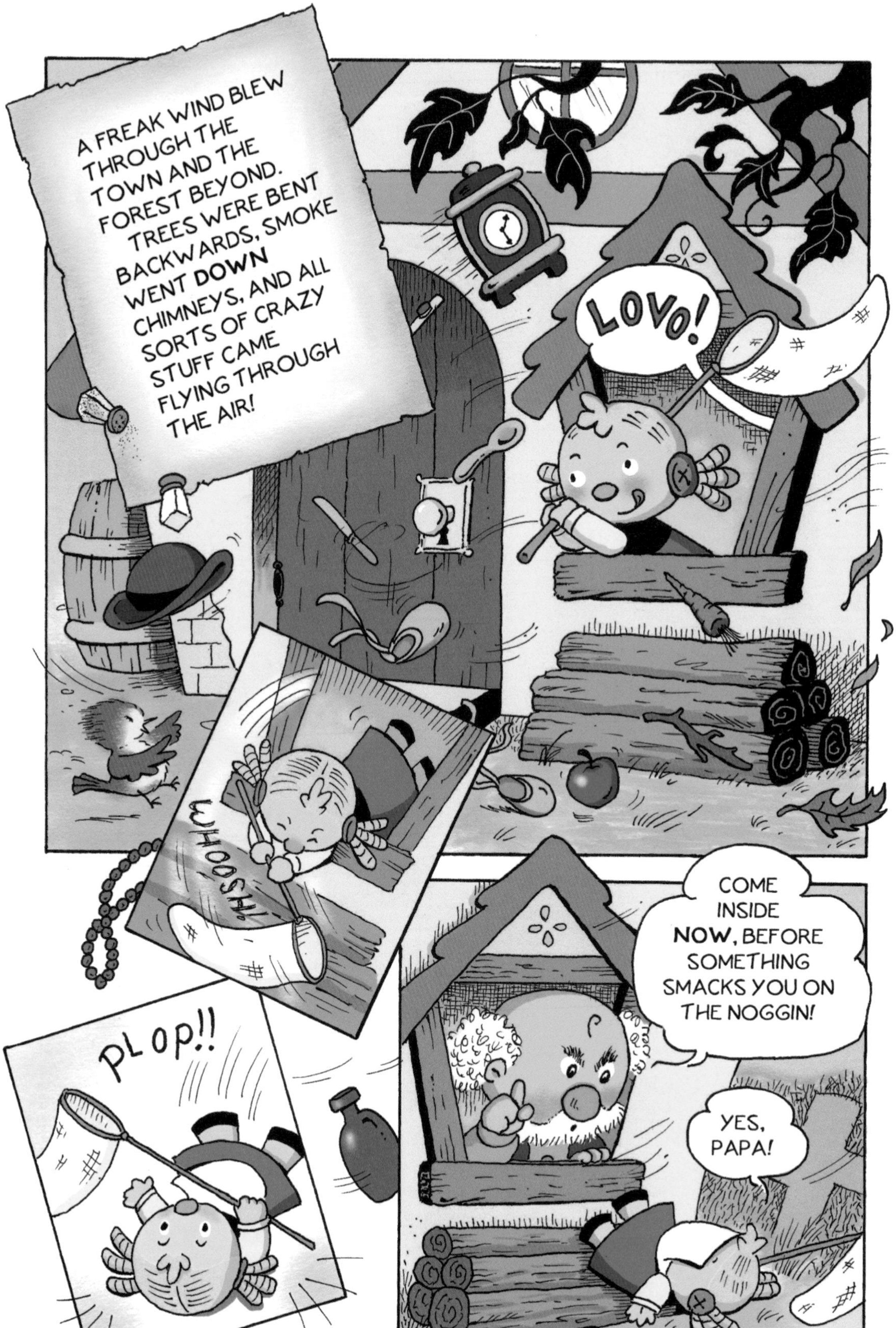
A FREAK WIND BLEW THROUGH THE TOWN AND THE FOREST BEYOND. TREES WERE BENT BACKWARDS, SMOKE WENT **DOWN** CHIMNEYS, AND ALL SORTS OF CRAZY STUFF CAME FLYING THROUGH THE AIR!
LOVO!
WHOOSH!
COME INSIDE **NOW,** BEFORE SOMETHING SMACKS YOU ON THE NOGGIN!
PLOP!!
YES, PAPA!

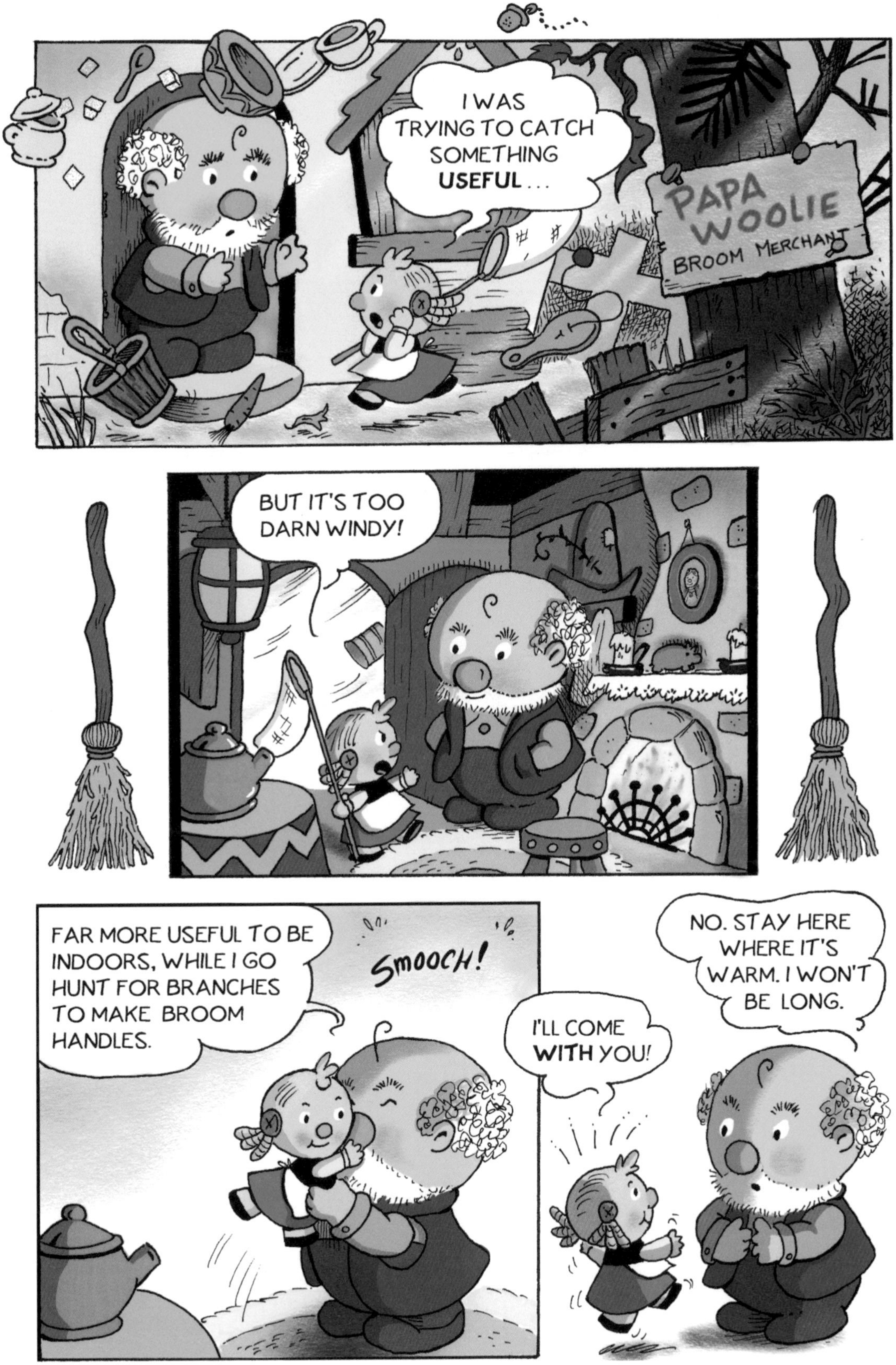
I WAS TRYING TO CATCH SOMETHING **USEFUL** . . .
PAPA WOOLIE
BROOM MERCHANT
BUT IT'S TOO DARN WINDY!
FAR MORE USEFUL TO BE INDOORS, WHILE I GO HUNT FOR BRANCHES TO MAKE BROOM HANDLES.
SMOOCH!
I'LL COME **WITH** YOU!
NO. STAY HERE WHERE IT'S WARM. I WON'T BE LONG.

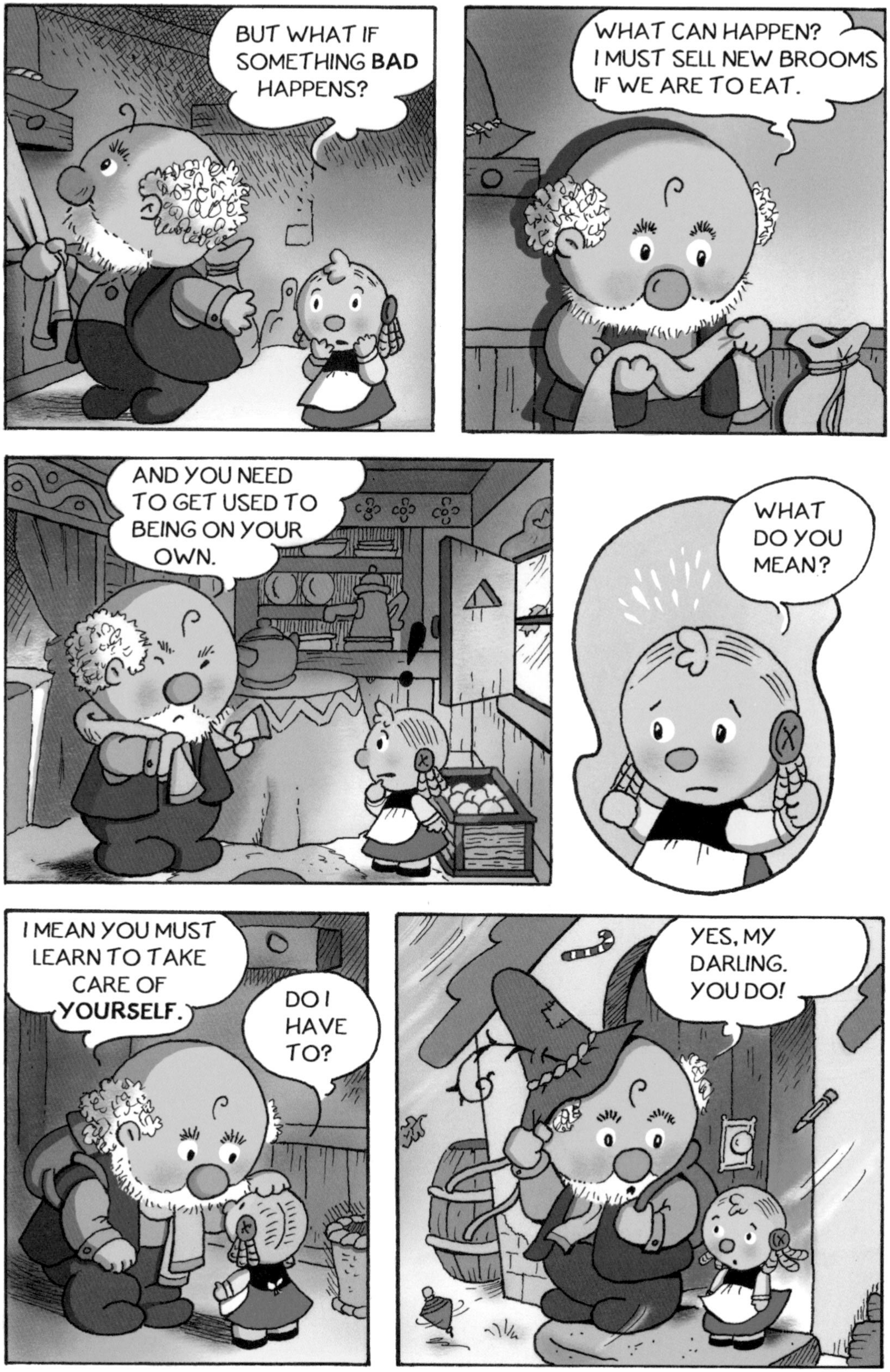
BUT WHAT IF SOMETHING BAD HAPPENS?
WHAT CAN HAPPEN? I MUST SELL NEW BROOMS IF WE ARE TO EAT.
AND YOU NEED TO GET USED TO BEING ON YOUR OWN.
WHAT DO YOU MEAN?
I MEAN YOU MUST LEARN TO TAKE CARE OF YOURSELF.
DO I HAVE TO?
YES, MY DARLING. YOU DO!

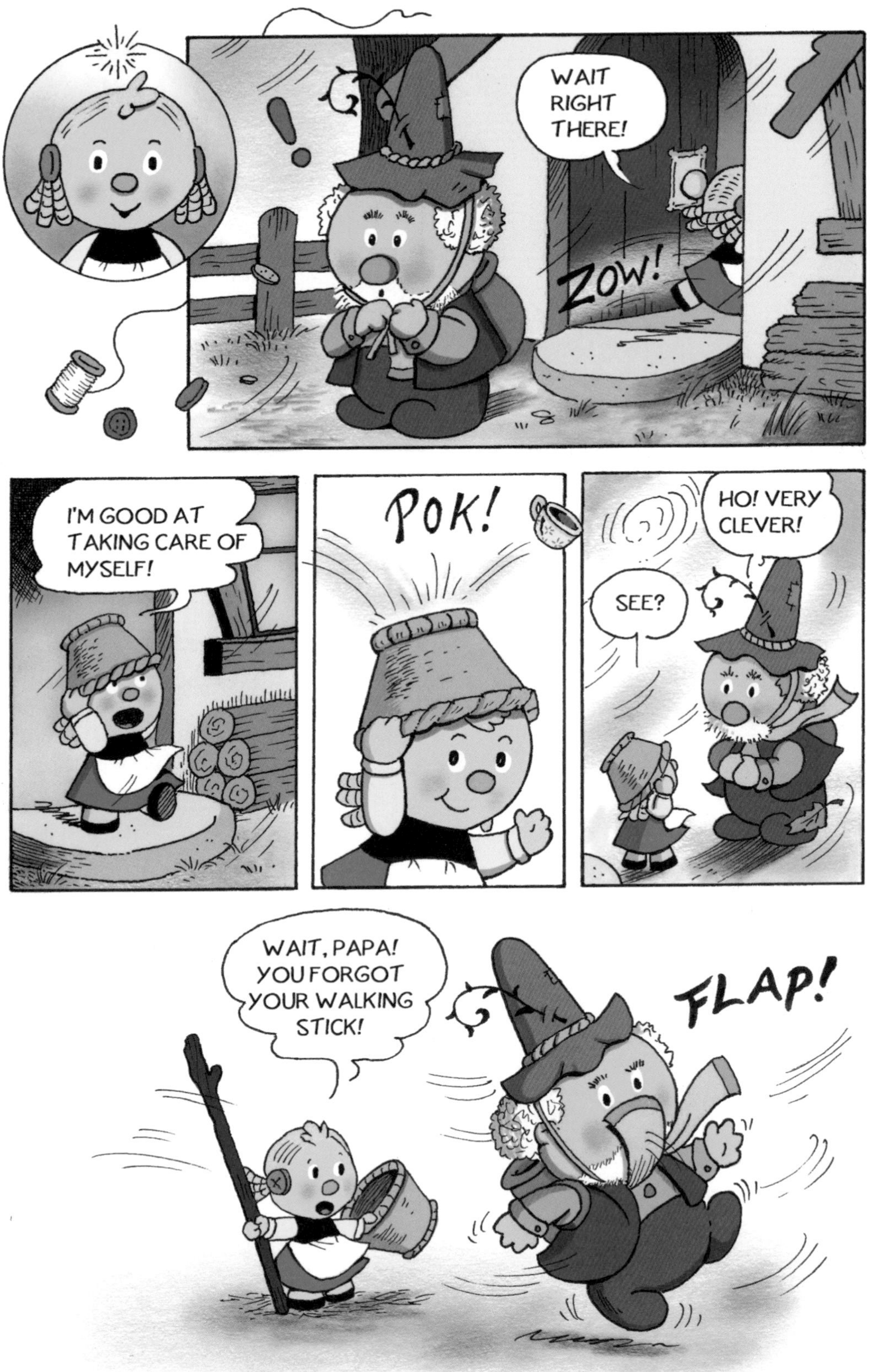
!
WAIT RIGHT THERE!
ZOW!
I'M GOOD AT TAKING CARE OF MYSELF!
POK!
HO! VERY CLEVER!
SEE?
WAIT, PAPA! YOU FORGOT YOUR WALKING STICK!
FLAP!

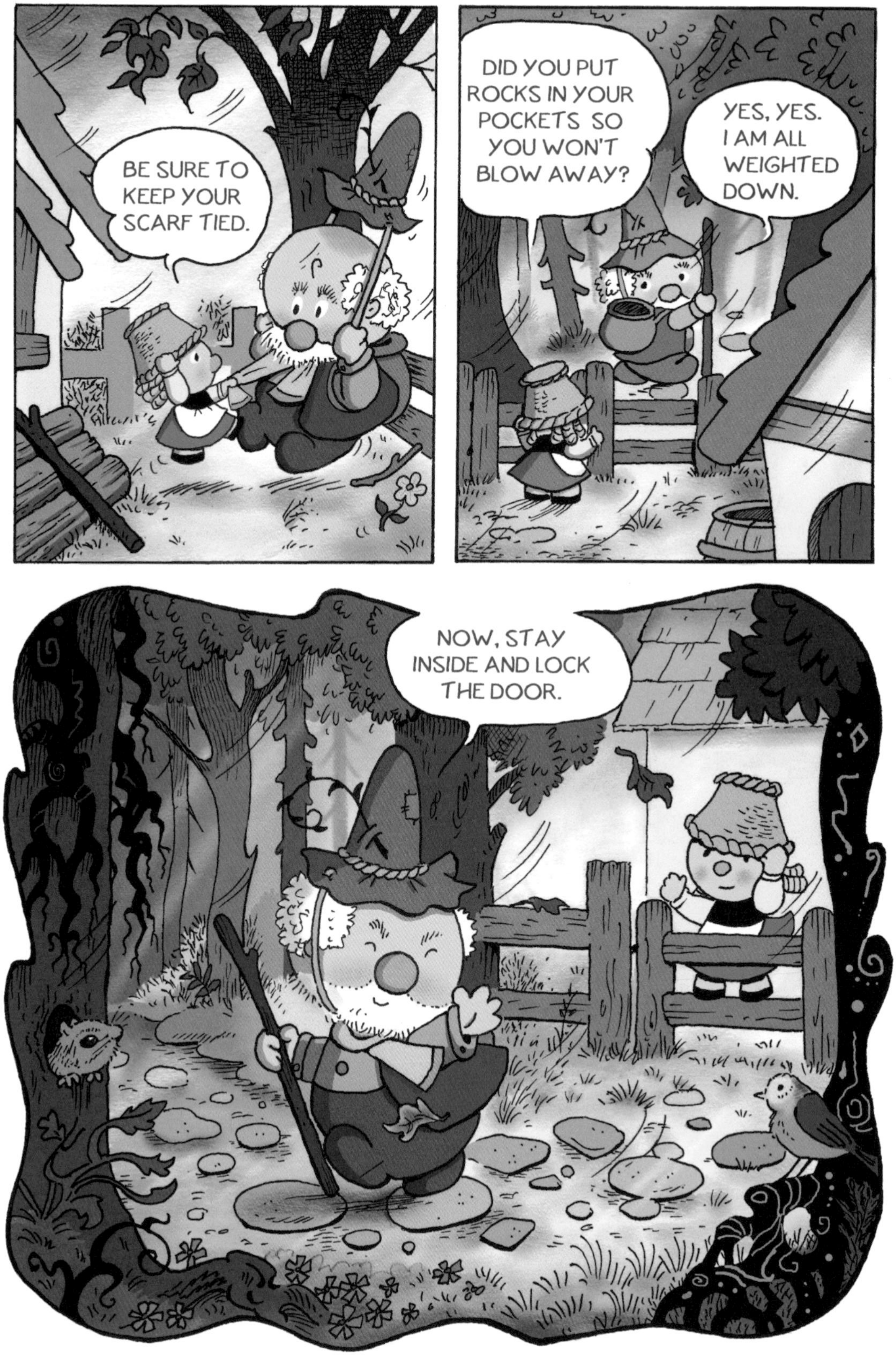
BE SURE TO KEEP YOUR SCARF TIED.
DID YOU PUT ROCKS IN YOUR POCKETS SO YOU WON'T BLOW AWAY?
YES, YES. I AM ALL WEIGHTED DOWN.
NOW, STAY INSIDE AND LOCK THE DOOR.

GEE! I HOPE HE'LL BE OKAY.

CHEEP!

HUH?

CHEEP!
CHEEP!

HELLO, LITTLE FRIENDS!

LOVO TAKES A PIECE OF BREAD FROM HER POCKET ∽∽

HERE, WE CAN **SHARE** MY BREAKFAST.

BUT SOME HUNGRY **CROWS** ALSO SPOT THE BREAD ∽∽

YOWZA!

AWK! AWK!

THE CROWS DO SQUAWK! THE BEGGARS ARE COMING TO TOWN!

OH, FOR A BITE OF A BAKER'S BUN WITH TEA TO WASH IT DOWN!

GOT ANY BATTER CAKE?

GO AWAY!

NO WORRIES, LOVE. **THIS** WILL DO!

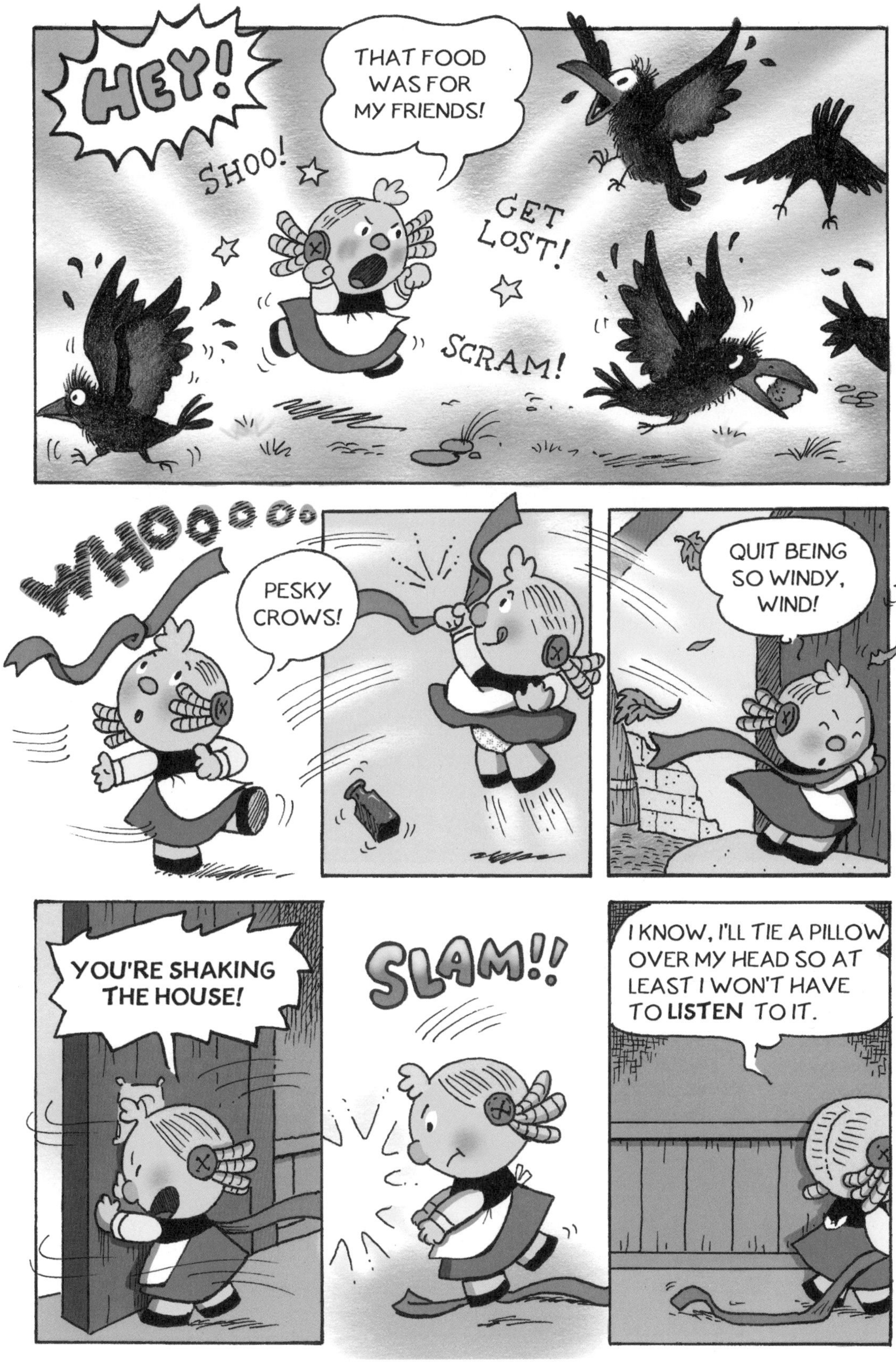
HEY!
THAT FOOD WAS FOR MY FRIENDS!
SHOO!
GET LOST!
SCRAM!
WHOOOOOO
PESKY CROWS!
QUIT BEING SO WINDY, WIND!
YOU'RE SHAKING THE HOUSE!
SLAM!!
I KNOW, I'LL TIE A PILLOW OVER MY HEAD SO AT LEAST I WON'T HAVE TO LISTEN TO IT.

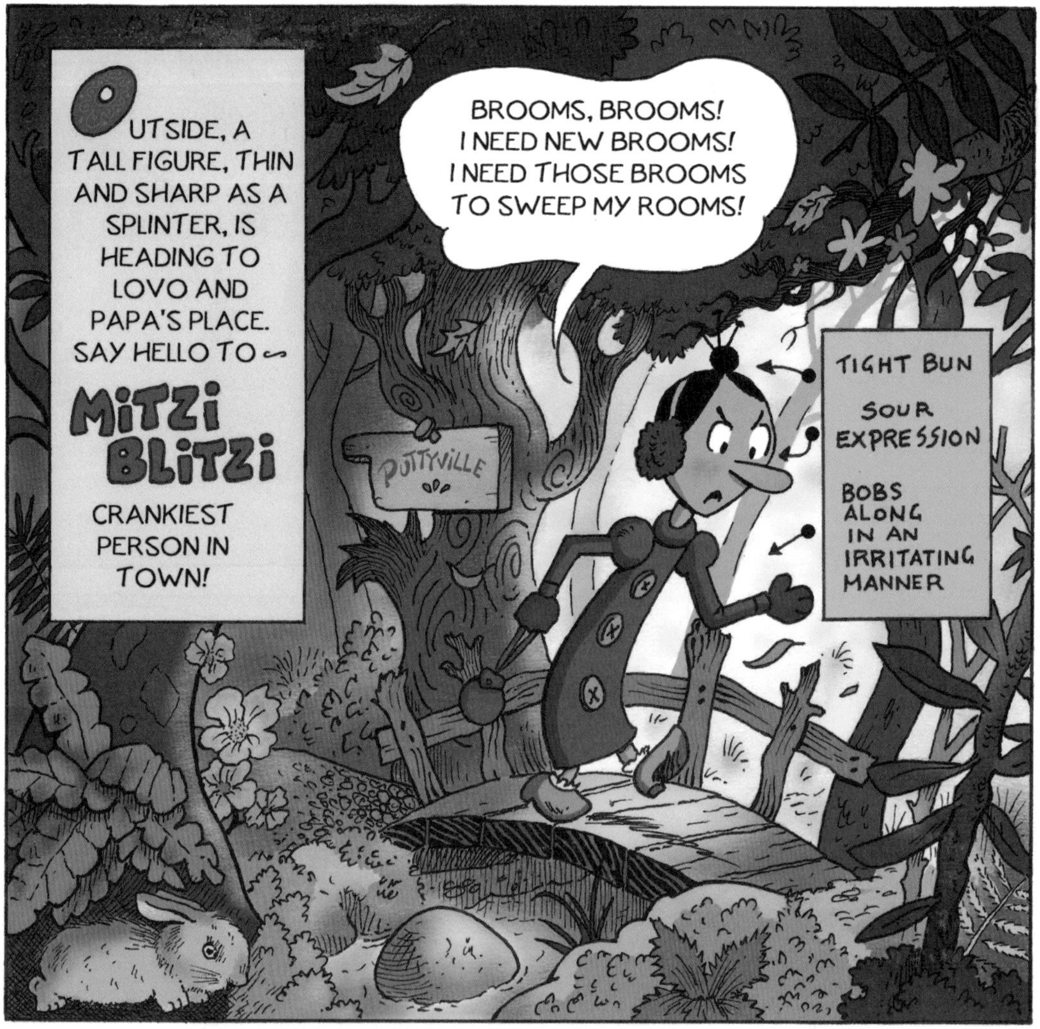
OUTSIDE, A TALL FIGURE, THIN AND SHARP AS A SPLINTER, IS HEADING TO LOVO AND PAPA'S PLACE. SAY HELLO TO ~
MITZI BLITZI
CRANKIEST PERSON IN TOWN!
BROOMS, BROOMS! I NEED NEW BROOMS! I NEED THOSE BROOMS TO SWEEP MY ROOMS!
PUTTYVILLE
TIGHT BUN
SOUR EXPRESSION
BOBS ALONG IN AN IRRITATING MANNER

MITZI ENJOYS MINDING HER OWN BUSINESS ~ AS WELL AS EVERYONE ELSE'S!

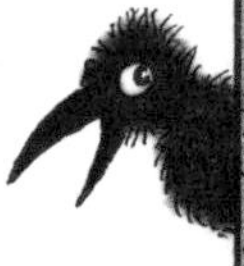

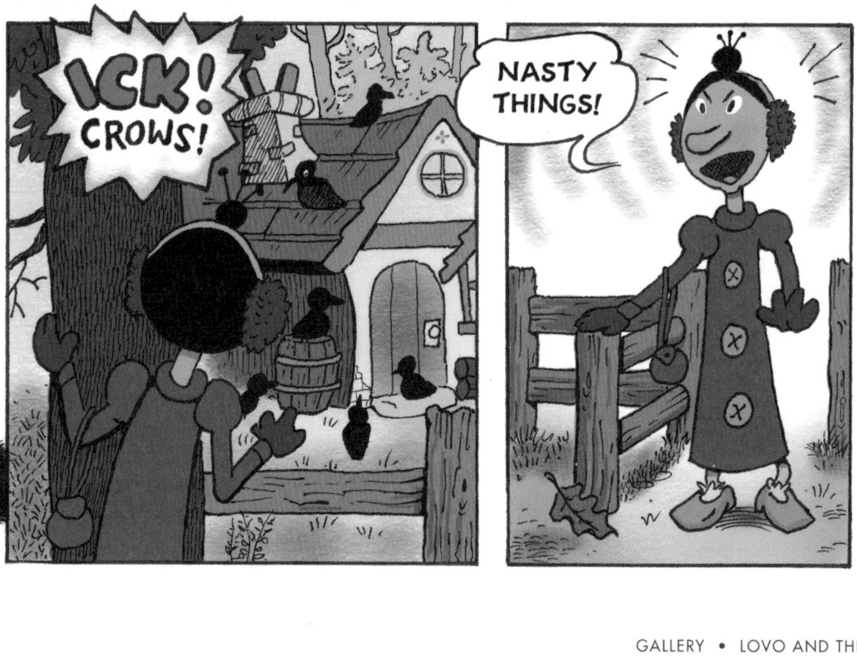
ICK! CROWS!
NASTY THINGS!

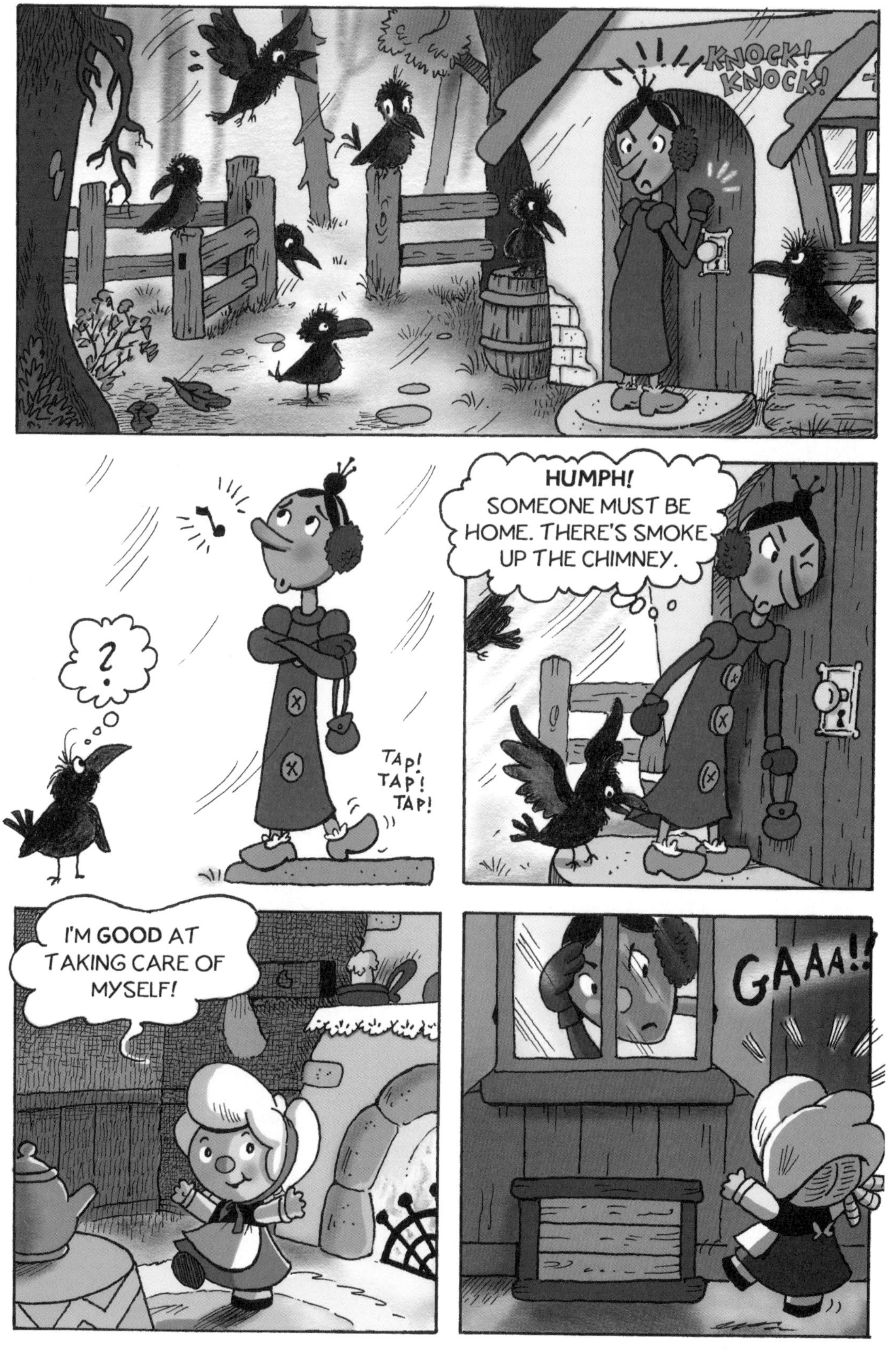
KNOCK! KNOCK!
TAP! TAP! TAP!
?
HUMPH! SOMEONE MUST BE HOME. THERE'S SMOKE UP THE CHIMNEY.
I'M GOOD AT TAKING CARE OF MYSELF!
GAAA!!

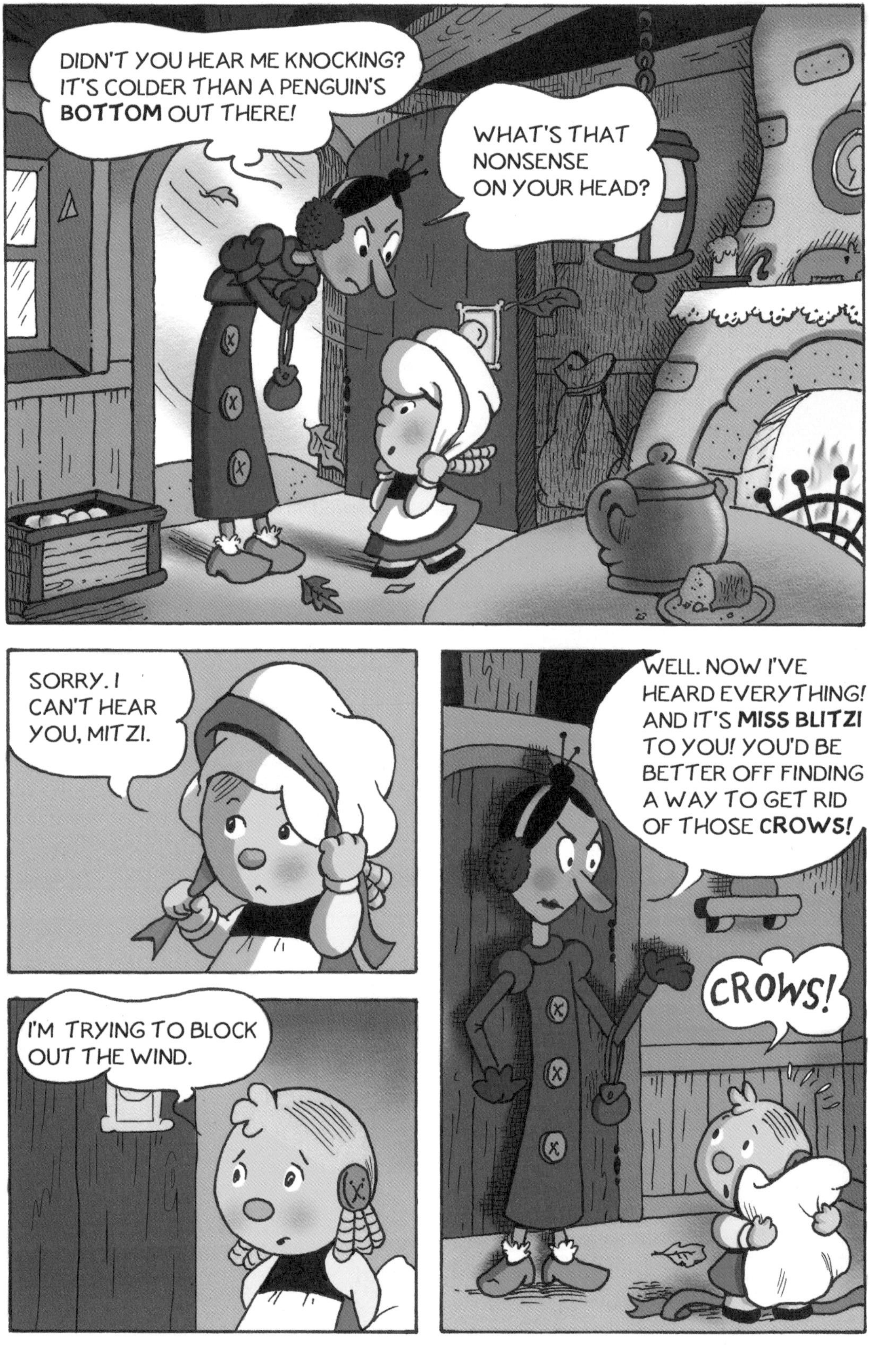
DIDN'T YOU HEAR ME KNOCKING? IT'S COLDER THAN A PENGUIN'S **BOTTOM** OUT THERE!
WHAT'S THAT NONSENSE ON YOUR HEAD?
SORRY. I CAN'T HEAR YOU, MITZI.
I'M TRYING TO BLOCK OUT THE WIND.
WELL. NOW I'VE HEARD EVERYTHING! AND IT'S **MISS BLITZI** TO YOU! YOU'D BE BETTER OFF FINDING A WAY TO GET RID OF THOSE **CROWS!**
CROWS!

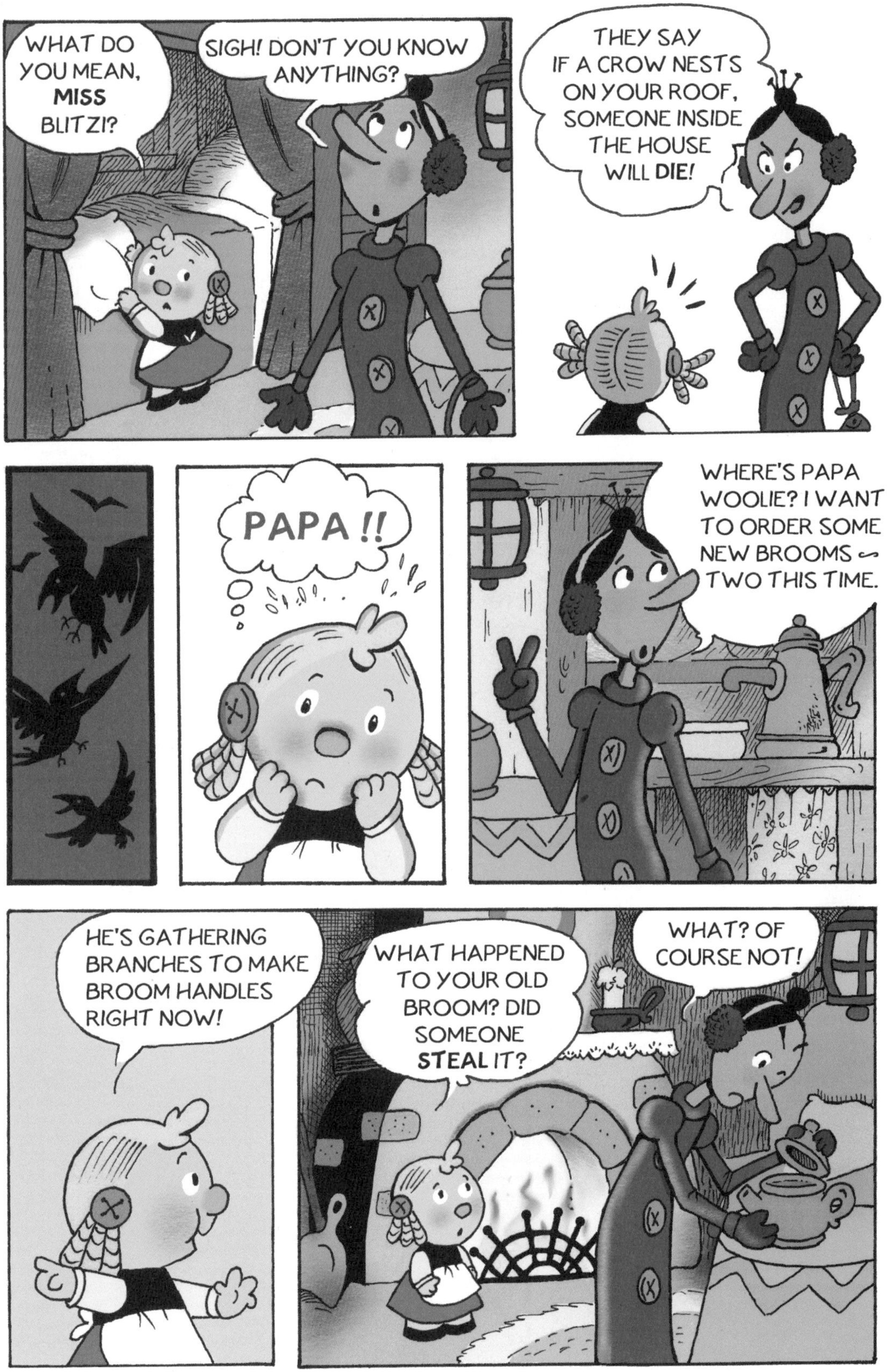
WHAT DO YOU MEAN, **MISS** BLITZI?
SIGH! DON'T YOU KNOW ANYTHING?
THEY SAY IF A CROW NESTS ON YOUR ROOF, SOMEONE INSIDE THE HOUSE WILL **DIE**!
PAPA !!
WHERE'S PAPA WOOLIE? I WANT TO ORDER SOME NEW BROOMS ~ TWO THIS TIME.
HE'S GATHERING BRANCHES TO MAKE BROOM HANDLES RIGHT NOW!
WHAT HAPPENED TO YOUR OLD BROOM? DID SOMEONE **STEAL** IT?
WHAT? OF COURSE NOT!

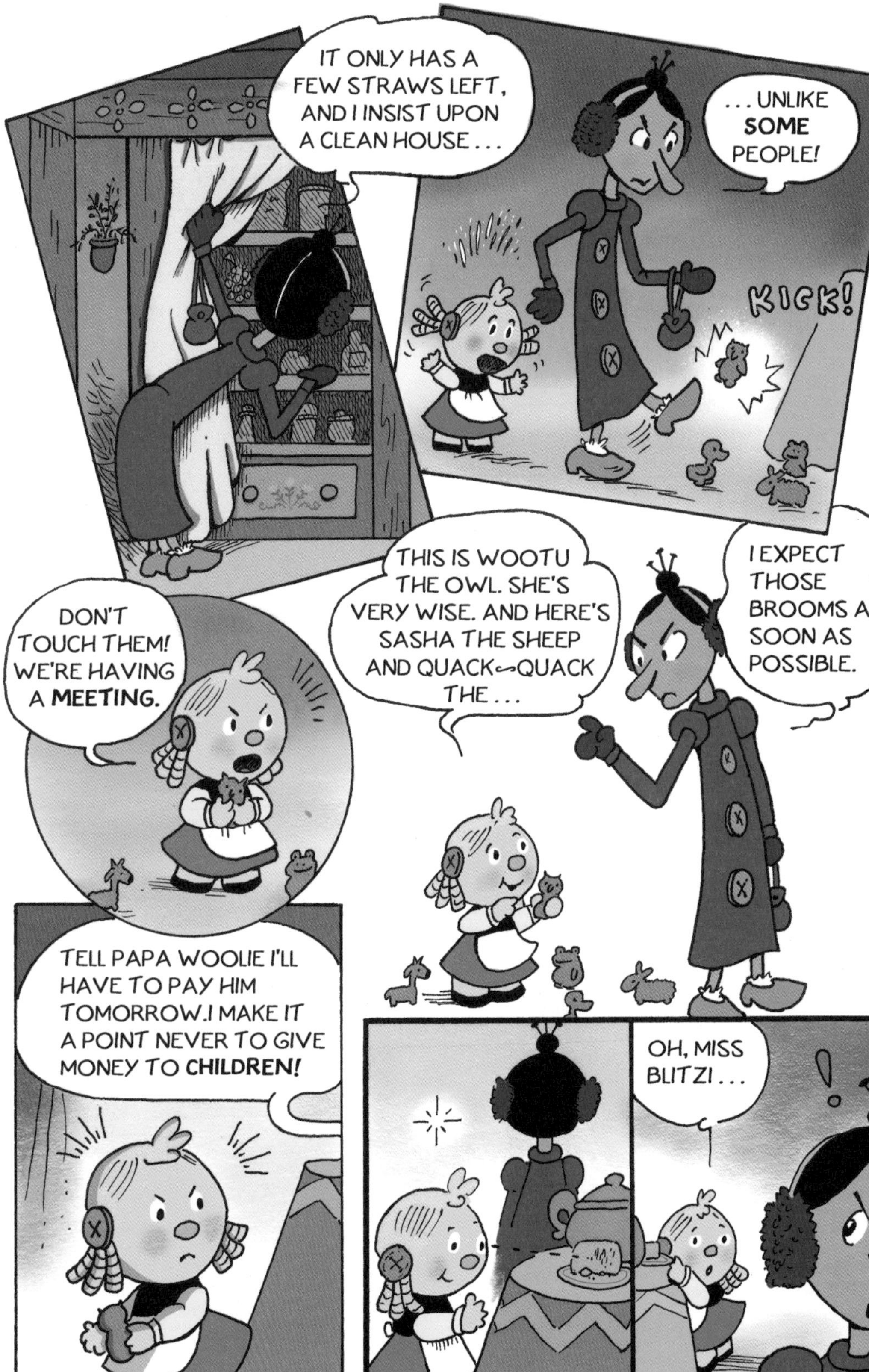
IT ONLY HAS A FEW STRAWS LEFT, AND I INSIST UPON A CLEAN HOUSE . . .
. . . UNLIKE **SOME** PEOPLE!
KICK!
DON'T TOUCH THEM! WE'RE HAVING A **MEETING.**
THIS IS WOOTU THE OWL. SHE'S VERY WISE. AND HERE'S SASHA THE SHEEP AND QUACK-QUACK THE . . .
I EXPECT THOSE BROOMS AS SOON AS POSSIBLE.
TELL PAPA WOOLIE I'LL HAVE TO PAY HIM TOMORROW. I MAKE IT A POINT NEVER TO GIVE MONEY TO **CHILDREN!**
OH, MISS BLITZI . . .
!

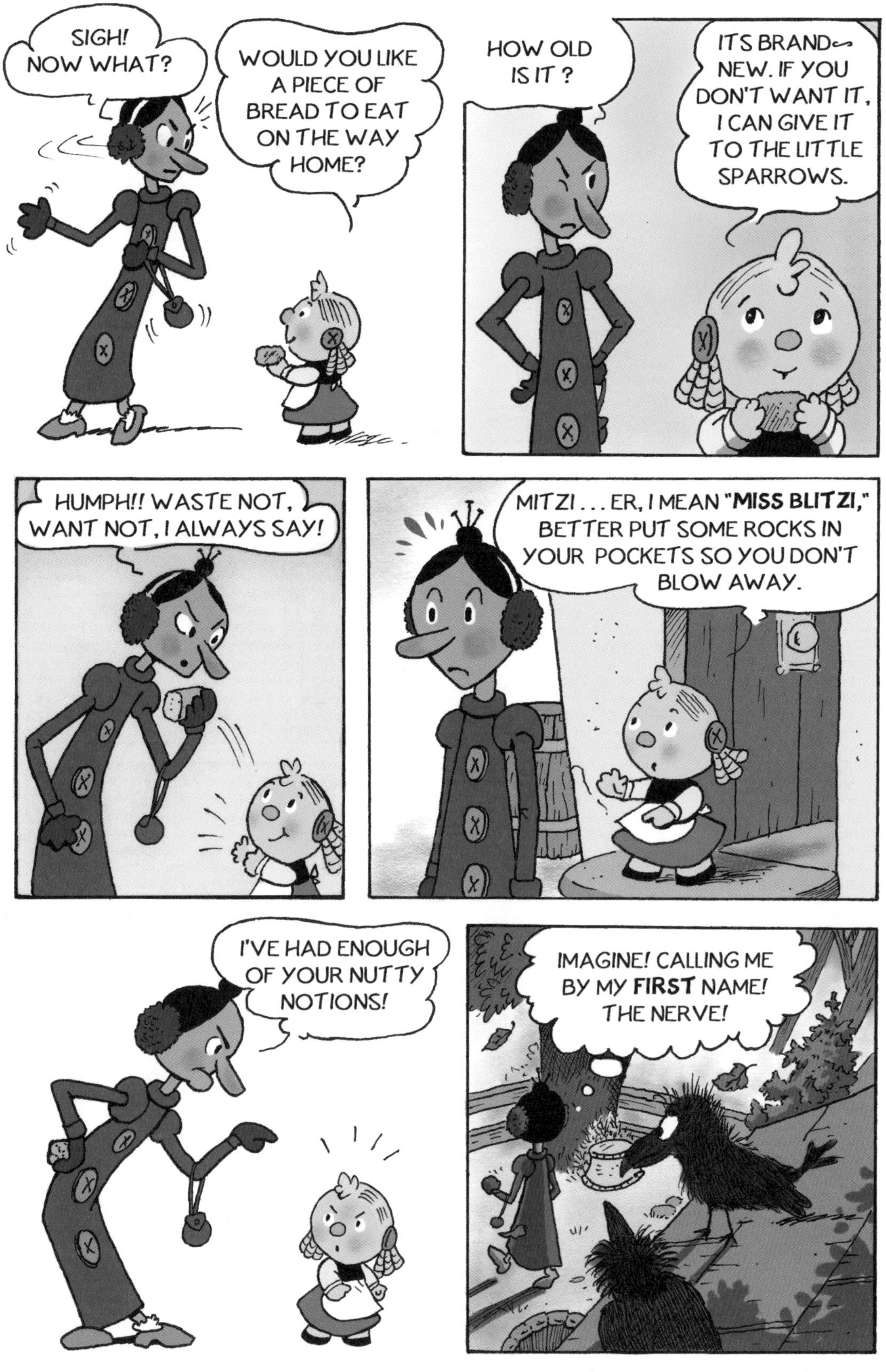
SIGH! NOW WHAT?
WOULD YOU LIKE A PIECE OF BREAD TO EAT ON THE WAY HOME?
HOW OLD IS IT ?
ITS BRAND-NEW. IF YOU DON'T WANT IT, I CAN GIVE IT TO THE LITTLE SPARROWS.
HUMPH!! WASTE NOT, WANT NOT, I ALWAYS SAY!
MITZI . . . ER, I MEAN "**MISS BLITZI,**" BETTER PUT SOME ROCKS IN YOUR POCKETS SO YOU DON'T BLOW AWAY.
I'VE HAD ENOUGH OF YOUR NUTTY NOTIONS!
IMAGINE! CALLING ME BY MY **FIRST** NAME! THE NERVE!

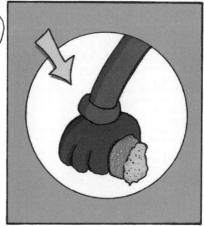

The sharp-eyed crows, who have been waiting for just such an opportunity, go wild when they see the bread.

Mitzi decides she needs to be elsewhere pronto!

There she goes!

Go away, nasty things!

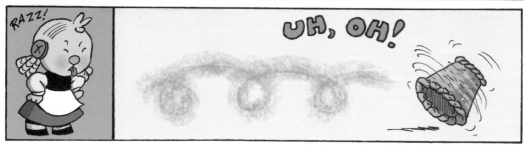

UH, OH!

... LOVO SEES HER BASKET TUMBLING INTO THE TREES.

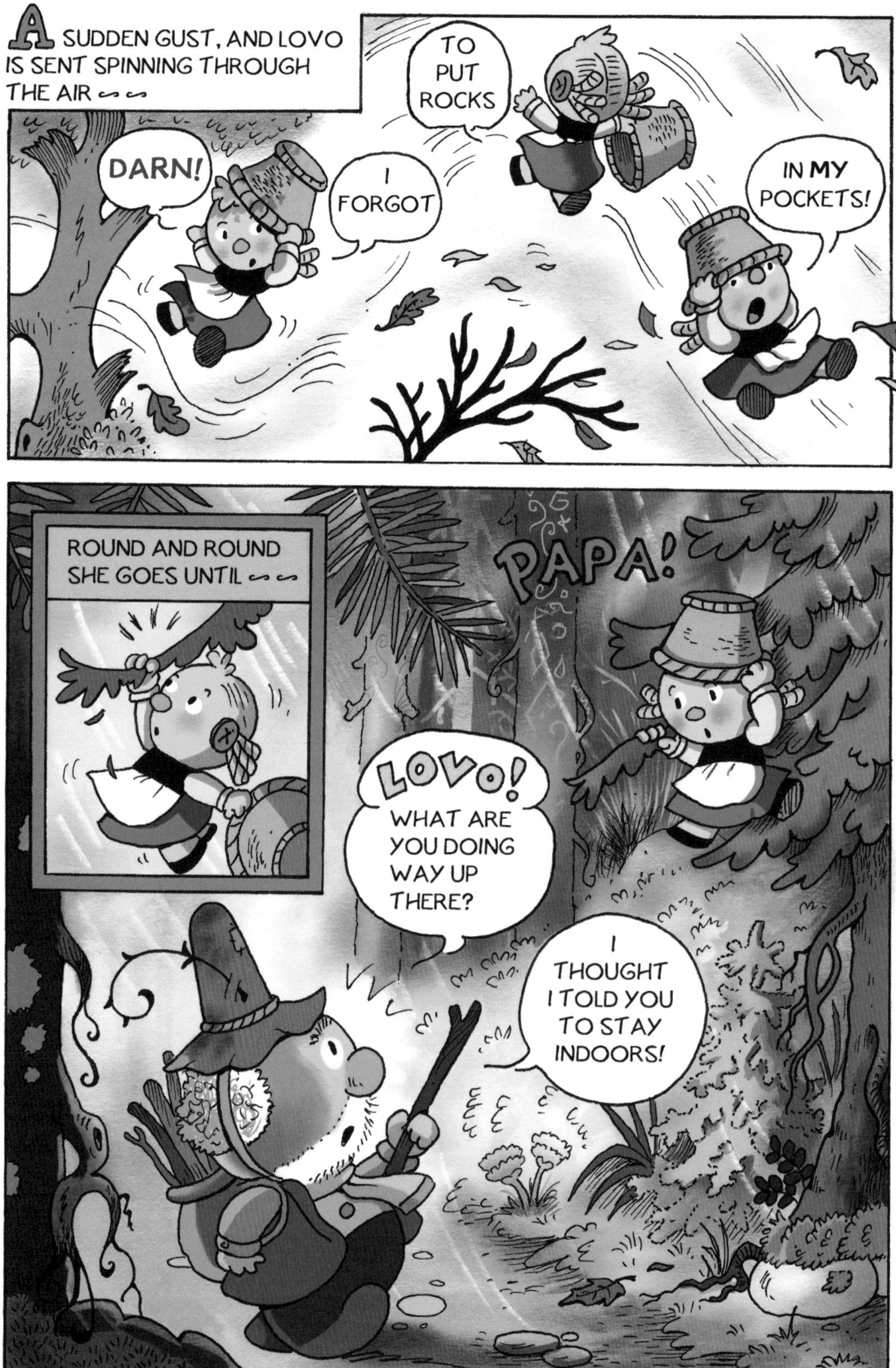
A SUDDEN GUST, AND LOVO IS SENT SPINNING THROUGH THE AIR ~~
DARN!
I FORGOT
TO PUT ROCKS
IN MY POCKETS!
ROUND AND ROUND SHE GOES UNTIL ~~
PAPA!
LOVO! WHAT ARE YOU DOING WAY UP THERE?
I THOUGHT I TOLD YOU TO STAY INDOORS!

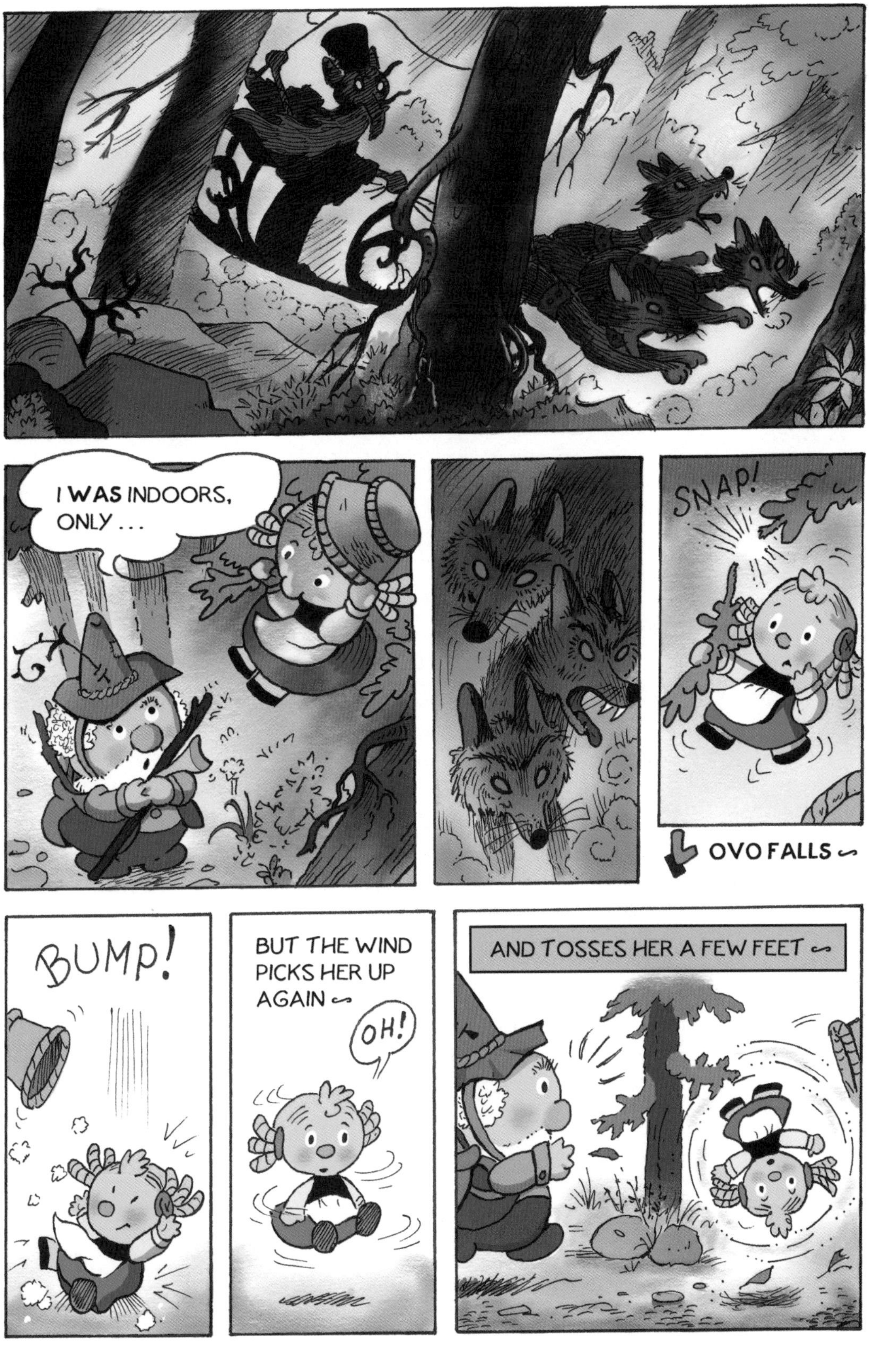
I WAS INDOORS, ONLY . . .
SNAP!
OVO FALLS ~
BUMP!
BUT THE WIND PICKS HER UP AGAIN ~
OH!
AND TOSSES HER A FEW FEET ~

...DIRECTLY IN THE PATH OF AN ONCOMING SLEIGH.
A DARK SLEIGH THAT RIDES ON AIR,
DRIVEN BY A CREATURE AS OLD AS THE KNOTS ON
THE TREES!

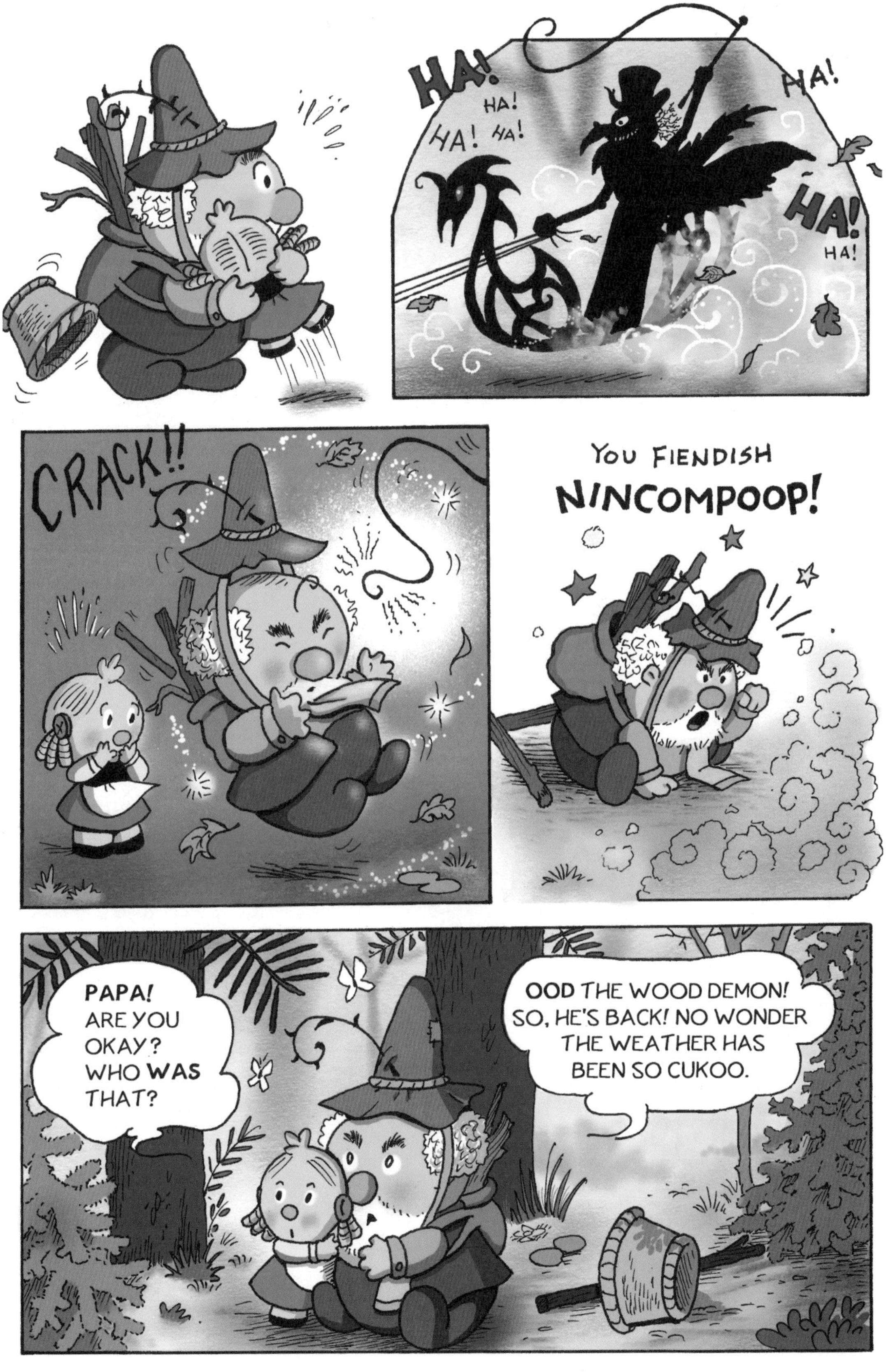
HA! HA! HA! HA!
HA!
HA! HA!
CRACK!!
YOU FIENDISH NINCOMPOOP!
PAPA! ARE YOU OKAY? WHO WAS THAT?
OOD THE WOOD DEMON! SO, HE'S BACK! NO WONDER THE WEATHER HAS BEEN SO CUKOO.

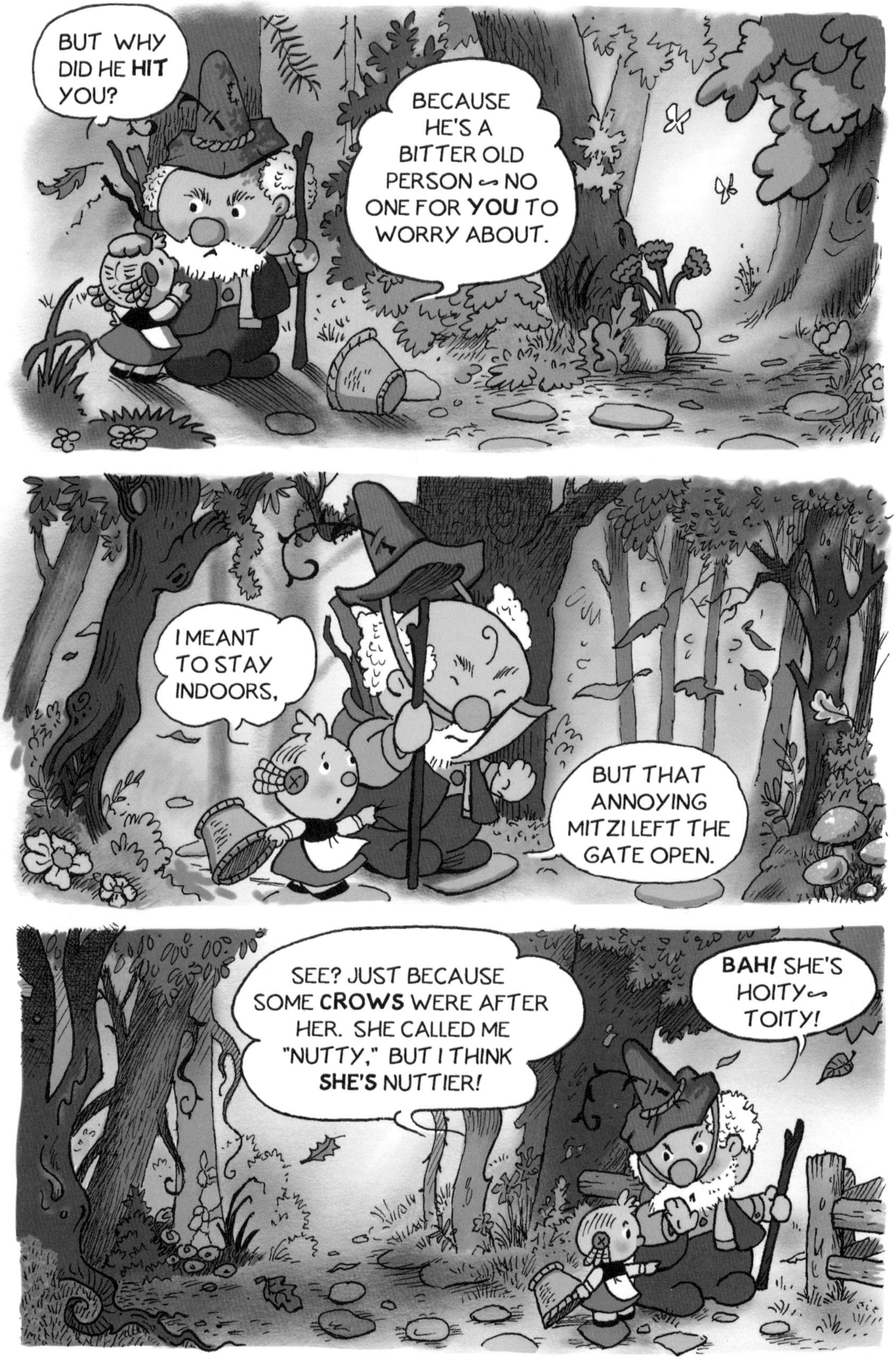
BUT WHY DID HE **HIT** YOU?
BECAUSE HE'S A BITTER OLD PERSON ~ NO ONE FOR **YOU** TO WORRY ABOUT.
I MEANT TO STAY INDOORS,
BUT THAT ANNOYING MITZI LEFT THE GATE OPEN.
SEE? JUST BECAUSE SOME **CROWS** WERE AFTER HER. SHE CALLED ME "NUTTY," BUT I THINK **SHE'S** NUTTIER!
BAH! SHE'S HOITY~ TOITY!

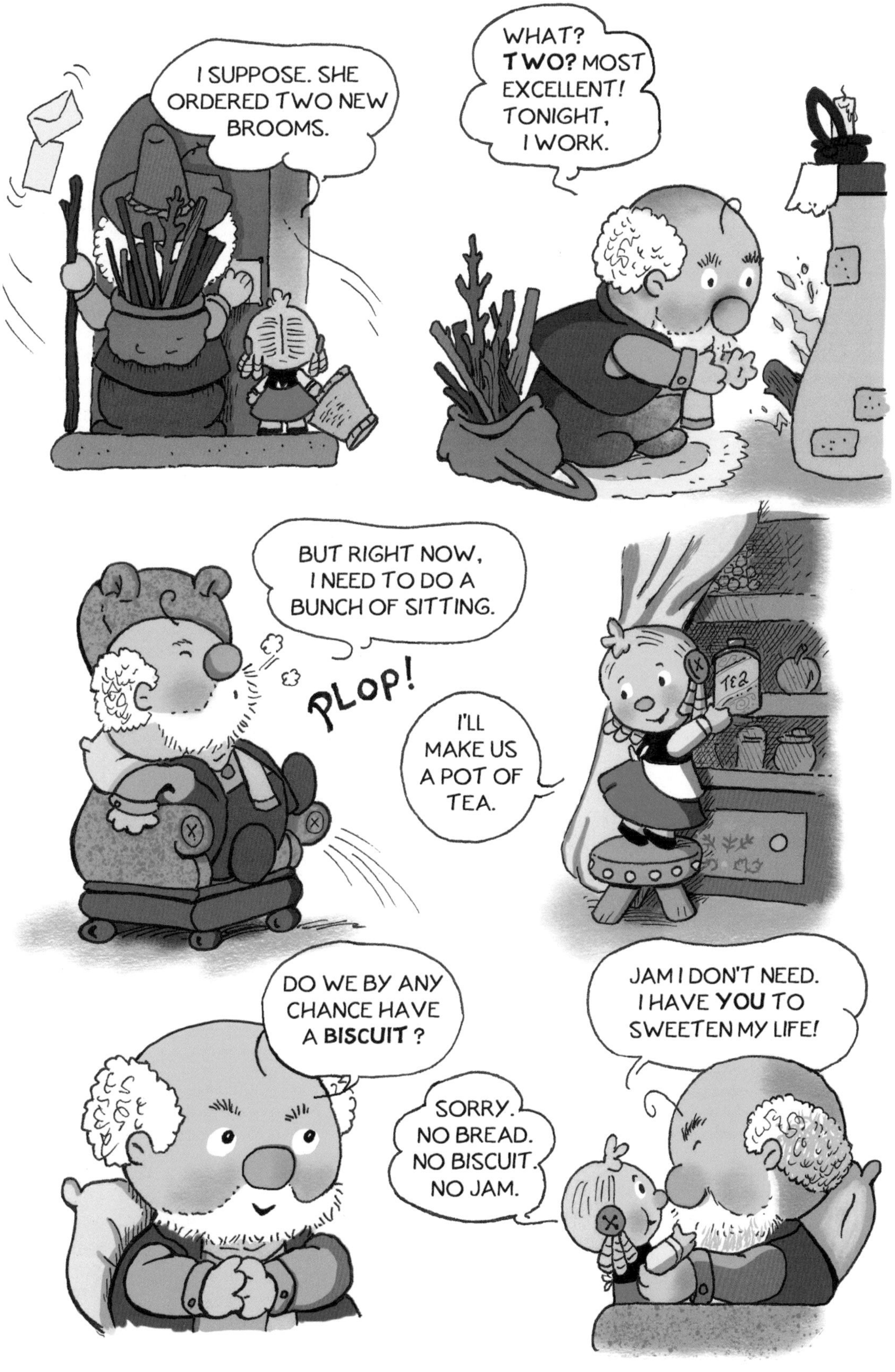
I SUPPOSE. SHE ORDERED TWO NEW BROOMS.
WHAT? **TWO?** MOST EXCELLENT! TONIGHT, I WORK.
BUT RIGHT NOW, I NEED TO DO A BUNCH OF SITTING.
PLOP!
I'LL MAKE US A POT OF TEA.
TEA
DO WE BY ANY CHANCE HAVE A **BISCUIT** ?
SORRY. NO BREAD. NO BISCUIT. NO JAM.
JAM I DON'T NEED. I HAVE **YOU** TO SWEETEN MY LIFE!

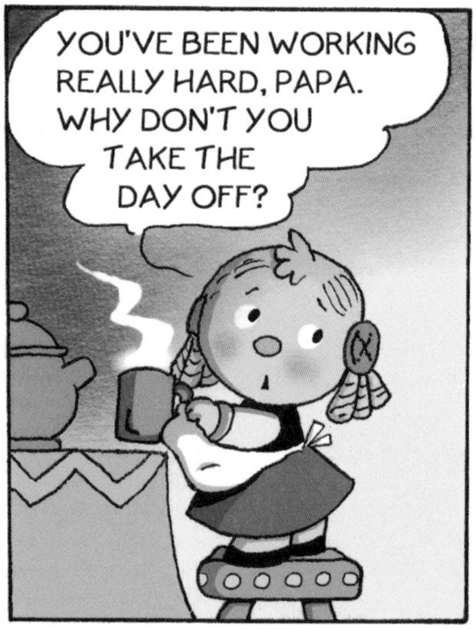
YOU'VE BEEN WORKING REALLY HARD, PAPA. WHY DON'T YOU TAKE THE DAY OFF?

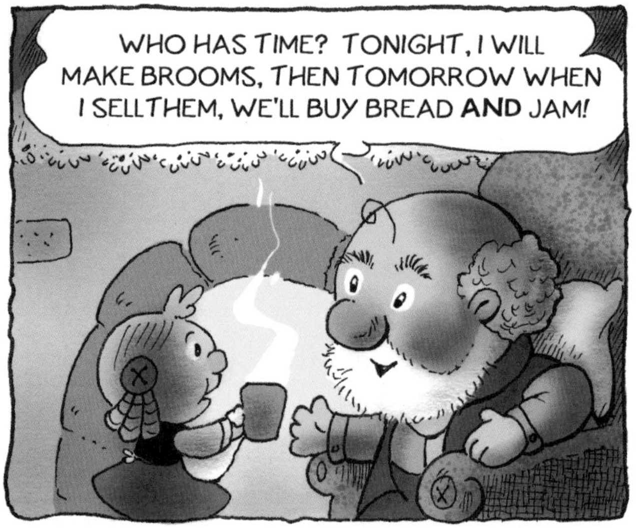
WHO HAS TIME? TONIGHT, I WILL MAKE BROOMS, THEN TOMORROW WHEN I SELL THEM, WE'LL BUY BREAD **AND** JAM!

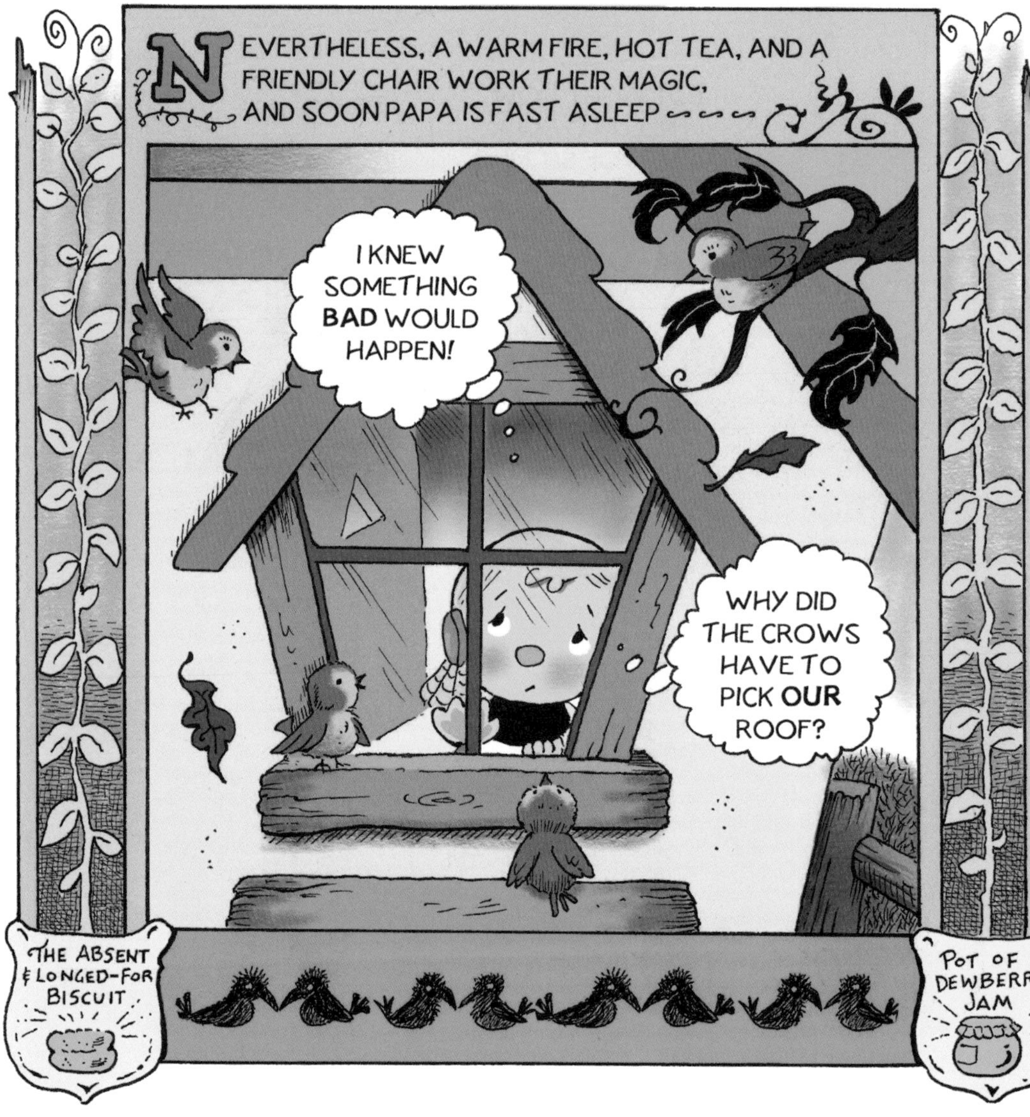
NEVERTHELESS, A WARM FIRE, HOT TEA, AND A FRIENDLY CHAIR WORK THEIR MAGIC, AND SOON PAPA IS FAST ASLEEP
I KNEW SOMETHING **BAD** WOULD HAPPEN!
WHY DID THE CROWS HAVE TO PICK **OUR** ROOF?
THE ABSENT & LONGED-FOR BISCUIT
POT OF DEWBERRY JAM

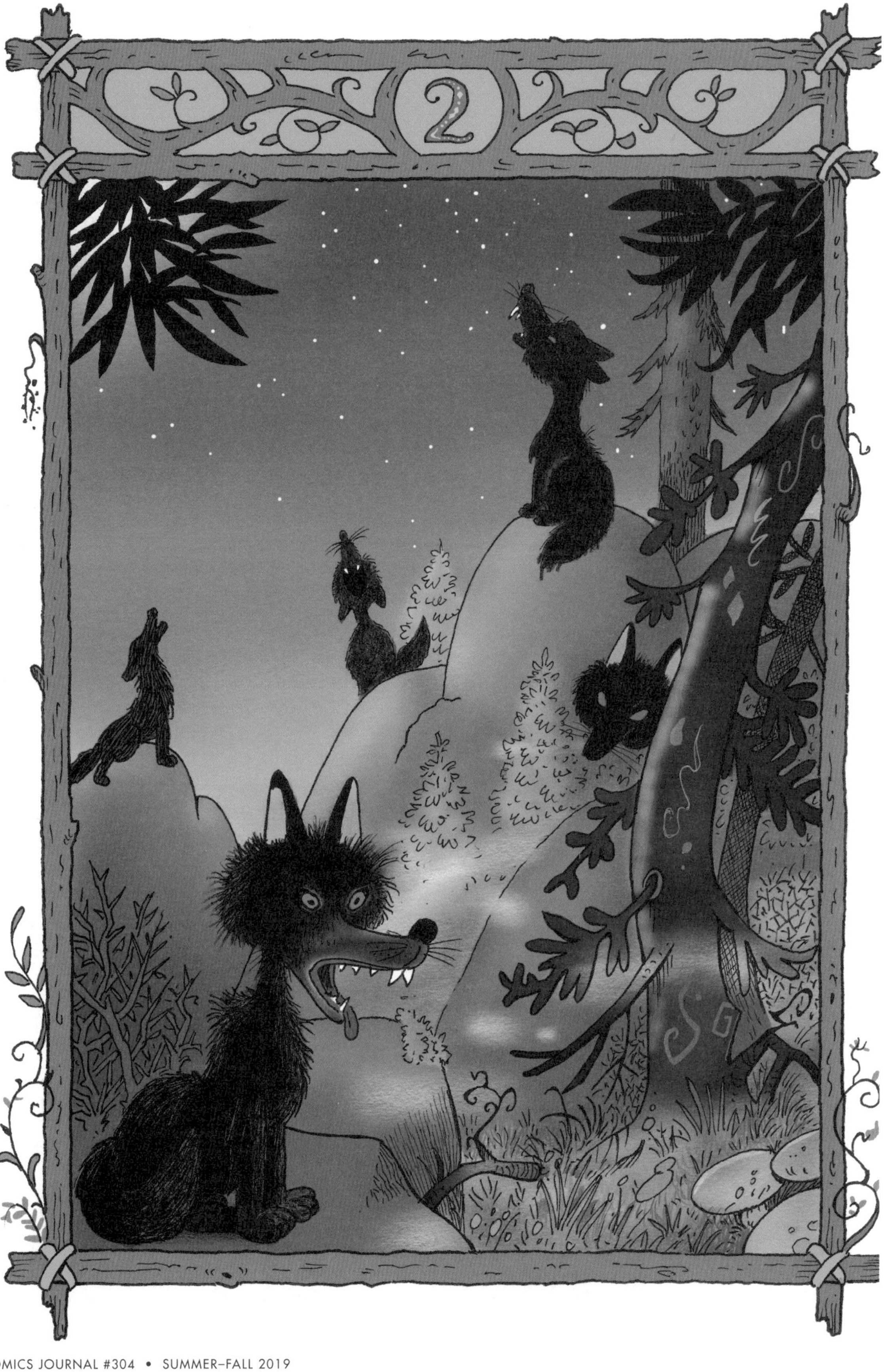
2

AFTER DARK, LOVO AND PAPA STAY CLOSE TO THEIR HEARTH, FOR IN THESE HAUNTED NORTHERN HILLS THE WOLVES HOWL LONG AND LOUD ALL NIGHT AND THE MOON IS A POOR LANTERN ◡◡◡

PAPA SANDS AND SHAPES THE BRANCHES HE HAS CHOSEN, ROUNDING THE ENDS.

LOVO SITS OPPOSITE, BREAKING AND GATHERING STRAW INTO PILES FOR THE BRUSHES.

SHADOWS DANCE UPON THE WALLS ◡◡◡

© Geoffrey Hayes

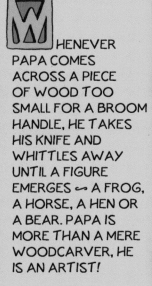WHENEVER PAPA COMES ACROSS A PIECE OF WOOD TOO SMALL FOR A BROOM HANDLE, HE TAKES HIS KNIFE AND WHITTLES AWAY UNTIL A FIGURE EMERGES — A FROG, A HORSE, A HEN OR A BEAR. PAPA IS MORE THAN A MERE WOODCARVER, HE IS AN ARTIST!

WOODEN FRIENDS

WOOTU THE OWL

BITTY THE BUNNY

PAVAL THE PIG

QUACK-QUACK THE DUCK

SASHA THE SHEEP

FEROOSH THE FOX

AN ENTIRE MENAGERIE OF WOODEN ANIMALS IS PROPPED IN CORNERS OF THE BEAMS OR ABOVE THE HEARTH.

IN THE FLICKERING LIGHT OF THE FIRE, THE TOYS ALMOST LOOK ALIVE, AND LOVO AND PAPA FEEL THAT THEY SHARE THE TINY HUT WITH MANY FRIENDS.

Krystal DiFronzo

Laurie Piña

A FEW YEARS AGO, I began collecting texts to develop a syllabus for an imaginary course I will likely never teach – on the budding sexuality and febrile imaginations of mischievous girl-children in literature. This list extends and dovetails into another which caters to stories on the strength and perseverance of women and their personal mythologies, like Eleni Sikelianos's *You Animal Machine* and Marie Redonnet's *Rose Mellie Rose*. If I were ever brave enough to instruct these courses, it is somewhere within these categories that much of Krystal DiFronzo's work falls. I first discovered DiFronzo the same way most people have stumbled upon their favorites – online through Tumblr. It was circa 2012 – back when the platform wasn't falling over itself to erase any instance of a nipple – when DiFronzo put out a call for submissions to a Kate Bush fanzine she was editing. I came for Kate Bush and stayed for DiFronzo's comics and reblogs. There are strong literary, fine- and folk-art influences present in DiFronzo's work and, in tandem with her multidisciplinary background, they combine to reflect a strong and personal vision – untempered by current artistic trends. Over the years, her comics have taken shape in a variety of styles and mediums but have retained an auteur-like consistency denoting a sharp, confident sensibility. Rough-hewn but deliberate pencil drawings, vibrant gouache paintings, lush colored pencils, rug work and collage are some of the many mediums she's used to bring her work to life – and I'll try my best to highlight the aspects I appreciate as a contemporary, and as a fan.

Looking through her work, I realized there are very few angles or sharp edges, if any, present in her comics. Her figures are soft and rounded – and I admire the way she draws limbs, almost like paper dolls conjoined by brads. If you could peel these characters off of their panels, they appear as though their arms and legs could swing: stiff, but with an implied flexibility. She gives weight and characterization to these figures through shading and, with varying degrees of value, hints at a rosiness which could easily be bruising or blushing. When these figures aren't nude, they are often dressed as if from a bygone era. DiFronzo shows us women in bonnets and aprons, languorous figures in gowns and togas. Their bodies and facial expressions are full of contradictions, or else exemplary of the Walt Whitman adage of humans containing multitudes; they appear beleaguered and strong, but also sensuous and stubborn. An issue I have with my own style is my characters are frequently taken at face value, and interpreted as simply *cute*. DiFronzo's characters, especially her animals, can be considered cute, but not as an empty descriptor or epithet – because her figures are prone to ugliness or foolishness while still retaining an air of beauty and depth of charm.

Another element to note is her mark-making. It's a delight to witness the presence of DiFronzo's hand in smudges or in the scritchy overlap of values in multidirectional shading – but also in her lettering. There is no regard for strict uniformity and it is this practice that makes the reader feel like a part of the creative process – while also encouraging people of all skill levels to make comics and embrace their imperfections.

* * *

THEMATICALLY, I have been interested in exploring the ideas of myth and memory in my own work. DiFronzo's comics stand out to me because, although our work and reference points are different, we draw from a similar well of literary and poetic inspiration – then go on to fashion our own myths and tales based on our own memories, interior worlds and personal fascinations. It's a sort of comics sorority that gives me that sigh-of-relief sensation you experience when you've come across someone who "gets it." In recent projects her writing is poetic and cryptic – but I'm a sucker for an evasiveness that invites interpretation. When carried out with sophistication, this type of writing flirts with the reader's mind and seduces their imagination. I love comics that are niche and operate on the conviction that they can use archaic language and find a home in the heart of a reader who understands subtext. Plus, I don't mind bringing a shovel to a narrative.

As aforementioned, DiFronzo's work draws from a folk-art sensibility and, in effect, folktales. Just as some people receive a sense of satisfaction in feeling recognized or seen when they read a straightforward autobio comic on Instagram, eliciting comments like "me AF" or "same," it is DiFronzo's penchant for preserving old tales through the synthesis of her own interests and experiences that I find myself thinking "me AF" and "same." In the Slavic folktale of the same name, Baba Yaga is a witch-like crone who lives

ABOVE: From *Seasonally Affected*, 2017–2018.

ensconced in the forest in a house mounted on chicken legs. Her chicken-legged hut has its own personality and can move about of its own will. DiFronzo's comic, *Baba Yaga's House* (2016) lends more personification to the hut through soliloquy. When the freewheelin' Baba Yaga bolts out into the world leaving her hut behind, it becomes a tale of separation anxiety. The hut waxes about its identity being tied to its sense of usefulness when occupied by Baba Yaga. Recalling that level of devotion and submissiveness in the lyrics to the Smog song "To Be of Use," it is the type of inferred connection made possible in the digital age – where one has access to their favorite artists' influences on social

ABOVE: From *Baba Yaga's House*, 2016.

media over the years. The comic is Riso-graph-printed in two colors, shades of blue and purple. The house's action and surrounding background is blue, literally and figuratively. Overlaid below, in purple, inside of rounded capsule panels, Baba Yaga's exploits set an emotional contrast as the house laments its loss until, at last, she returns again, quelling its fears.

In this comic and others, DiFronzo exercises an intuitive sense of pacing. The manner in which her panels and pages are structured gives me the impression that they're formulated off the cuff. That is not to propose that there is a lack of thought put into the layout, but to suggest that it seems like visual rhythm comes naturally to her. This formal ability is especially useful when creating works without words. As a cartoonist who relies heavily on writing, it's inspiring to look at DiFronzo's silent comics with messages can be translated across tongues. This is exemplified in *Murder/Moon* (2016), which also possesses a mythic quality. The story follows a family of crows and their struggle for survival under the sun and moon. That there is no dialogue or narrative voice, except for three segments denoting "Myth," "Day" and "Night," leaves more room for reader interpretation. The depictions of the birds are beautifully rendered and the measured pace of the four-panel structure they occupy in "Day" – punctuated intermittently by single rectangular expanses – seems to underscore their fate.

Additionally, her forays in color possess a rich, material quality that produces the illusion that the work is scented with perfume or stained with something earthy or visceral, like wet soil or blood. Another standout body of work can be found in her colorful *Seasonally Affected* series (2017–2018), which collects several mixed-media pieces meditating on the seasons: winter, in "My Green Tesselated Boudoir," and spring, in "Demeter in the Supermarket." They are excellent examples of DiFronzo's organic synthesis of interests and personal emotions in dialogue with each other, illustrating a portrait of a specific time. In "Demeter," there is a smaller comic stapled within the book. It begins with the line "I feel like the mother of the world," which is the title of a Smog song. For those who recognize the lyrics, the comic initially appears to be a visual accompaniment to the lyrics, but turn the page and it's delightful to see that DiFronzo riffs off of it and forges her own narrative. It's a practice reminiscent of the way people used to use Tumblr, reblogging an image, or a YouTube video of a song, building on something that exists with their own stories. It's another kind of language – one of modern folklore – and this is how DiFronzo inhabits it.

Above all, I admire DiFronzo's ability to blend beauty, tragedy and humor. She's

skillful at elucidating the cruelties of nature and antiquated depictions of desperation in survival – that are all at once funny and sad because it's all still so relatable. Not because of the usual zeitgeist-y trappings, but because it's deeply human. DiFronzo has been on a steady course that exists, hovering, above the traditions of folktale and Greek chorus. She navigates it with the unpredictable but sharp nature of a bird of prey – watching below and diving down to snatch up a rodent or feast upon carrion in a brilliant display. Readers should all be like baby birds in a nest, waiting to gaze upon her next bounty. ☼

ABOVE: From *Murder/Moon*, 2016.

In the next issue...